How to Leverage AWS and Google Cloud for SAP & Oracle Environments

By

Shaun Snapp with Ahmed Azmi & Mark Dalton

Table of Contents

Introduction

This book will cover many individual topics. These topics may seem overwhelming at times, but the book attempts to provide just enough coverage to understand the topic to see how it fits into the overall cloud picture. However, in addition to covering technical topics, this book emphasizes a new way of thinking. Moreover, new ways of thinking are not so easily adopted as covering specific topics.

How do we know this?

Well, new technologies have a history of being applied with the methods of thinking from previous technologies. Cloud services are different from the on-premises modality of IT. Very different in fact. It's easy to "say the words" but something else entirely to understand something really new. A good example of this is a similar change in thinking that came from containerization in the shipping industry. Malcolm McLean is widely credited with coming up the first successful implementation of containers on ships. The "technology" of containerized shipping had preceded McLean's application to his trucking company.

This is explained in the following quotation.

> "McLean wasn't the only one who had the idea to use containers on ships. Many others tried it, too, and almost all gave up on the idea soon after -- not because they were too stubborn to accept a great idea, but because they lost too much money on it. The idea was simple, but it wasn't easy to put it efficiently into practice. In hindsight, we know why they failed: The ship owners tried to integrate the containers into their usual way of working without changing the infrastructure and their routines. They tried to benefit from the obvious simplicity of loading containers onto ships without letting go of what they were used to. Only after aligning every single part of the delivery chain, from packaging to delivery, from design of the ships to the design of the harbours, was the full potential of the container unleashed."[1]

---

1   https://www.amazon.com/How-Take-Smart-Notes-Nonfiction-ebook/dp/B06WVYW33Y

It's not sufficient to adjust only the ship so that it can hold containers. To leverage containers, McLean needed to think of the impact of the container on overall supply chain. Today containers are placed on the rail and go deep inland. However, if one stops at just the ship in thinking about how to use the container, much of its efficiency is lost.

The first rail cars that could handle containers were single stack. Later rail cars were adjusted to accommodate double-stacked containers. The eventual full benefits of containers did not arrive until years after Malcom McLean' initial innovation.[2]

This is the same issue with cloud. Cloud is not an "add-on" to on premises. Although many on-premises vendors would like their customers to think that cloud is merely a minor adjustment to on-premises. Cloud, if leveraged properly, can change everything in how enterprise software is sold, implemented, maintained, tested, and other items.

The impression currently given is that cloud projects bring great success to companies that use it. That usually is the case. Companies don't publicize errors they made or how they sub-

---

2   https://ogrforum.ogaugerr.com/topic/o-scale-freight-car-guide-intermodal-cars

optimized an implementation. However, there are still many areas that can be improved so that these companies take full advantage of cloud rather than received an isolated benefit.

Cloud companies are currently growing rapidly. However, the vast majority of IT expenditures are **still** for on-premises solutions. The change to cloud modality is dramatic, and it will require the adjustment of how people in IT operate. There is nothing that the advanced of the cloud will leave untouched. While cloud is a technology, even those removed from the technology will need to adjust. For example, cloud is something that sourcing departments and contract negotiators need to change their mindsets around in order to accommodate appropriately.

Cloud Versus the On Premises Model

While SAP and Oracle can't stop talking about the cloud, what tends to be little discussed is that historically SAP and Oracle environments have built their entire business model based upon on premises. They have been two of the most successful software vendors under the on-premises model. However, AWS, Google Cloud Platform or GCP is the official name for the Google cloud offering (but we will refer to it as "Google Cloud" for this book) Azure and others are changing things very rapidly. This allows for the testing of software in a way that was not possible just a few years ago. AWS has the lead over all other cloud entities regarding size and growth. However, AWS's lead is now shrinking, at least in usage like the following graphic displays.

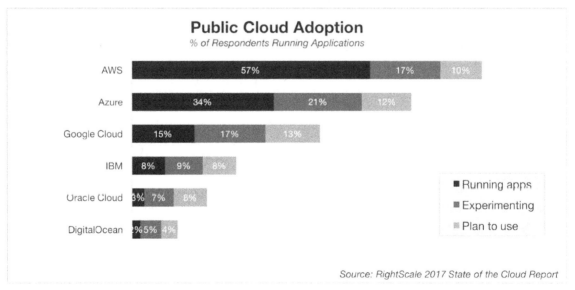

This graphic is consistent with other analyses that Azure is even hotter on AWS's tail than Google Cloud.

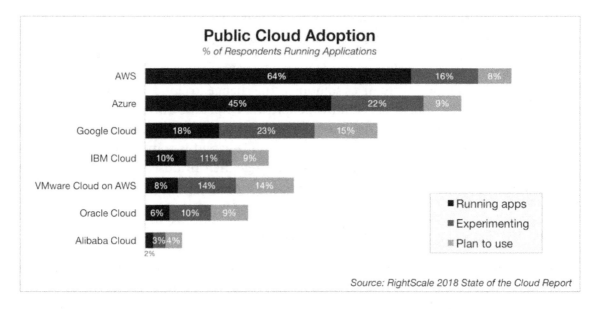

Source: RightScale 2018 State of the Cloud Report

Notice the change from 2017 to 2018.

Under the multicloud model, companies don't have to choose one cloud provider, but instead use multiple cloud providers, picking and choosing the services from each that best fit their needs. Using one cloud versus another can also come down to more than just the service's capabilities or its pricing.

AWS and Google Cloud have many similarities, but they are also born from different backgrounds. As observed by Lynn Langit, an AWS Hero and trainer/educator, Google Cloud is very developer focused, while AWS is a "DevOps" (a combination of development with operations) cloud.[3] For example, many of Google Cloud's services are a logical selection when the desire is for straightforward and more mature services than AWS.[4][5] AWS, on the other hand, is the standard choice for the latest or most innovative services. Google Cloud has a strong orientation around releasing things that were developed to run Google, but in

---

3   https://read.acloud.guru/serverless-superheroes-lynn-langit-on-big-data-nosql-and-google-versus-aws-f4427dc8679c

4   *"GCP has quite a different product philosophy to AWS. When new GCP features and resources are released into general availability, they are usually very high quality. This is in contrast to AWS where it can sometimes feel like you are the first person to use a feature. A quote I have seen which rings true to me is "Google's Beta is like AWS's GA."* - https://www.deps.co/blog/google-cloud-platform-good-bad-ugly/

5   Interestingly, Azure's rise occurred after they embraced Linux? How strange it is for Microsoft that paid so mightily to undermine Linux so aggressively in the press that their success only occurred after they offered open source. This brings up a question that Microsoft would prefer not to address – which is better open source or closed source. If Azure had to make its customers run Windows instead of Linux, Azure's market share in cloud would collapse.

many cases, those services are not necessarily a good fit for the customers which do not run at Google's scale, which is, of course, most of the known solar system.

This industry is in a transition from a time when lock-in in IT environments was the norm (with SAP and Oracle being the best at it) to an opening of options, and the ability to test in a small way before making a more significant commitment. Furthermore other providers, like Heroku, which offer a far more complete PaaS service than AWS or Google Cloud use AWS or Google Cloud as the IaaS are preferred over by some developers and companies over using AWS or Google Cloud for PaaS. Moreover, as we will cover in the book, that is just the beginning of the choices to be made.

Leveraging cloud services is a very different model and way of thinking from leveraging on-premises hardware and software. One example of this is that cloud has low access and testing overhead. One can start up an account with a cloud provider very quickly, and the primary limitation to using any cloud offering is knowledge, not the ability to gain access. This allows one to get hands-on experience in a way that was not possible under the on-premises model. This translates to there not being a reason to become an "Amazon shop" or a "Google shop" exclusively. Furthermore, each of these providers is coming up with new things all the time, so one never knows what might come up, or what service will be adjusted or repriced that can be leveraged. Also, the benefit of including both in a book is that many things that can be said for AWS can often also be said about Google. There are differences between the two such as how replication is allowed between the region, how the network has been set up, pricing, and many more items. We will illuminate these differences throughout the book. However, AWS and Google Cloud are quite comparable in many ways.

It is difficult not to be impressed by AWS and Google Cloud. However, some of the things we write in this book can also be extended to Azure as well as other IaaS providers, although we will not cover Azure or these other providers in this book specifically concerning using their services. We do discuss Azure as one part of the overall cloud market and as one of the "big three" hyperscale cloud providers.[6] AWS, Google Cloud and Azure are called "hyperscale" providers because of their enormous scale, which is based upon their extensive

---

6   The list of IaaS providers by Wikipedia is extensive. *"Amazon Abiquo Enterprise Edition, CloudStack Citrix Cloud, CtrlS, DigitalOcean, EMC, Atmos, Eucalyptus, Fujitsu, GoGrid, Google Cloud Platform, GreenButton, GreenQloud, IBM cloud computing, iland, Joyent, Lunacloud, Mirantis, Nimbula, Nimbus OpenNebula OpenStack Oracle Cloud OrionVM Rackspace Cloud Safe Swiss Cloud SoftLayer Zadara Storage, libvirt, libguestfs, OVirt, Virtual Machine Manager, Wakame-vdc, Virtual Private Cloud OnDemand"* - https://en.wikipedia.org/wiki/Infrastructure_as_a_service

investments into infrastructure.[7] Currently, these are the only three cloud providers that are discussed in these terms, and as we will explain, their CAPEX investments support this framing. However, there are others that offer other differentiated services. They can also be good options depending upon the requirements. Moreover, as we will describe in the book, there are many more choices to make than merely among the predominantly IaaS focused providers. One of the most challenging features of leveraging the cloud is choosing the best combination of items that fit the requirements of a particular company.

The things we will discuss **cannot** be extended to either SAP Cloud Platform or Oracle Cloud. This is because those offerings are so far behind the leaders of AWS, Google, Azure, and other true IaaS offerings. SAP and Oracle have huge installed bases. This installed base gives SAP and Oracle the ability to push those customers to their cloud offerings SAP Cloud or Oracle Cloud. Moreover, even with that factor, both the SAP Cloud and Oracle Cloud are still quite small in usage.

What are AWS and Google Cloud?

AWS and Google Cloud are frequently referred to as PaaS/IaaS. We use the terms SaaS, PaaS, and IaaS in the book. Also, we often refer to AWS and Google Cloud as IaaS. The problem is this is not accurate. We debated this point before publishing the book and picked up some good insight from Dan Woods(#1), an enterprise architect.[8]

> *"I assume compute (server or serverless), storage and networking is IaaS. DB is at the very least PaaS. But look at their product list and it's stacked with SaaS... literally littered with GUIs. Just because it's not a CRM system doesn't mean it doesn't count. In response to your question, I'd call AWS an internet application platform provider. An unsurpassed one at that."*

---

7   *"IBM and Oracle's CAPEX suggest they are not in the same class as Amazon Web Services, Microsoft Azure and Google Cloud. While I have written about their CAPEX spending before (IBM, Oracle), if derisively due to the paltry sums involved, in this post we will look at their investments systematically and compare them to the hyper-scale cloud players. Because, unlike marketing, CAPEX doesn't lie. In cloud computing, CAPEX is the ultimate form of putting your money where your mouth is, because no amount of jawboning alone will conjure up data centers or pack them with millions of servers."* - https://seekingalpha.com/article/4178206-ibm-oracle-separating-clowns-clouds

8   There are two Dan Woods referenced in this book. One is Dan Woods an enterprise architect that we refer to as "Dan Woods #1" and a second Dan Woods who covers data warehousing topics, whose material we references from Forbes and we refer to as "Dan Woods #2."

LAYER	COMPONENTS
Hardware	Server Hardware / RAID / Network Protocols / Block devices
OS	Linux / Mac OS X / Windows Server / CoreOS
Virtualization	Xen / VMware / KVM / VirtualBox
Hosting	Azure / AWS / Linode / Rackspace cloud
Containers / PaaS	Google appengine / Docker / Heroku
Scaling	Load balancing / Partitioning / CDNs
Package management	apt / rpm / brew
Server management	Bash / GCC / Make
Web servers	Apache / Nginx
Databases	MySQL / SQL Server / MongoDB / Redis
Search	Elasticsearch / SOLR / Facets
Config management	Puppet / Composer / Chef / Kubernetes
Programming	PHP / Java / Swift / Go / Ruby / Python / Javascript
Frameworks	Wordpress / Flask / Symfony / Rails / Django / AngularJS
Frontend dev	HTML5 / CSS3 / SASS / LASS
Security	XSS / SQL Injection / SSL
Frontend design	UI / UX / Photoshop / Illustrator / Photography
Business requirements	User requirements gathering / Project management

A "stack" is a combination of software components that interoperate with one another. It is called a stack because the components are viewed as stacked on top of one another. Which components are provided determine if the provider is a SaaS, PaaS, IaaS provider or some combination of the three. The problem with defining AWS or Google Cloud as IaaS providers or IaaS and PaaS providers is that these service providers provide access to all of these components in the stack.[9] [10]

We have Heroku listed as a PaaS connecting to AWS or Google Cloud as an IaaS. However, now, as AWS and Google Cloud have so many services, they are vendors, but they don't

---

9   https://medium.com/swlh/the-full-stack-developer-is-a-myth-4e3fb9c25867
10 Companies often use the term "full stack developer" as a job description. We found the following interesting quotation while researching this topic. *"Full stack for companies… is only a matter of finances, nothing else. Companies don't care about the future of the developer. Companies don't care about what it takes to be constantly beating in your craft and trying to be awesome. They care about having one person… that they pay 1/10 of the money and does the job (kind of) of 3, 4, or 5 people.*

I'm completely against the term full stack and the meaning that it brings… one day ur coding… the other day ur washing the dishes … and the next ur doing SEO… that u probably don't even have any idea what it is. The English term "jack of all trades master of none" applies in full." - https://medium.com/swlh/the-full-stack-developer-is-a-myth-4e3fb9c25867

transfer a license. There is a lot of grey area here. AWS and Google Cloud offer a range of services. Internally, they organize teams around products not layers like IaaS/PaaS/SaaS. Both AWS and Google Cloud offer SaaS, PaaS, and IaaS.

Furthermore, they also offer more than just access, because they also offer unique products that they developed (Google BigTable, Google Spanner, AWS DynamoDB, AWS Redshift). They don't transfer a license, but they do allow these products to be accessed. However, if we think of AWS's data warehouse/data lake/analytics offering, we can observe the following services.

Category	AWS	Google Cloud
Storage Bucket	S3	Google Multi Regional Storage Bucket
Data Warehouse	Redshift	BigQuery
ETL	Glue	Data Flow
PaaS/FaaS/Compute	Lambda	Functions
Analytics	QuickSight	Data Studio

As can be seen above, AWS and Google Cloud provide the entire stack for data warehousing and analytics. The data can be imported into AWS and Google Cloud, and never has to leave before being consumed by the user through QuickSight and Data Studio. This means that AWS and Google Cloud are providing the full stack.

Now, this does not necessarily mean that the customer uses every component of AWS's stack, but it says that in this case AWS can provide the full stack. This is why particularly as AWS and Google Cloud grow their services, they should be considered full stack providers.

The distinction between a software vendor versus a service provider touches on a story that is poorly covered in the IT media. This story is that AWS and Google Cloud are **fundamentally** different from SAP Cloud Platform and Oracle Cloud because neither AWS nor Google Cloud is a software vendor. AWS and Google Cloud are software and hardware service providers. That means they sell access to software and to hardware; they do not **transfer ownership** of software in return for income. Being a service provider rather than a software vendor has many advantages. These advantages include the following:

1. *Open Source Promotion*: The ability and the incentive to promote open source (along with their own "home grown" products). AWS and Google Cloud can do this because they do not care about license revenues. They do not benefit from license revenues (those revenues go to a software vendor, not to AWS or Google Cloud).

2. *Leveraging Open Source to Improve the Value Proposition*: The lack of licensing costs and licensing restrictions with open source products makes AWS and Google Cloud's value proposition even stronger. It is this license revenue or commercial software model with the closed source software vendors using their large income streams to promote their software over open source alternatives that has led to the overuse of commercial products and the corresponding underuse of open source.

3. *The Incentive to Introduce their Own Products*: AWS and Google Cloud have introduced many inventive and important software products. This software is mostly not open source, but AWS and Google Cloud treat their own products as if they are open source. That is they only charge for access to the service.

4. *The Incentive to Introduce Products That Work*: The short-term nature of on-premises software sales has promoted many salespeople to become "quick hit artists" and to sell products that they know do not work (or at least they have little evidence that they do work). Many salespeople are attracted to on-premises software sales because they can "get paid up front," as soon as the software sells. That is before the customer tests the software or gets value from the software. SAP customers are often filled with very marginal SAP applications that seemed like a good idea at the time. People who work for companies that still own licenses for SAP PLM, MDM, CRM, PP/DS, SNP, SRM and many other previous SAP applications will know something about this. AWS and Google Cloud cannot introduce products that do not work, because the customer can deactivate the service at any time. Therefore, ineffective services won't be able to retain subscriptions.

Moreover, the differences don't stop there; This is because unlike SAP and Oracle, AWS and Google Cloud developed their capabilities by building something of **significance internally** before they ever began offering services to customers.

- For AWS this was the Amazon store.

- For Google, this was the Google search engine.

And today, Amazon and Google operate the most extensive network of data centers in the world. Furthermore, they don't only manage these data centers, both companies have been primary innovators in the data center and data center networking space. They collectively changed the way that data centers are configured. Some people are fans of Azure; however, Microsoft has never been the innovator in the cloud. Azure is what it is today by copying AWS and Google Cloud. Microsoft struggled with the cloud until they began embracing and copying AWS and Google Cloud. Microsoft wanted something impossible, for its cloud to be based on Windows. As long as Microsoft held to that self-centered doctrine, Azure would have never broken through.

There are many things that make AWS and Google distinct from other companies in the enterprise software space. Google innovated in the scale of data centers by shunning the use of proprietary hardware and software and building its infrastructure on open source and commodity hardware. However, this is a bit misleading, as the hardware components are commodity, but both AWS and Google custom build their hardware. Google even produces their server power supplies. Furthermore, these two companies did not come up with these ideas independently from one another. Google was the initial innovator in this area, and Amazon (before they had expanded into AWS of course) was impressed by Google's approach and decided to follow suit.

Google developed the approach of vast numbers of inexpensive redundant Linux based servers. This decision was made when everyone told Google to purchase hardware from the established vendors like HP instead. This is observed in the following quotation from Google.

> *"Our hardware must be controlled and administered by software that can handle massive scale. Hardware failures are one notable problem that we manage with software. Given the large number of hardware components in a cluster, hardware failures occur quite frequently. In a single cluster in a typical year, thousands of machines fail and thousands of hard disks break; when multiplied by the number of clusters we operate globally, these numbers become somewhat breathtaking. Therefore, we want to abstract such problems away from users, and the teams running our services similarly don't want to be bothered by hardware failures. Each datacenter campus has teams dedicated to maintaining the hardware and datacenter infrastructure."*[11]

1. SAP and Oracle don't know anything about this. They sell software to companies, and they don't even implement most of their software, as partners implement the majority, and of far less than advertised quality.

2. Neither SAP nor Oracle is well versed in how to run what AWS and Google run.

3. The world does not use an Oracle search engine or purchase from SAP's online retail outlet.

---

11 Site Reliability Engineer: How Google Runs Production Systems

SAP and Oracle have been able to convince Wall Street that selling and supporting software puts them in an excellent position to sell cloud services. We don't think it does.

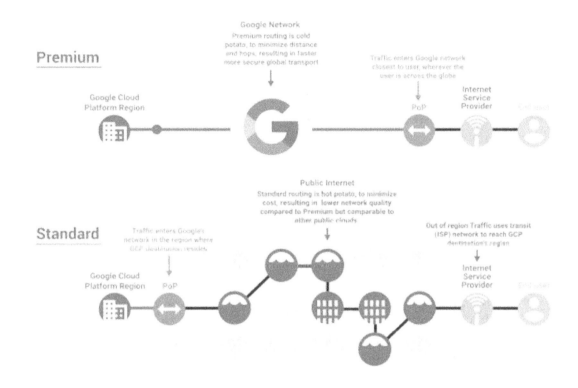

Outbound and Inbound traffic delivery

How the data centers are designed is not the only area of innovation on the part of AWS and Google Cloud. At a premium tier (top) customers can access Google's network, which is significantly faster than the public Internet. Google has laid its own undersea cables.

The more you know about AWS and Google Cloud, the more different their entire set of capabilities and philosophy appears from either SAP or Oracle. This extends to their documentation, which have entirely different "voices."

SAP and Oracle sales reps are very aggressive about asserting an equivalence between their cloud offerings and AWS and Google Cloud. In our view, using SAP and Oracle applications that are hosted on the SAP and Oracle clouds will increasingly **disadvantage** those applications. We predict that SAP and Oracle will continue to make exceedingly slow progress in the cloud. Therefore while SAP and Oracle have been aggressively pitching their cloud to customers, our view is that companies that go with either SAP or Oracle clouds will end up regretting that decision. This is why one of the authors of this book, Mark Dalton's company AutoDeploy, migrates Oracle JDE to AWS for clients and has a migrator that speeds the process. This way customers get the JDE ERP application on a highly effective cloud, without having to deal with Oracle's seemingly never-ending "cloud promises."

Oracle has had over a decade to get their cloud Fusion program to deliver results, and today, companies run the on-premises versions of Oracle's applications. This issue of ineffectiveness in the cloud and an inability to do much more than product marketing statements about the cloud brings up the question, "why wait for SAP and Oracle when you can migrate some of their items to the cloud, and to the best clouds?"

As we will see, not every item can be migrated as JDE to AWS or Google Cloud.

Choosing Simple Over Complex

Something we find to be less discussed as a philosophical difference is the tendency to choose complexity. SAP and Oracle tend towards making things complex, which (in part) explains the high TCO of SAP and Oracle installations. Several years ago SAP tried to dispel this accurate description of SAP environments with their Run Simple marketing campaign which we covered in the article Is SAP's "Running Simple" Real? The issue? There was nothing beyond marketing to the Run Simple program.[12]

Conversely, AWS and Google Cloud tend towards simpler approaches. The topic of Google's focus on simper approaches is explained here by Google.

> *"Google's network hardware is controlled in several ways. As discussed earlier, we use an OpenFlow-based software-defined network. Instead of using "smart" routing hardware, we rely on less expensive "dumb" switching components in combination with a central (duplicated) controller that precomputes best paths across the network. Therefore, we're able to move compute-expensive routing decisions away from the routers and use simple switching hardware."[13]*

This quotation of how Google works goes back to 2006.

> *"This growth is driven by an abundance of scalable technology. As Google noted in its most recent annual report filing with the SEC: "Our business relies on our software and hardware infrastructure, which provides substantial computing*

---

12   http://www.brightworkr.com/saphana/2016/09/02/saps-running-simple-real/
13   Site Reliability Engineer: How Google Runs Production Systems

resources at low cost. We currently use a combination of off-the-shelf and custom software running on clusters of commodity computers. Our considerable investment in developing this infrastructure has produced several key benefits. It simplifies the storage and processing of large amounts of data, eases the deployment and operation of large-scale global products and services, and automates much of the administration of large-scale clusters of computers."

Google buys, rather than leases, computer equipment for maximum control over its infrastructure. Google chief executive officer Eric Schmidt defended that strategy in a May 31 call with financial analysts. "We believe we get tremendous competitive advantage by essentially building our own infrastructures," he said.

Google does more than simply buy lots of PC-class servers and stuff them in racks, Schmidt said: "We're really building what we think of internally as supercomputers."

Because Google operates at such an extreme scale, it's a system worth studying, particularly if your organization is pursuing or evaluating the grid computing strategy, in which high-end computing tasks are performed by many low-cost computers working in tandem."[14]

In essence, Amazon and Google were two enormously successful implementations or test cases for approaches that rejected proprietary software and hardware, which happens to be the bread and butter of SAP and Oracle. Naturally, not only SAP and Oracle but HP, Dell and Fujitsu would prefer not to talk about AWS's and Google's success with their homegrown hardware model.

SAP and Oracle and the rest would have said that Amazon and Google could not have did what they did. They would have come up with a litany of reasons that what they accomplished was impossible. All of this would have fit very nicely in the conventional wisdom at the time. All of these reasons would have pushed Amazon and Google to become customers of the traditional proprietary model. However, Amazon and Google accomplished what they set out to do, and they legitimized their mold breaking approaches because of their success. Therefore the only response available from the promoters of conventional wisdom on enterprise software is to avert their eyes.

After AWS and Google Cloud mastered these capabilities internally, they opened up their internal capabilities and offered the world a different way of doing things through what amounts to opening their infrastructure and innovative software to customers as a service.

This is stated as much by Google.

---

14   http://www.baselinemag.com/c/a/Infrastructure/How-Google-Works-1

> *"Because of the size and scale of these services, Google has put a lot of work into optimizing its infrastructure and creating a suite of tools and services to manage it effectively. Google Cloud Platform puts this infrastructure and these management resources at your fingertips."*[15]

This rapid rate of change is causing previous assumptions to be challenged. IT directors and CIOs that previously were tied up just managing on-premises environments must now consider how to and whether they should leverage the cloud for their companies.

That is where we wanted this book to come in.

This book is written to help people without much time to study the subject to get up to speed on the options that are out there. For this goal, we combined three different authors with different exposures to AWS, Google Cloud, SAP, and Oracle. The primary author of the book is Shaun Snapp, a long-term SAP consultant, and SAP researcher. Shaun combined with Ahmed Azmi, an experienced technical resource in the areas of development, Oracle, SAP, and AWS migration, and Mark Dalton, the CEO of Autodeploy, a company the migrates Oracle JDE customers to the cloud among other cloud deployments. We also used several technical reviewers, including very prominently Denis Myagkov, who has many years of experience in SAP programming and infrastructure. Therefore, this book is based upon both first-hand experiences and research. We found many areas of this book that overlapped with many years of Brightwork Research & Analysis' research. Hence there is are numerous links to the Brightwork Research & Analysis website to substantiate assertions that would be far too expansive to include in the book.

We brought a combination of SAP, Oracle, AWS and Google Cloud experience to bear on the question of how to best leverage the cloud for SAP and Oracle environments.

All three of the authors agree that AWS and Google Cloud are "shaking the tree" of IT and that there are so many areas of opportunity for Oracle and SAP customers to leverage. In our collective view, the most significant limitation in leveraging AWS for Oracle and SAP customers is understanding what is available combined with how AWS can change the way companies with on-premises experience have been doing things. It has been pointed out previously that incorporating the cloud into your IT environment is about both gaining additional domain expertise, as well as adopting a new way of thinking. One example of this is leveraging "serverless" or self-configured server computing (we place the word "serverless" in quotation marks in the book because it's not an accurate term for describing what occurs as of course a server is still used). We think it should be called "auto-configured services computing." When "serverless" is accessed, it means that the old paradigm of accepting

---

15 https://cloud.google.com/docs/compare/aws/

specific batch job times based upon semi-static hardware is virtually gone. "Serverless" is particularly beneficial when the load is difficult to estimate. With things like "serverless," it means that the assumptions have changed.

Reviewing Other Books in the Field

When reviewing the literature before writing this book, we examined the AWS and Google Cloud books published up to that point. Also, we found that the vast majority of the books presently written on AWS and Google Cloud are of a technical nature and focused on a particular technology. That is they tell the reader how to do a **specific thing** with AWS and Google Cloud.

Here is a brief sampling of books we found on AWS.

- AWS Certified Solutions Architect Official Study Guide: Associate Exam
- Architecting for the AWS Cloud: Best Practices (AWS Whitepaper)
- AWS Security Best Practices (AWS Whitepaper)
- Microservices on AWS (AWS Whitepaper)
- AWS Certified Advanced Networking Official Study Guide: Specialty Exam
- Learning AWS Lumberyard Game Development
- Google Cloud Platform for Developers
- Google Cloud Platform for Architects
- Data Science in the Google Cloud Platform
- Google Compute Engine
- Hands on Machine Learning with Google Cloud Platform

We could list another 20 books, but the pattern is not much different from what is observed above.

As you can see with AWS and Google Cloud, books that cover a specific technology is the norm. Providing a specific focus is necessary to use a service, and we have read several of them ourselves. However, this is not at all one of those types of books. This is not a "how-to" book, but instead provides an overview of the technical landscape. This book focuses on why AWS and Google Cloud are so advantageous for customers generally and SAP and Oracle customers specifically.

AWS's Advice on Migration

AWS is seeing substantial growth, but SAP and Oracle are going to resist leveraging the AWS cloud as this reduces their control over the account. Secondly, neither AWS nor Google are companies that "holds people's hands." They both have growing partner networks, but AWS and Google Cloud are still much more "do it yourself" than SAP or Oracle, which provide an army of consultants that are available to provide large amounts of expensive consulting. Instead, AWS and Google provide clear documentation for how to leverage their offerings.

AWS has published the following migration graphic.

Figure 3: Comparison of cloud migration strategies

Their definition of these strategies are as follows:

1. *Re Host*: AKA lift and shift which is where applications are moved without changes.

2. *Re Platform*: AKA lift, tinker and shift. This is where parts of the application are changed by it is mostly kept the same when migrated. The example AWS gives is switching out WebLogic for the open source Apache Tomcat. This makes sense as when companies move to AWS they find they can access many open source items very quickly and easily.

3. *Re Factor/Re Architect*: One example of this AWS gives is migrating from a monolithic architecture to "serverless." We cover monolithic versus microservices later in the book.

4. *Re Purchase*: This moves from an on premises license to SaaS.

5. *Retire*: This decommissions the application that is no longer needed.

6. *Retain*: This keeps applications that are critical for the business but must be refactored.

Amazon Web Services – **AWS Cloud Transformation Maturity Model**

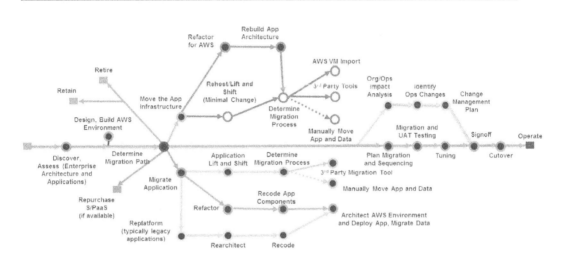

Figure 3: Application migration dispositions and paths identified from migration strategy

AWS provides this decision point diagram which fits in with the different options.[16]

---

16 https://d1.awsstatic.com/whitepapers/AWS-Cloud-Transformation-Maturity-Model.pdf

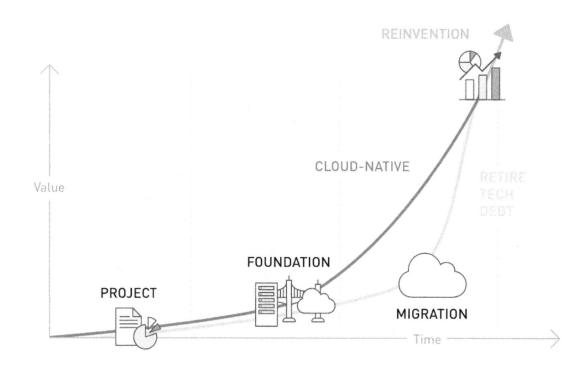

Notice the term "retire technical debt." On premises environments have an enormous amount of technical debt. They are filled to the brim with applications they don't get value out of, high overhead support costs. They also have too many skills required for the items they are trying to control, which means many components are not managed properly. This prevents these companies from gaining the full benefits from their purchases.

Consistent with AWS's recommendation to start simple, rehosting opportunities should be evaluated as one of the first items for companies to do. They are the "low hanging fruit." SAP and Oracle have been exaggerating their cloud capabilities for years now. Companies that are using SAP or Oracle for hosting should ask themselves why. It only takes a brief evaluation of either SAP or Oracle Cloud to easily tell that this is not something that SAP or Oracle have been good at doing. Both SAP and Oracle receive roughly 16% of their revenues from the cloud, but for SAP at least, most of this is from SaaS acquisitions and not from SAP Cloud. Oracle coerces customers into purchasing cloud licenses, so their reported figures are unreliable, as we will cover further in this book. When we discuss IaaS rather than SaaS, SAP and Oracle shrink to a very small component of what each company's revenues.

AWS proposes migrating consistent with the maturity of the customer, as is covered in the following graphic.

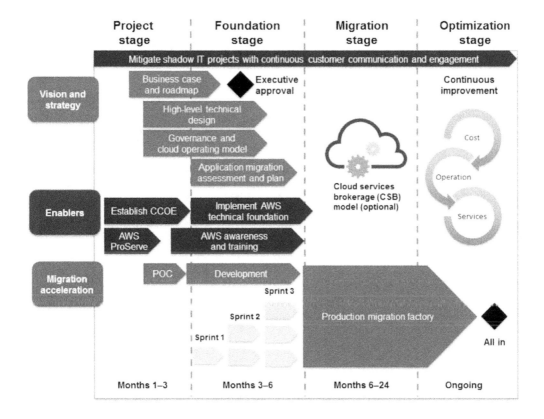

Figure 1: AWS Cloud Transformation Maturity Model –
stages, milestones, and timeline

AWS sees these factors as determining what and when and even if to migrate different components to the cloud.[17]

When migrating, AWS proposes the following steps.

1. *Test Systems at Production Scale*: This can be accomplished on AWS because it is so easy to spin up a production sized environment. Furthermore, it can be brought up for just a short period of time, and deactivated in between usage periods. This can be considered "test on demand."

2. Automate to Make Architectural Experimentation Easier: *A big part of this is replicating systems.*

---

17   https://d1.awsstatic.com/whitepapers/AWS-Cloud-Transformation-Maturity-Model.pdf

3. *Allow for Evolutionary Architectures*: This is "build to change." This is where automation and testing on-demand come into play.

4. *Drive Architectures Using Data*: Where data collection comes into play based upon the workloads you apply.

5. *Improve Through Game Days*: This is simulation. You simulate as many realistic factors as you can on planned days.[18]

Making the Business Case for Migration

AWS proposes that there are five areas that make up the case for migration. These are the following:

1. Business Agility

2. Operational Resilience

3. Cost Avoidance

4. Workforce Productivity

5. Operational Costs

---

18   These steps were rewritten as a synopsis of AWS's explanations of these items that can be found at this document link - http://d0.awsstatic.com/whitepapers/architecture/AWS_Well-Architected_Framework.pdf

Table 4: A case for migration

BUSINESS AGILITY	OPERATIONAL RESILIENCE	COST AVOIDANCE	WORKFORCE PRODUCTIVITY	OPERATIONAL COSTS
77% faster to deliver business applications	98% reduction in P1/P0's	52% average TCO savings	15 automated bots developed	35% reduction in compute assets (792)
Rapid experimentation	Improved security posture	80% cloud first adoption	8 cloud migration parties	50 applications decommissioned
Reduced technical debt	15 cloud services created		Shift to self-service culture	$14M YOY savings
Streamlined M&A activity	Improved performance		DevOps in practice	
$14.2M Investment +	18 Months +	Focus	= 300+ Apps Migrated &	$14M YOY Savings

AWS provides the case study above as an example of the case for migration.

We see several things left out of this, one of the most important being the ability to test. This book will frequently refer to the enhanced ability to test solutions before committing to solutions as this is a primary distinction between on-premises and cloud. In traditional SAP and Oracle on-premises implementations, one must invest time in things like hardware sizing. The sizing process often becomes so time-consuming that the sizing became a large percentage of the final hardware price that was purchased.

SAP was notable for providing a "Quick Sizer" that was quite inaccurate. The problems with sizing SAP and Oracle extend beyond just the time-consuming nature of sizing exercises and inaccuracy. For example, with SAP's HANA database, SAP deliberately released information that would cause customers to undersize the HANA, so that the initial purchase would be based upon false pretenses. This topic is covered in the article Understanding Pricing in S/4HANA and HANA.[19]

None of these things happen with AWS or Google Cloud because of the ability to test without making anything but a short-term commitment. AWS and Google Cloud's capacity is an "ocean" where the customer can access any percentage of this ocean of capacity. There

---

19   http://www.brightworkr.com/saphana/2017/03/18/understanding-pricing-s4hana-hana/

is simply no comparison in this area with SAP or Oracle. For example, SAP has the SAP Cloud, and Oracle has the Oracle Cloud which SAP and Oracle tout as being this "ultra-flexible" IaaS/PaaS. SAP and Oracle are trying to pretend that they offer to customers what AWS and Google Cloud provides.

The growth of AWS and Google Cloud versus SAP Cloud and Oracle Cloud illustrates that companies are clearly choosing AWS and Google Cloud (as well as Azure). Google's growth is, of course, slower than AWS that leads everyone. Moreover, as we will discuss, Google Cloud is a better fit for some types of customers and for some scenarios. AWS and Google Cloud share many similarities, but they also have important differences that we will illustrate in this book.

What is Being Migrated to or Accessed in AWS and Google Cloud?

This book discusses migration, but migration is only part of the story with leveraging the cloud for SAP and Oracle. Increasingly, companies will place more custom components into the cloud that will integrate back to on-premises systems, all while leveraging cloud services. AWS's software will even be used to manage on-premises resources, and co-managed with open source cloud management projects like OpenStack and CloudStack. That is why the book is titled "how to leverage" rather than "how to migrate."

A Brief Overview of AWS and Google Cloud Services

We have discussed a few services already, but to put some firm roots down, let us review what AWS and Google Cloud offer customers concerning specific services.

The list below includes some of the most popular services provided by either AWS or Google Cloud.

Google	AWS	Layer	Description	Features
Google Compute Engine	Amazon (Elastic Computer Cloud) EC2	Application	Virtual machines, or a virtual "computer," and allows the running of an operations system. Could, for instance be used as a web host.	Multiple CPUs, choice of operating systems (Windows or different flavors of Linux), static or dynamic IPs, can be configured from a file, allows adjustment of instances. Must run within an availability zone (AZs), or a Google or AWS physical location. AZs operate within an account.
Google Kubernetes Engine	Amazon EC2 Container Service	Application	A container service for applications which allows applications to be isolated from infrastucture. Manages underlying cloud resources, and grealty increases the portability of code aka "run anywhere."	Autoscaling, autodeployment, container cluster monitoring. Containers are considered as "VM 2.0" as they do not virtualize the hardware, just the software. They can be used along with VMs.
Google App Engine	AWS Elastic Beanstalk	Application	Self configuring server for coding that works with the data sources of (for AWS) either RDS or Virtual Private Cloud. (also allows for manual override of auto configuration). Allows for fast application development.	Load balancing, provisioning, application health monitorying, autoscaling. Containers can be managed by Docker.
Google	AWS	Layer	Description	Features
Google Cloud Functions	AWS Lambda	Application	A self configuring server. Extremely low maintenance solution for customers. Essentially requires code combined with a data source, which can be Cloud SQL/RDS. Does not change anything related to the coding.	Plugs directly into integrated development environments. Local work is saved to AWS and GCP.
Google Cloud Storage	Amazon S3	Storage	A high availability and performance storage bucket or elastic container designed for frequent access. Called a bucket as it stores data with or without a hierarchy. Considered to be almost unlimited in capacity. For long term storage, for instance data and databases are moved from EC2 to S3. S3 is used by Dropbox and Netflix. Holds Gmail data.	Can be configured for higher or lower uptime, and frequency of access. Data is encrypted when ingested. Storage class is if the bucket is multi-regional, regional, nearline (rarely accessed), coldline (rarely accessed). Buckets must be uniquely named. Supported by an SLA.
Google Nearline or Google Coldline	Amazon Glacier	Storage	Long term archival "considered as tape replacement" storage with queued downloading (i.e. non immediate) Named "Glacier" to represent "cold" storage.	Cost optimized to be extremely rarely accessed. Due to cost they are great first option for AWS & GCP testing.

Google	AWS	Layer	Description	Features
Cloud SQL	Amazon RDS	Database	Managed relational database. This means that the maintenance of the database is taken over by Google or AWS. Cloud SQL or RDS is setup in Google Cloud Storage and S3.	Cloud SQL has the choice of MySQL and PostreSQL. Amazon RDS has the choice of 6 databases. Google is considered to offer better security/more complete encryption.
Google Cloud Bigtable or Google Cloud Datastore	Amazon DynamoDB	Database	Managed database service for unstructured data aka "No SQL." For Google often used with Google App Engine.	Define number of requests to be processed per second. Stored on SSDs for performance.
	Amazon Redshift	Database	Managed large scale high performance data warehouse. Primarily column oriented storage.	Scalability and reduced complexity over on premises data warehouses.
Google BigTable and BigQuery		Database	Greater than 1 TB databases, designed for mass scalability. (For BigTable built on Google File System, used by GMail and YouTube at Google.)	Good for lots of read write operations and analytical applications, Non relational..
Google Cloud Memorystore (Simply renamed Redis)	Amazon Redis	Database	A managed in memory database, as well as a cache and a memory store service.	Scalability and high availability.
Google VPC	Amazon VPC	Network	Allows AWS resources to be launched from a private isolated cloud.	Creates a shared private IP space for teams working globally.

Most of the most commonly used AWS services map very well to those offered by Google Cloud. A primary difference between AWS and Google Cloud is that AWS has far more services. If we provided a more extensive list the difference would become obvious. But many of AWS's services don't have nearly as much usage as the services listed in this table.

Storage solutions for any workload

A single API for all storage classes

Constant options are a feature of AWS and Google Cloud. Furthermore, the ability to adjust the service is unprecedented in the history of IT. Lengthy sizing exercises are a feature of on-premises implementations. Furthermore, once an application/database license and the hardware were purchased, there was a forward momentum to using the solution "as planned."

In many cases, lengthy sizing exercises have resulted in sunk cost decision making orientation that kept solutions in place that did not add value.

SAP and Oracle's High TCO

Something critical is how SAP and Oracle do everything they can to hide the TCO of their databases and applications. One of the authors of this book, Shaun Snapp wrote the only book on enterprise software TCO calculation titled Enterprise Software TCO,[20] and Brightwork Research & Analysis has the most complete Enterprise Software TCO calculators.[21] (available online and free)

---

20 http://www.brightworkr.com/scmfocuspress/it-decision-making-books/enterprise-software-tco/
21 http://www.brightworkr.com/softwaredecisions/all-enterprise-software-tco-calculators/

As part of the research for this book on author, Shaun Snapp found that both vendors and consulting companies provide either inaccurate or incomplete TCO. SAP has paid Forrester on multiple occasions to create misleading TCO studies for SAP applications.

We conclude that consulting companies and vendors want their customers to know the TCO of their offerings about as much as any person in sales want their customers to know the TCO of their purchase. That translates into not at all. Moreover, as most sales, on-premise software sales is about emphasizing the license purchase. This is true even though research at Brightwork Research & Analysis indicates that the average application's license is only (on average) **10% of the TCO of its lifetime costs**. Knowing this, is it somewhat shocking how often we have observed software buyers focus most of their attention on the initial purchase price.

Once again, AWS and Google Cloud are not software vendors, so they work a bit differently. Both AWS and Google Cloud are predicated **upon massive infrastructure investments**. These enormous investments and overall low overhead sales and access approach lower costs, and AWS and Google have the highest orientation around cost reduction and economies of scale of any of the entities we have studied in enterprise software. Also, because they offer a low TCO, they have a unique incentive to allow customers to calculate the TCO of using their services.

They offer an easy to use TCO calculator.

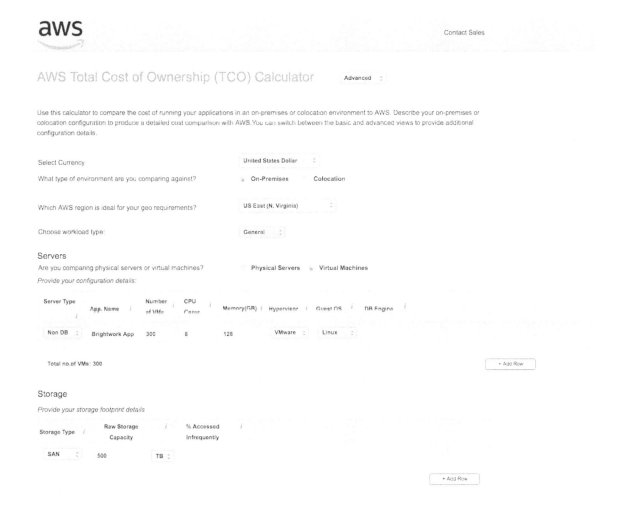

This is the basic version of the AWS TCO calculator.

The overall transparency with AWS and Google Cloud is significantly increased. AWS customers are notified of their monthly charges by email, even if they don't login to their AWS consoles. We will get into this topic in more detail in our chapter on pricing.

Furthermore, as we cover in other parts of this book, we predict that AWS and Google Cloud infused SAP and Oracle environments will lower their TCO. For one reason, companies pick up **a great deal of flexibility in their infrastructure.** Secondly, using AWS and Google Cloud makes the implementing company less reliant on SAP and Oracle consulting partners. The self-service nature of AWS and Google Cloud make it a simple matter to project that the consulting multiple versus costs. This is in our view the most significant opportunity for releasing IT funding to be applied to higher level uses.

How This Book Differs from Other Information Available About AWS and Google Cloud

AWS and Google Cloud's many services and the explanations of these services and how these services interact with other components makes up an overwhelming amount of information. And it is very easy to get lost in the details. It means that in addition to understanding a technical topic in detail, a primer on how the topics fit together is one of the most important but missing areas in the field. This is the target we aimed for.

A Book or AWS and Google Cloud Focused on SAP and Oracle

This is the only book focused on leveraging AWS and Google Cloud for **SAP or Oracle**.

A Book That is Independent and Clear Eyed on SAP, Oracle, AWS and Google Cloud

Most books written on either SAP or Oracle are written by employees, consultants, and employees of companies that are official partners with SAP or Oracle. Because of this, very little of the full reality for customers regarding SAP and Oracle get into books. One of the authors of this book, Shaun Snapp wrote a book for SAP Press. During the process of writing the book, portions that were not sufficiently flattering to SAP were removed from the book by the publisher, as we covered in the article Reading Propaganda About SAP Support from SAP.[22] SAP Press never tells its readers that they censor any information that while it may help customers in dealing with SAP and that they do what SAP tells them to do. The reader

---

22 http://www.brightworkr.com/sapprojectmanagement/2016/11/reading-propaganda-support-sap-press/

may be buying the book, but the books are edited to the liking of SAP, placing SAP's interests ahead of the reader's interests.[23]

This is indeed not only a problem with SAP and Oracle but is a pervasive problem in software and information technology books where the authors frequently only write the book to obtain consulting business and where the best way to achieve that consulting business is to write as Pollyannaish-ly about the subject as possible. The Brightwork Research & Analysis website does not do this and is never compensated by any vendor for any content, book or article. There is no other book like this that covers how to leverage AWS and Google Cloud for SAP and Oracle because knowing the IT publishing market the way that we do, that book would spend most of its time trying to convince readers to use SAP and Oracle clouds.

SAP HANA on AWS (AWS Quick Start) Oct 26, 2016
by AWS Whitepapers and Amazon Web Services

Kindle Edition
$0⁰⁰
Get it TODAY, Oct 11

SAP S/4HANA Cloud: Use Cases, Functionality, and Extensibility (SAP PRESS) Sep 28, 2017
by Michael Jolton and Yosh Eisbart

Hardcover
$56⁸⁵ $69.95 *prime*
Get it by **Sat, Oct 13**
FREE Shipping
Only 12 left in stock - order soon.

More Buying Choices
$35.00 (73 used & new offers)

SAP Cloud Migration: Landscapes and Infrastructures (SAP PRESS) Mar 25, 2016
by André Bögelsack and Galina Baader

Hardcover
$45⁶⁷ $69.95 *prime*
Get it by **Sat, Oct 13**
FREE Shipping
Only 3 left in stock - order soon.

More Buying Choices
$30.82 (61 used & new offers)

Books like those listed above explain how to leverage SAP's cloud offerings. They don't break the wall and demonstrate how to harness the non-SAP cloud to improve SAP. The top book

---

23 Anyone questioning this, we encourage you to think through how many times you have read anything critical in a book that focuses on a software product, versus how often the book is promotional in nature. Now think of how many times problematic things come up when working with a software product. How could the books on these topics be unbiased if they don't cover problems with the application much less problems with the vendor?

is the republishing of a white paper (so not a book) and does explain how to leverage HANA for AWS, but it does not question the official agreed upon partnership between SAP and AWS regarding how SAP HANA is used. This book does examine that topic, and because we have no relationships, we are free to question everything.

Similarly, this book will tell the reader the reality of SAP and Oracle (as well as AWS, Google Cloud and all other entities), with the only concern being that we provide accurate information. We are not here to carry water for any entity and will call out things as we see them. No doubt some feelings will be hurt at SAP and Oracle and others in the course of reading this book, but we are used to that. Complaints and otherwise can be directed to the book page where we will reply to them, or to our contact details at the end of the book.

SAP and Oracle are fighting aggressively to control the cloud so that the transition to the cloud occurs as much on their terms as possible. That is SAP and Oracle would not want a little thing like the cloud coming between them and their account control. For example, Oracle doubled the cost of their database license for AWS. This was done in order to increase the cost of running Oracle on AWS versus Oracle Cloud. After this Oracle then declared that **it was less expensive to run the Oracle DB on the Oracle Cloud** -- leaving out the matter of their doubling of the database license.[24] (it is still not less expensive to run the Oracle database on the Oracle Cloud for reasons we will discuss in this book).

Most books on SAP and Oracle whitewash how these vendors operate. Again if you as an author have a relationship with SAP or Oracle, or care what they think, you would not be free to write the truth on topics that relate to these vendors. Whitewashing SAP and Oracle's behaviors will not help customers learn the best path forward, but it assists authors in SAP and Oracle meet their career objectives. It is nearly impossible to find books that write the slightest thing critical about either of these vendors. Both of these vendors use the most aggressive/predatory control tactics in the software industry, including the use of audits by both Oracle and SAP, and something called indirect access by SAP, which is an assertion of the right to charge extra for what amounts to application integration (And which is covered in the article Type 1 Versus Type 2 Indirect Access.)[25] Indirect access is an illegal hypothesis that violates US antitrust law as we cover in SAP Indirect Access as a Tying Arrangement Violation.[26] If truths like these are not acknowledged, then it's impossible to defend the company against these vendors. Do you recall hearing about these things from SAP consulting companies? Of course not, and whose interests do the consulting companies support (it's a bit of a trick question, but it goes 1) Their own, 2) SAP's, 3) Their clients….. in that order.

---

24 https://oracle-base.com/blog/2017/01/28/oracles-cloud-licensing-change-be-warned/
25 http://www.brightworkr.com/sap/2017/04/type-one-versus-type-two-indirect-access/
26 http://www.brightworkr.com/sap/2017/02/saps-indirect-access-violate-us-laws-tying-arrangements/

One commenter described how Oracle is more of a conglomerate or holding company than a software development company.

> *"I don't think it's generally a bad place for engineers, but it has transitioned from being a tech company into being just a "buy 'em and milk 'em" company (a la the old Computer Associates business model of buying companies and jacking up the prices and maintenance/support), which is a lot less interesting to most engineers."*[27]

As a customer of SAP and Oracle, you are going to "get milked." SAP and Oracle have substantial lock in control over their customers and they have been and will continue to use it. And this gets to the next topic the book is about, which is lock in.

A Book Focused on Lock In

The authors of the book have a lot of experience on SAP and Oracle projects. Something curious about these projects? Well, the term "lock-in" is almost never used. With on-premises projects with SAP and Oracle, lock-in is simply accepted. It is almost encouraged through the use of terms that are meant as endorsements of the principle that you hear when someone says "we are an Oracle (or SAP) shop."

The cloud is very different. The term lock-in is considered distinctly pejorative, and how to stay away from it is frequently mentioned in literature on the topic. SAP and Oracle accounts are entirely too locked-in. So when we provide information in this book, lock-in, and how to avoid it is always in the back of our mind.

A Book That Explains Where SAP and Oracle Really Stand on the Cloud

While currently, both vendors cannot talk enough about the cloud, both vendors fought against the cloud for many years (and we have the evidence in this book). These vendors behaved this way as they knew that the cloud cut against their on-premises business model. Moreover, once they embraced the cloud (not that they wanted to, but Wall Street told them they did not have an alternative) their approach to the cloud has **not been to improve IT efficiency or to reduce prices**. Instead, it has been to merely to lift and shift their business model to the cloud, and then to deceive their customers and prospects as much

---

27   https://www.quora.com/Whats-so-bad-about-Oracle-Whenever-engineers-I-know-say-Oracle-it-seems-to-mean-the-worst-place-to-work-and-you-should-never-do-that-Why-is-that

as possible about the cloud. For instance, for years, Oracle has been crediting cloud sales to customers who use the same on-premises version of the application. Information from actual projects as well as Oracle sales reps is that the cloud version of the Oracle application is not implemented (but booked as revenue) while the on-premises version is no booked as revenue, but is used.

This is explained also by Seeking Alpha.

> *"Oracle management likes to talk a lot about new customers and competitive wins. I get that. I am sure that there are workloads new to Oracle on the cloud. How much these are I cannot say. But the fact is that core IT applications are simply not growing by all that much-they have long since been saturated. Most of the time when Oracle sells a cloud application, it is selling it to someone who has the selfsame application running on-prem."*[28]

Thus the customers of both of these vendors are prime candidates to harness AWS and Google Cloud to improve their value.

A Book That Addresses SAP and Oracle and Consulting Partner Information Quality

Migrating from SAP and Oracle, or portions of SAP and Oracle to AWS has many implications. Some of them are related to corporate strategy, contracts, and related factors. We will cover as many of these as we can.

Customers have for decades chosen SAP and Oracle applications and databases. In some cases the selections made sense. However, in many cases when there was no logical reason to select the options presented by SAP or Oracle except they felt like safe choices. This is buying on the basis of brand rather than an actual analysis of the pros and cons of the purchased items. SAP and Oracle has not only extensive sales and marketing budgets, but an army of consultants built up that both implement, but also serve to promote more and more SAP and Oracle sales.

Brightwork Research & Analysis frequently performs analysis of statements by SAP and Oracle consultancies to their clients is that the average information quality provided by them is low. As it happens, right now, we are aware of Oracle partners who are lying to companies about Oracle Cloud. They are falsifying the customers they have live on Oracle Cloud. They are doing this so they can sell Oracle Cloud and get experience in Oracle Cloud.

---

28 https://seekingalpha.com/article/4006820-oracle-company-hardest-working-spinmeisters-planet

SAP and Oracle spend mightily to influence people, and it works which we cover in How SAP Controls IT Media. The vast majority of SAP sales reps and SAP consulting firms spend their time talking about how SAP "could be used" (according to a brochure), not how it is used. Brightwork Research & Analysis is one of the only entities that discuss how it is used in reality. Moreover, discussing this topic is **very bad** for sales, which could cause you to "lose the deal" and to then get fired as a sales rep for these companies.

The problem is financial bias.

Implementation companies don't implement things from many vendors. They implement software from a few vendors. If the consulting company has a financial bias, it is logical and is borne out by observations that they will recommend what is best for them financially. SAP and Oracle consulting companies are not fiduciaries as we cover in Do Consulting Companies Have a Fiduciary Duty.[29] They are under no obligation to place their client's financial interests ahead of their own.

While they may be safe politically, they are in many cases not safe in reality. Here are several examples of why this is the case.

- *Immature Products*: SAP has a history of bringing out immature applications that have major implementation failures and have to be written off. SAP implementations have so undermined some companies that they were sufficiently weakened to become acquisition targets.

- *High Cost and Maintenance Database*: The Oracle database (Oracle 18, 12, 11) has many upper-end features, but it also historically has the highest maintenance overhead of any database in its class (until SAP released HANA that is, which took the crown). Furthermore, many of the Oracle DB's more advanced features go unused by customers. Like SAP, Oracle accounts suffer from high TCO. SAP and Oracle's high TCO is how they can pay at the top of the market for sales reps.

- *A History of Overpromising*: Both SAP and Oracle have a long established history of overpromising what their applications and databases can do often promoting the upper level of functionality that is very rarely reached by customers because of the effort and maintenance overhead in getting their offerings tuned. The result is the "average usage" is far below the potential theoretical usage. So what customers see in the sales phase is not anywhere close to what customers get.

---

29 http://www.brightworkr.com/enterprisesoftwarepolicy/2013/11/09/fiduciary-liability-it-consulting-companies-have-no-fiduciary-duty/

All of this is possible because, under the on-premises model, the application or database **is purchased first and then tested after**. Customers buy cloud services by the SLA not by the sales pitch.

This leads to the next orientation of the book.

A Book That Highlights the Change from the On Premises and the "No Testing Paradigm"

In the past, under the on-premises "no testing" paradigm, software buyers had no way of verifying vendor claims until after they were into the implementation. The time before the Internet was "even better" for sales teams as they could offer the information that suited the needs of the sales team without a good way for customers to validate the information. This had the consequence of placing the sales team in the driver's seat. Sales reps have regaled us with stories of the "good old days." One stated the benefits to us succinctly.

> *"You could tell customers anything you wanted!"*

The on-premises sales time lag had and still has an enormous impact in allocating purchasing dollars to vendors that **make exaggerated promises versus those that exaggerate less**.

In our view, this gap has allowed software failures like Lidl (with SAP) to occur where the project is eventually canceled seven years the project commences, with the customer reverting to their original systems. This is a clear indicator that there were significant variances between what was proposed in the sales stage and what eventually came to light during the implementation.

SAP consultants primarily perform the post-mortems of failed SAP implementations as they provide the bulk of quotations to media outlets. Therefore, they are resistant to point to the exaggerations of SAP sales as a contributing factor to software project failures.

The following quote attests to this.[30]

> *"Apparently one of the biggest problems was a "but this is how we always do it" mentality at Lidl. Changing the software necessitated reassessing almost every process at the company, insiders say. But Lidl's management was not prepared to do that." - **Handelsblatt**

---

30   https://global.handelsblatt.com/companies/lidl-software-flop-germany-digital-failure-950223

However, our question is that if this is true, why did it take Lidl's management **seven years** to figure out that they wanted the SAP system to work the way Lidl worked? Secondly was Lidl told during the sales process that the SAP software could account for nearly all of their requirements "out of the box?" We ask because as we cover in the article The Myth of 90% Out of the Box, SAP and other ERP vendors routinely tell prospects that 90% of their requirements will be met without any customization.[31]

One way or another, Lidl could have tested the SAP software earlier with their processes, money could have been saved. It is less likely that SAP would have been chosen in the first place and then Lidl may have opted to go the custom route and upgrade their existing systems. How can we be so sure that SAP and Oracle make exaggerated claims in the sales process? Well, each of the authors of this book has participated in sales processes where SAP and Oracle have repeatedly made exaggerated claims. We also have the exaggerations stated directly in the website announcement by Lidl's consulting company called KPS as we documented in the article KPS Continues to Keep Promote HANA for Retail for Lidl After Failure.[32]

Now let us contrast the lengthy unverified on-premises sales process that burned Lidl so badly with a "seven-year and 500 million Euro cost for nothing" to the cloud.

- Cloud services customers can test everything for themselves.

- Cloud services customers are able to experiment with free tier accounts to test performance metrics like availability, latency, and data transfer rates.

- Cloud services customers can make their buying decision is based on guaranteed SLAs. For instance, if the nearest region, or content delivery network (CDN), is 3000 miles away, latency will be a significant problem for modest workloads even if the entire DC is dedicated to a single customer and running 100% bare metal.[33] Some cloud buyers no longer spend time evaluating vendor claims or sales pitches. They sign an SLA that guarantees performance metrics. How vendors deliver less of their concern because they can't inspect data centers for themselves. By the time they're ready to sign, they'd have tested and verified everything is live.

---

31 http://www.brightworkr.com/erp/2018/08/30/the-myth-of-erp-being-90-out-of-the-box/

32 http://www.brightworkr.com/sap/2018/08/kps-continues-to-keep-promote-hana-for-retail-for-lidl-after-failure/

33 https://aws.amazon.com/cloudfront/ Cloudfront is AWS's content delivery network.

A Book Designed for Reference-ability

You will notice a very large number of references in this book. We purposely wanted to include quote and references so that everything can be traced back to the source. We also ran into so many quotes that we wanted to use, but which we placed the book as footnotes to have them available to read, so they did not distract from the primary direction of the book.

Somewhere along writing the book, we concluded that we wanted to use the book as a reference for sources ourselves. Having the links included with the context is very useful as it provides the context of each quotation. There are hundreds of sources that we included, and now we have these sources in the overall thread of how it applies to the book's specific subject matter. In fact, we started using it as a reference after we got the book up to around 50,000 words and we think this is the most referenced book (that is pointing out to references) covering the area. This topic has a fantastic number of interrelated topics, and without a repository, it's difficult to keep it all straight. One of the risks in this area is that one begins to get attached to something (a tool, service, fill in the blank) while another selection or way of using the item is not properly illuminated. And if we find this valuable, we think readers will also find them valuable. Therefore, also consider using the book as a resource as this book can save you a lot of time in researching related topics. This book is a great starting point to jump into a large number of more specific areas.

For Kindle customers, Kindle has a great search function which we have used in our previous research to great effect.

Honest and Realistic Information About Leveraging Cloud for On-Premises Environments

Cloud has been presented as simplifying IT environments. However a decade and a half in, this has proven to be not true.

This is highlighted in the following quotation from Constellation Research.

> *"The cloud has not simplified IT for almost all organizations because they are operating on a fluid automation pane that includes the public cloud and on-premises computing resources. Business priorities, timing, and write-down cycles all determine at what time what load may be moved to the public cloud or should remain on-premises. Changes in executive management often result in a shifting workload mix (for instance, due to software-as-a-service, or SaaS, portfolio changes) that affects the overall computing portfolio. A greater diversity*

in workloads and new next-gen application use cases create more heterogeneity and increase the complexity of IT operations."[34]

Nothing can be simplified if the information provided about that topic is inaccurate. This book has been written by an entity focused on research. That means that the book is filled with what we believe to be true, without any consideration for what sounds good, what makes the most readers feel good, what promotes a vendor, IaaS provider, etc.

Who is This Book For?

Usually, a book that covers IT can specify if it is more directed towards decision makers, or programmers or project managers. However, for this book, it's difficult for us to see who this book isn't for. If of course there is an interest in cloud and the reader works in an SAP or Oracle environment, the book will be of interest to anyone. Top level decision makers can breeze past the more technical aspects of the book, and technical resources can breeze past the method, and financial issues brought up in the book. Our approach has been to write a book that weaves together all the aspects as moving to the cloud is an integrated decision. Therefore we see the book as of universal interest to those interested in the subject of cloud and SAP or Oracle. This book is targeted towards people that have worked in SAP and Oracle environments but want to access AWS and Google Cloud for may capabilities that cannot be obtained from SAP or Oracle. The book is focused on weaving together many disparate areas, from the various cloud and on-premises components that can be used, to how the on-premises model employed by SAP and Oracle works, to pricing and financial implications and much more. The one thing the book is not is a deep dive into any one particular technical area.

Now let us jump into chapter one.

---

34 https://www.oracle.com/assets/next-gen-enterprise-computing-5104870.pdf

Chapter 1: What are Oracle and SAP Really Investing in Cloud?

Both Oracle and SAP have tried to argue that they have made major investments in the cloud. Let us take a closer look at these claims. SAP's lack of investment in the cloud has been well documented, one source being the book SAP Nation 2.0.[35]

- SAP's Steve Lucas stated that they were not going to open their application to the cloud as it would be a "race to the bottom."[36] [37] But then SAP introduced their multi-cloud strategy as covered in the article SAP's Multicloud Announcement, where they essentially changed strategy from proposing that they would not open their solutions to the other cloud providers, to doing a 180 and stating their solutions would be to being complimentary with AWS, Google Cloud and Azure.[38] Currently, SAP Cloud connects to AWS, Google Cloud and Azure.

- Oracle, on the other hand, has promoted its investment into the cloud and to directly challenging AWS. As we will discuss further on in detail, Oracle has had to answer pointed questions as to why for a company which such enormous resources their investment in the cloud has been so small compared to the major cloud providers.

Our conclusion is that neither Oracle nor SAP have any particular technology interest in the cloud. (Of course they have a very real monetary interest in the cloud, but this is to

---

35 https://www.amazon.com/SAP-Nation-2-0-empire-disarray-ebook/dp/B013F5BKJQ

36 https://diginomica.com/2015/12/09/saps-steve-lucas-on-why-hana-beats-oracle-ibm-microsoft-and-aws/

37 Steve Lucas' statements around the cloud in 2015 are so comical they deserve their own laugh track. In 2015, he stated the following. *"We built our own data centres for the HANA Cloud Platform, this is really important. The reason that we have not put the HANA Cloud Platform on something like AWS, is because AWS doesn't adhere to all the global privacy laws where we operate. We actually own and operate our own data centres. That's incredibly critical. The HANA Cloud Platform is not meant to compete with AWS, we are not in a race to the bottom. It's not our goal. Our goal is to provide a business oriented platform-as-a-service that integrates with the world of machines, with IoT interfaces."* - https://diginomica.com/2015/12/09/saps-steve-lucas-on-why-hana-beats-oracle-ibm-microsoft-and-aws/

38 http://www.brightworkr.com/sap/2017/05/best-understand-saps-multicloud-announcement/

defend their on premises ecosystems.) Rather they rightly viewed the cloud as a threat to their account control within their enormous respective account bases. And this is why both companies have a history of being so dismissive to cloud, particularly in the cloud's early period.

This video from 2009 shows Larry Ellison getting a lot of laughs applying a straw horse logical fallacy where he implies cloud is simply hosting.

In this amusing rant, it is difficult to critique the performance. However he misses on the shared resource aspect of cloud, the multi tenancy of cloud, the sever-ability of cloud terms. Instead Larry prefers to focus on arguments that were not particularly prevalent at time related to the cloud having "no hardware".[39]

Moreover, nine years later, the Oracle Cloud is a non-factor on Oracle accounts. At the time of this video in 2009, while Oracle and SAP were "running down" (a bit of deliberate FUD perhaps?) cloud, AWS, and Google Cloud were investing in their offerings. Larry thought he and Oracle could ride the on-premises model forever. Now after doing little aside from cranking up the cloud marketing machine for over a decade, Oracle is lost in making progress in its cloud. In September 2018, Thomas Kurian, the head of Oracle Cloud stepped down. Thomas Kurian's exit from Oracle (it is at least strongly rumored) was due to his view that existing Oracle customers should be able to choose which IaaS they wanted to run their software on, which conflicted with Larry Ellison's vision. After all this time, and so little progress, Oracle is still trying to figure out its strategy, and appears headed in an unsustainable direction with respect to the cloud.

---

39   https://www.youtube.com/watch?v=KmXJSeMaoTY

The Threat to SAP and Oracle from the Cloud

How is cloud a threat to both Oracle and SAP? Well, cloud **naturally undermines** the on-premises assumptions around which both these vendors developed their business model. That is everything from their internal skills to their contracts and internal incentives. Cloud companies are not configured like Oracle or SAP and would impose a great deal of unwanted change if they had to adapt. Change, particularly when one is so financially successful doing things for decades one way, is historically put off as long as possible.

Cloud also threatens their consulting partners that **are also based around the on-premises model**. Once the cloud is employed, the number of consulting resources drops and hence consulting revenues. This is a primary reason why SAP and Oracle partners fought the cloud. Behind closed doors they still fight the cloud, although they can't admit it publicly. SAP and Oracle and their consulting partners would like to move with the times, but the problem is they want to move with the times while keeping their inefficient and dated methods of operation, and their margins, perhaps even increasing them as we will see later in the book. We have reviewed internal SAP consulting company slides that promoted the idea that cloud would help them increase their revenues. Perhaps this consulting company does not fully appreciate how the cloud works, but the cloud **reduces** the number of resources required for a project. Moreover, consulting companies function by the following formula.

Deloitte Revenues = The Number of Resources on the Project x The Number of Weeks on the Project

Cloud reduces both of the inputs.

Fewer resources are required, and they are required for a shorter period of time. This is **not good news** for consulting companies. Senior members of SAP and Oracle consulting partners have stated to the authors that they would **never** recommend the cloud.

Why?

Because if they did, they would not be able to staff a sufficient number of resources, to bring in enough money, to maintain their position in their companies.

The marketing these same companies do around the cloud looks much different. In public communications, SAP, Oracle, Accenture, Deloitte, etc.. are "all in on the cloud."

However, what do all of these entities really want, and how do they plan to react to the cloud?

It is all very simple. They will superficially promote the cloud while keeping everything else the same, which means defending their on-premises revenue model. If a customer is utilizing entities that only have a history in on-premises software, the likelihood that they will benefit from real cloud efficiency rapidly shrinks. There are **no precedents** where entities passively accept lower revenues without fighting that change. As we will discuss, the fact that so many people are still employed in IT consulting is evidence that we are still early in the cloud transformation of IT.

SAP and Oracle can only slow the process and they must do what they can to either co-opt cloud (i.e., pretend they are more involved in it than they are) or adopt it. So far they have chosen to co-opt the cloud rather than become true cloud vendors.

What is the Difference Between Real Cloud and Faux Cloud?

While SAP and Oracle and their partners dislike the arrival of cloud, they are financially incentivized to "pretend to move to the cloud." They have spent most of their efforts trying to cloud wash or to co-opt the cloud, which means to miscommunicate either their on-premises revenues or support revenues as the cloud. SAP and Oracle will tell Wall Street anything they want to hear. If cats are popular on Wall Street, SAP and Oracle loooove cats. If its dogs….well you get the picture. The fact is that most of what SAP and Oracle offer customers is a faux cloud, as we covered in the article How to Understand Oracle as Faux Cloud Versus AWS.[40]

We have investigated true cloud versus faux cloud in depth for several clients. What we discovered was shocking to us. The vast majority of notably bigger companies that say they are cloud/SaaS are not cloud. Salesforce, a company that started as cloud, now has restrictive cancellation clauses and other account control terms & conditions. Cloud computing has a specific meaning and a particular set of requirements. While reviewing all the marketing literature, it is very tempting to forget what the actual definition of cloud, which is why we always refer back to earlier research we performed on this exact topic.

Cloud is frequently diluted to mean the service merely is off premises. So, let us take this opportunity to get clear on what the cloud is, and what features are necessary for an offering to be considered cloud.

The following eight conditions must be met for a service to be cloud.

1. One code base
2. No customization
3. Vendor provides the hosting (i.e., the vendor provides and maintains all infrastructure for the application)
4. Flexible cancellation
5. Published and transparent pricing
6. Using a cloud salesforce
7. Using self-guided demo systems
8. Vendor-provided Software maintenance

One code base is what allows for multi-tenancy. This means that multiple customers use the application logic and in some cases the same database. Multi-tenancy flows directly into the topic of no customizations. No customization is necessary because if different customers were allowed to make customizations, then the application could no longer be multi-tenant.

To provide the IaaS capabilities, vendors invest in their own data centers. However, as we will cover further on in the book, only a few companies are interested in making these investments. If we look at SAP, while they tout cloud, in many cases they have other entities

---

40   http://www.brightworkr.com/saaseconomy/2018/04/09/oracle-as-faux-cloud-versus-aws/

hosting their applications and databases. In the past, this was more commonly a consulting partner like CapGemini. Also if your hosting is with Deloitte or Accenture, that have shown no cloud true capabilities, even to manage multitenancy one has to wonder about the effectiveness of this strategy.

Definition: This is the first time we have used the term multitenancy. Multitenancy means more than one "tenant," the tenant, in this case, being a customer. Multitenancy is critical to understanding cloud. Multitenancy can be considered the core characteristic of the cloud. It allows resources and costs to be shared across a pool of users. It means that in the case of database multitenancy, the data from many customers can be kept in a single database instance, and the database can be maintained at very low overhead and high economies of scale. At the application level, it means that updates can be implemented for all users at once. We will discuss multitenancy in depth further in the book.

Think about it in these terms, does anyone go to Deloitte or Accenture or CapGemini for cloud IaaS if they are not pushed there by SAP? This appears more geared toward **giving business to partners** rather than doing something that is in the customer's best interests.

In summary, it seems that SAP is not all that interested in investing in data centers. This raises questions about how a vendor like SAP deals with third parties hosting their software.

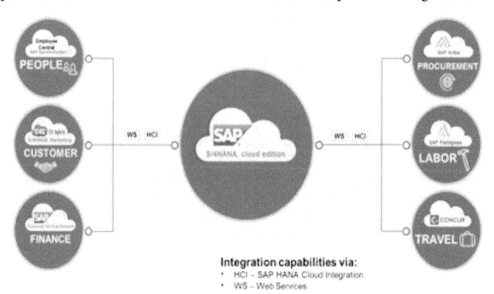

SAP's marketing materials show many cloud acquired applications. SAP's marketing investment into cloud is certainly large. However, SAP maintains what has been described by others as a

"puny" data center investment and capability. SAP's acquired application typically suffer from habitual data center underinvestment.

This is explained in the following quotation.

> "There is another concern about SAP's S/4 public cloud. The data center in Sankt LeonRot Germany, while close to SAP's impressive Walldorf headquarters, does not itself inspire much confidence. It has been called puny and primitive compared to the data centers of infrastructure as a service providers like Amazon, Microsoft Azure and Rackspace. Indeed competitors like Info and Unit4 are using infrastructure-as-a-service (using data centers from Amazon and Microsoft respectively) rather than trying to compete with their scale."

> "Even where SAP offers public cloud options-for example with its SuccessFactors and Concur customers-- the individual data centers are undersized and often supported by co-location vendors around the globe. SAP's about 82 million cloud users are fragmented across products and across geographies. Little attempt appears to have been made to date, to consolidate data centers that support them. While compliance requirements dictate regional diversity in such facilities, they are further reminders of Balkanization in the SAP economy."[41] [42]

Most of SAP's database and applications revenue is from on-premises applications. S/4HANA is an internally developed application. There is an on-premises and a cloud version of S/4HANA. Yet out of 1500 "live" implementations we estimate around 10% are S/4HANA Cloud. On quarterly calls, SAP does everything it can to distract from this reality. The reality is that outside of the acquired applications, SAP does not have cloud application business of any significance.

The cloud customer should have a month-to-month contract with the software vendor or service provider which allows for flexible cancellation. This relates to preventing lock-in, although it should also be acknowledged that some applications have more lock-in than others. ERP systems, by their nature, have more lock-in than other applications, like CRM applications which are far easier to switch between. Although regardless of the application, there is some stickiness factor that reduces the actualized flexibility in switching to a different system.

---

41 https://www.amazon.com/SAP-Nation-2-0-empire-disarray-ebook/dp/B013F5BKJQ
42 We use this quotation later in the book as well. Out of enormous numbers of articles by SAP and SAP partners promoting SAP's cloud capabilities this is one of the few that exist that describe any investigation on the topic.

AWS and Google Cloud offer highly flexible cancellation terms. It is the ability to bring up and bring down services and to pause services. For example, we can close down any one of our AWS or Google Cloud services at any time. The services are billed in hours or minutes or second or millisecond. When the service is turned off, the billing no longer runs. This is not a "month-to-month" cancellation capability, but an **immediate** canceling capability. The account stays active at AWS and Google Cloud, but that is separate from the services that are billing or not billing as the case may be. We have become used to this type of flexibility, but it is easy to forget how unusual this is in the history of enterprise software.

SAP and Oracle are not experienced in working this type of business model.

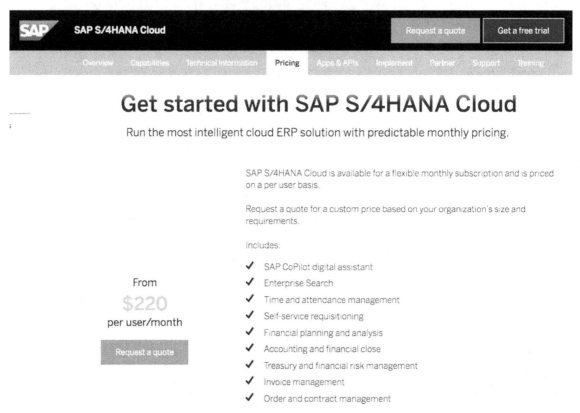

SAP has only very recently begun to offer month to month subscriptions to their products. We reviewed this same pricing page in June of 2018, and at that time the price was listed as monthly, but it had a yearly term. The vast majority of SAP's products have secretive pricing. We were not able to verify if a monthly term applied to S/4HANA Cloud if a discount was applied. SAP responded that they would only answer that question if we provided a customer name.

Clearly, SAP is having to respond to market pressures. SAP could have done this years ago, but they didn't. SAP is being forced to adjust to the cloud; and these changes are being fought tooth and nail by SAP (and by Oracle). And, as our example of SAP's unwillingness to verify the interaction between a discounted price and the monthly cancellation term, often when one gets into the details, it turns out that the promised cloud terms are not cloud at all.

Even now SAP and Oracle operate on the on-premises model where projects are made about software capabilities, usage, implementation difficulty, product maturity, and other product features without testing the item. Some might respond to this by contradicting the statement and pointing to proof of concepts. However, proof of concepts are run by the vendors. Vendors run the POC to "prove the concept" not to "test the concept." The POC intends to convince the customer to purchase the software. It is not at all like when the customer tests the software themselves. By contrast, cloud puts the customer in the "driver's seat" rather than trying to control the process of evaluation.

On the topic of the necessity for a self-guided demo system, generally, on-premises application sales teams tightly control exposure to the application. The prospect is only allowed to see a demo of the system for short periods of time. Specialized resources called pre-sales consultants to walk prospects through a demo. This approach does not provide or allow a thorough evaluation of the usability of the system. Demonstration consultants, who are very familiar with the application, can do many things that average users often cannot. Alternatively, when cloud vendors provide access to a cloud demo environment, the experience becomes self-guided. This gives the prospect more control and allows them to understand whether the application is a good fit for them in a shorter period.

Published pricing is a fundamental feature of cloud providers. For AWS and Google Cloud, they chose to outsource much of the pre-sales effort to its customers. They do this by doing what was in the past unthinkable; that is by publishing their pricing and making it virtually non-negotiable. In doing so, AWS and Google Cloud remove an enormous obstacle for customers to adopt their services. Also, then customers can begin testing the capabilities and the cost without even needing to, in many cases, interact with AWS or Google Cloud representatives.

As any reader of this book will likely know, SAP and Oracle have unpublished pricing. Just a few pages ago we showed an example of published pricing for SAP's S/4HANA, but this is new, in part faux cloud pricing, and most of SAP's product catalog is still secret. The same applies to Oracle. And when we say secret, we don't just mean unpublished. We mean secret. On the first page of SAP's pricing page, it states that sharing the pricing spreadsheet could expose the person sharing the pricing sheet to legal jeopardy.

Interesting isn't it? According to SAP, its pricing is protected information. Furthermore, if one is in possession of this pricing spreadsheet, the recipient has certain responsibilities.

"This SAP Software Price List may only be distributed by an employee, agent, or representative of SAP AG / SAP subsidiary. If you have received it by any other means, you are hereby notified to return it to SAP AG to the attention of the Contracts Manager."

Oh yes, a company that writes these types of clauses around its price list is TRULY ready for the cloud!

Both SAP and Oracle's pricing is so complicated that sales reps for each company seem to spend at least as much time working out pricing as focusing on technology. For example, we had to completely revamp the SAP pricing sheet before we were able to use it because as it is originally given to salespeople and pricing consultants it is extremely difficult to use. Secondly, even if the pricing sheet is obtained, there are so many discounts that it the pricing can't be known with certainty. This applies equally to Oracle. We cover this in more detail in the section Why the Price Paid for Oracle is Often Unknowable.

It even goes even beyond this. If you go through an official SAP representative, there are still frequently problems getting a firm price. At clients that we advise, SAP sales often postpone giving out pricing even when the customer specifically asks for a price. For some reason, the pricing has to be run up to the higher levels in SAP….or at least that is what customers are told. It is quite odd when you can't even get a price for weeks because of a large number of behind the scenes mechinazations and scheming that have to take place. However, this is the world that SAP and Oracle have created for their customers. And these are the type of things people outside of the field don't find out because it is not the sort of thing that is published.

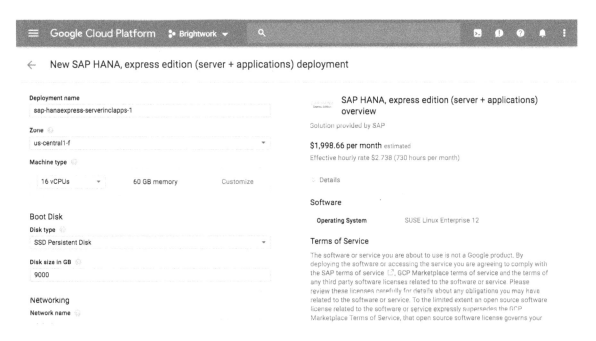

*AWS and Google Cloud have estimates per configuration. The example we have in this screenshot is for SAP HANA, express edition. This for the HANA database that can be run without a base edition, platform edition or enterprise edition license. SAP does this to encourage development on HANA. Because the only charge here is from Google Cloud, the pricing is transparent. However, as soon as one switches to the SAP HANA "Bring-Your-Own-License," while the **hosting costs are the same**, the overall pricing immediately becomes secret. In that case, neither AWS or Google Cloud have anything to do with the pricing of the license. That license pricing is set by SAP, and now "the games begin," as one must work through an archaic and time-consuming process called the on-premises sales model.[43]*

The original cloud vendors followed a low-cost distribution and sales model. This means employing fewer salespeople, focusing less on relationships and on manipulating relationships. It means cloud salespeople are closer in many ways to presales resources than sales resources. This **dramatically lowers the cost of sale**, and it also reduces the amount

---

43　We (Brightwork Research & Analysis) has the largest amount of research on HANA. Our conclusion is that HANA will underperform open source databases available on AWS or Google Cloud. Concerning Oracle, PostgreSQL is an excellent substitute for the Oracle DB. AWS and Google Cloud present a severe problem for many software vendors. Through the easy of choice and deployment, AWS and Google Cloud are exposing the fact that open source alternatives are in many cases better options than the commercial offerings. This is more restricted to infrastructure items presently, but we predict this will increasingly grow into applications in the future. SAP and Oracle do not like the way that AWS and Google Cloud are educating customers. The servers the that run the web run Linux. Not Windows Server. The wave of open source is becoming too obvious to ignore.

of inaccurate information being communicated to customers. This also happens to be how AWS and Google Cloud operate.

When considering this context, while SAP and Oracle declared they were moving more to the cloud, **they did not reduce their sales force**.

SAP and Oracle are both highly aggressive sales cultures with vast numbers of salespeople. Oracle employs 35,000 at last count. That should tell anyone who is paying attention that SAP and Oracle are not migrating to the cloud anywhere near as fast as they are saying.[44] If a company is following a cloud model, the need for salespeople steeply declines, as the primary means of interaction is through the website, not through phone calls and on-site visits. (And the skills of the salespeople also change.) If one compares the revenue to employees in AWS and Google Cloud versus SAP and Oracle, AWS and Google have a higher ratio or revenues to employees.

Cloud began with the cloud vendors providing the maintenance. This means that this is taken off of the customer's plate. Under SaaS, the customer only uses the application; they don't worry about the infrastructure, database, updates, etc. The updates are supposed to be so automatic and well managed that the customer does not notice the update being made. An excellent example of this is Gmail, which is a cloud application that most people use. Gmail has gone through many updates, but Gmail users do not observe the changes occurring. The story with AWS and Google Cloud is a bit more complicated because customers are not using AWS and Google Cloud just for applications (SaaS), but for their development and infrastructure (PaaS, IaaS). But this applies very readily to AWS RDS and Google Cloud SQL, where much of the maintenance of these databases is managed for the customer, and the customer can focus on using the database.

The following quotation explains this from Google.

> *"Let Google manage your database, so you can focus on your applications. Cloud SQL is perfect for Wordpress sites, e-commerce applications, CRM tools, geospatial applications, and any other application that is compatible with MySQL or PostgreSQL."*[45]

---

44 That is in addition to reviewing the sales numbers that were associated with the cloud for both vendors – even though those values are "enhanced" for perception purposes.

45 https://cloud.google.com/sql/

Getting Real on SAP & Oracle's Cloud

Here are the eight cloud criteria, which we will list again:

1. One code base

2. No customization

3. Vendor provides the hosting (i.e., the vendor provides and maintains all infrastructure for the application)

4. Flexible cancellation

5. Published and transparent pricing

6. Using a cloud salesforce

7. Using self-guided demo systems

8. Vendor-provided Software maintenance.

It should be easy to see that SAP & Oracle do not meet any of these criteria. This may be surprising to many readers, but it is only surprising in comparison to SAP and Oracle's claimed adherence to the cloud.

Larry Ellison once commented on the topic of cloud computing:

> *"The interesting thing about Cloud computing is that we've redefined Cloud computing to include everything that we already do."*

And...

> *"We'll make Cloud computing announcements because, you know, if orange is the new pink, we'll make orange blouses. I mean, I'm not gonna fight this thing ... well, maybe we'll do an ad. Uh, I don't understand what we would do differently in the light of Cloud computing, other than market ... you know, change the wording on some of our ads."*[46]

Yes, one can see how dedicated Larry Ellison is to the cloud.

---

46 http://www.cbronline.com/news/cloud/he-said-what-5-things-larry-ellison-actually-said-about-cloud-45633

Hasso Plattner is also on record critiquing the cloud and stating that most of SAP's customers would **not be interested in cloud**.[47] Thus, one wonders why Wall Street has been so accepting of the 180 degree change in position on the part of SAP and Oracle. Except for a few cracks here and here, such as the response to Oracle changing its reporting in June or 2018 in an obvious attempt to obscure their extremely weak cloud growth, Wall Street appears to have bought SAP and Oracle's cloud story hook line and sinker.[48]

A recent case brought by the City of Sunrise Florida Firefighter Fund, a pension fund, against Oracle for exaggerating their cloud revenues brings some of these issues to the fore.

> *"In truth, Oracle drove sales of cloud products using threats and extortive tactics. The use of such tactics concealed the lack of real demand for Oracle's cloud services, making the growth unsustainable (and ultimately driving away customers). Among other things, the Company threatened current customers with "audits" of their use of the Company's non-cloud software licenses unless the customers agreed to shift their business to Oracle cloud programs."[49]*

There are public examples of Oracle offering "audit or purchase cloud" options to customers. This is where the expense of the audit is used to coerce a purchase.

The following quotation regarding Southern California Edison explains how this works.

> *"Within the past year, Oracle signaled it might audit Southern California Edison. As an alternative, Oracle offered Edison a deal worth $21 million a year that included $4 million to $5 million of Oracle cloud services, said one person briefed about the discussions. Edison said it did not "see the ROI"—return on investment— from such a deal. It decided to instead pay several million dollars to cover any potential shortfall Oracle might find in an audit of its existing licenses. A Southern California Edison spokeswoman declined to comment."[50]*

Certainly there would be no ROI to $5 million in Oracle cloud, but the ROI is not being audited!

---

47 Hasso has tried to obscure this opposition by supporting a "private cloud." The concept of the VPC now used to make public clouds protected was unknown to Hasso. Apparently it is still unknown to Hasso as SAP Cloud still does not use VPC (to be discussed later in the book). Brightwork Research & Analysis has read a very large number of Hasso Platner's statements and books, and when Hasso makes technology projections, they have low accuracy. Although they can't be considered purely forecasts, and they are always in line with SAP's revenue objectives.

48 https://www.wsj.com/articles/oracle-results-beat-revenue-and-earnings-targets-1529444704

49 http://www.brightworkr.com/saaseconomy/2018/08/13/oracle-sued-for-making-false-claims-about-cloud-growth/

50 https://www.theinformation.com/articles/oracles-aggressive-sales-tactics-are-backfiring-with-customers

The toymaker Mattel received a similar offer from SAP.

> *"Mattel, a longtime Oracle customer with around 28,000 employees, was recently warned it could be audited. Oracle offered Mattel a $20 million to $25 million deal that included cloud services. Similar to Edison, Mattel decided to pay several million dollars to ensure it was complying with Oracle's licensing terms on existing software and agreed to a small deal involving Oracle cloud services, as well as to continue its relationship with rival Microsoft Azure. Mattel told Oracle that the software giant was "not strategic" as a cloud partner, said an Oracle employee."*

This is reinforced by a company with quite a bit of exposure to Oracle customers.

> *"I don't have to take off my shoes to count the number of House of Brick customers I am aware of that have actually implemented anything in the Oracle Cloud. On the other hand (er, other foot), I'd probably need a bunch of people with shoes off to count the number of customers with Oracle cloud credits on the shelf. This is Oracle Cloud inventory customers were compelled to purchase in order to receive additional on-prem software at the same discount level they used to get."[51]*

> *"I am not at all compelled by Ellison's announcement a month ago about how he's now got a bigger, better deal and will best AWS' performance. He'd have to make it free to compete with the price of all the cloud credits sitting on licensee's shelves. Even with the software costs sunk, these licensees are not implementing their Oracle Cloud credits. Oracle has not produced an implemented market share anywhere near the scale that induced VMware to strike a deal with AWS."[52]*

> *"Sometimes however, you may have a rep say something like "I heard that you are on the list for an audit. If you make this purchase, I can probably make that go away." Not surprisingly, rejecting their proposal will likely trigger an audit. Once we began our assessment, we quickly identified tens of millions of dollars of unneeded expense that could be trimmed from their Oracle budget. The client was thrilled, and their right sizing of expenses was validated when they received an audit notice from Oracle.*

> *Avoiding an audit with Oracle is not necessarily a good thing. As was the case with our client in this story, if you are not being audited there is a good chance you are paying Oracle too much money and that is why they are leaving you alone."[53]*

---

51 http://houseofbrick.com/will-this-latest-suit-against-oracle-ever-see-a-court-hearing/
52 http://houseofbrick.com/an-opinion-on-oracle-open-worlds-single-message-cloud/
53 http://houseofbrick.com/curses-foiled-again-audit-defense/

And reinforced by this comment on an article from Slashdot.

> *"Oracle, in the meantime, is on a mission to push existing customers to their weird and overdue cloud thing. It started about 4 years ago, and their tactics started with stripping their own salesforce of commissions on on-prem solutions. Then price hikes. Now, I hear, auditing. (We've since cancelled all our licenses so luckily that's not one of my problems anymore).*
>
> *As to why people stick and swear by Oracle - Exadata offers support for insanely bad queries and still manages to make a pretty good job running them. This is a good solutions for companies with incompetent, outsourced dev teams that don't mind paying for the licenses. But the number of such companies is going down and Oracle must see the writing on the wall - they are going the IBM way of being relegated to niche solutions, US gov't contracts and the like. And by looking at IBM numbers, it's not exactly a pleasant place to be."*[54]

AWS and Google Cloud have a history in the cloud that SAP and Oracle does not. All customers have is vague promises from SAP and Oracle that they will change and that they have big plans. These are all projections of what they will do. And after over a decade of making these types of statements, the evidence is that they are not becoming more cloud, and they are also not reconfiguring their internal organizational design to become so in the future. Even publishing pricing information is beyond them.

How Prepared are SAP and Oracle to Live with Cloud Margins?

There will be massive internal impediments to change, including the fact that both SAP and Oracle are internally incentivized around the on-premise software model. Furthermore, if SAP and Oracle were to race to the cloud, they would notice their margins quickly eroding. They would need to **lay off a sizable percentage of their workforce**, and the cloud implementations would cause massive dislocations in their consulting partners. As soon as that happened, their consulting partners cease recommending their software. Wall Street is quite confused on this issue. Here are some critical truths about the cloud.

- The highest margin software vendors are on premises vendors like SAP and Oracle, **not cloud vendors**.

- The largest cloud application vendor is Salesforce, and they have not been profitable.

---

54   https://developers.slashdot.org/story/18/05/27/1925236/oracles-aggressive-sales-tactics-are-backfiring-with-customers

- AWS is one of the few cloud entities that has been profitable, but competition is coming, and most analysts predict naturally that AWS's margins will decline.

- Because of how they report cloud revenues it's very difficult to determine the profitability of Google Cloud and Azure (for Microsoft). However, it is broadly thought that the profitability for both is low. We have contacts within Microsoft that tell us Azure is not profitable and is a loss leader for Microsoft.

We predict that SAP and Oracle won't change or won't be able to adapt fast enough. The changes for both of them will be wrenching, and they won't be undertaken voluntarily. All three authors of this book are all in on AWS and Google Cloud as the future, and think SAP and Oracle customers should be evaluating how to incorporate these entities into their IT strategy. Increasingly when we analyze options available for SAP and Oracle customers, we end up looking to see if AWS or Google Cloud have something we can leverage. There are just so many ways to unlock value in SAP and Oracle customers.

With all of this background in mind, let us dive into one of the "killer apps" for AWS and Google Cloud, which is their managed database services.

Real Versus Faux Marketplaces

One important area of distinction between AWS and Google Cloud and SAP and Oracle are their marketplaces. Marketplaces for vendors and cloud service providers are where users go to add components to their cloud.

Let us review the following marketplace screenshot from SAP.

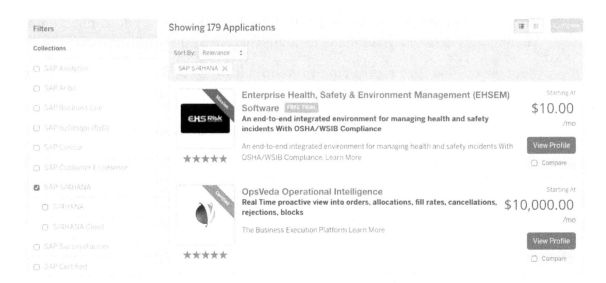

This is the SAP App Center, which is SAP's marketplace. It is meant to conjure images of the Apple App Store or the Google Play, the Android store. However, these applications cannot be directly installed on SAP, therefore the App Center is misleading. This "marketplace" is nothing like what it appears to be, which is a directory of pluggable applications.

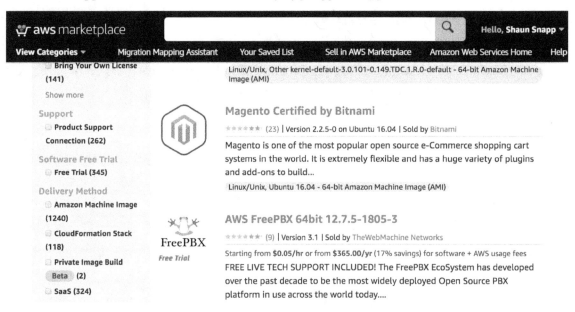

By contrast, this is the AWS Marketplace. The AWS Marketplace is filled with offerings categorized into infrastructure software, developer tools, and business software. Unlike the SAP App Center, these applications can be installed on AWS.

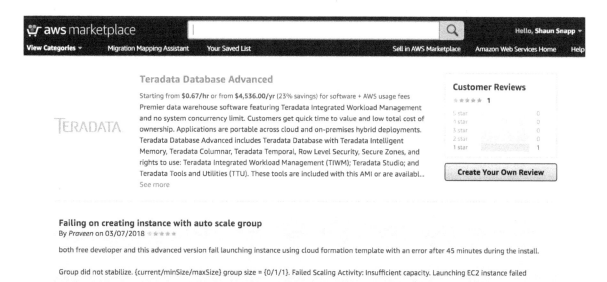

Failing on creating instance with auto scale group
By *Praveen* on 03/07/2018 ★★★★

both free developer and this advanced version fail launching instance using cloud formation template with an error after 45 minutes during the install.

Group did not stabilize. {current/minSize/maxSize} group size = {0/1/1}. Failed Scaling Activity: Insufficient capacity. Launching EC2 instance failed

As with the AWS store, reviews are allowed. And apparently they allow negative reviews, which is a good indicator of accuracy (web entities like G2Crowd may have a few negative reviews, but the overall score always ends up being 4 or higher).[55]

AWS and Google have become so popular that the major vendors have to provide offerings for them or risk losing out on market share. Teradata has done exceptionally well under the on-premises model. We doubt they really want to be on AWS's marketplace and face competition from open source offerings in such an easily comparable way. However, they don't want to lose out on AWS's customers. Teradata has also seen the future and has migrated their focus to the cloud. It turns out leveraging cloud services greatly enhances data warehousing, Teradata's core market, which is something we will cover later in the book.

---

55   This topic is covered in the article Why G2Crowd Has False Information on S4HANA. - http://www.brightworkr.com/saphana/2017/12/18/g2crowd-false-information-s4hana/

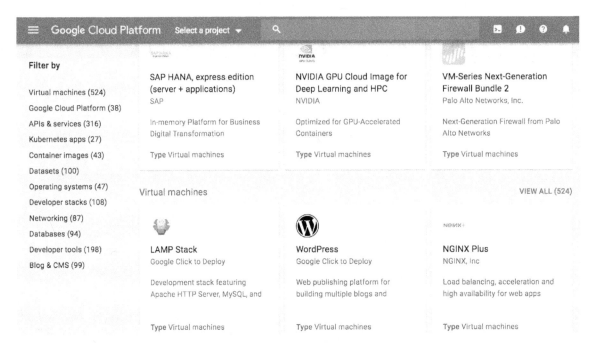

*The Google Cloud Platform Marketplace is another example of easy to implement components. None of these items is brochure ware. They are **immediately available** for installation.*

The ability to immediately install components on a marketplace is a critical distinction between SAP and Oracle's marketplaces and AWS and Google Cloud's marketplaces. AWS and Google Cloud's marketplaces are designed to get you to spin up the service as quickly as possible. There is no one you have to talk to, there is no back, and forth on secret pricing, there is no waiting while price estimates are run up different hierarchies and where customers are told: "we want to get you the very best price." Instead, the customer just begins using the service. Usually, a tiny instance is activated for testing, and the billing usually is small until later in the process when the instance is grown.

All of this translates to the usage is immediate. Or that is close to immediate as the service does of course have to install on the account, which is normally in just a few minutes. This is fantastic, and a genuine innovation in the industry. The efficiency differences between this way and the old on-premises way is stark. And not all the cloud providers have mastered this equally, as will be explored as this book progresses.

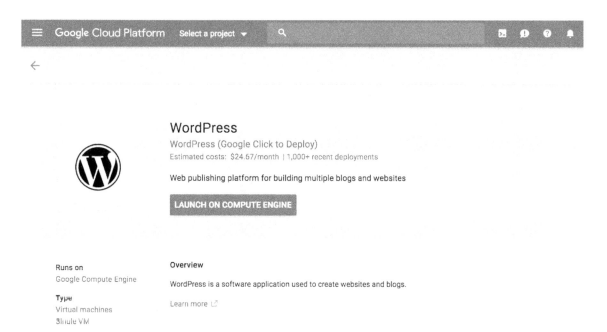

As soon as the item is selected, the cost is estimated, and it can be immediately launched. This is WordPress, which is a web application, but notice, it is launched as its virtual machine. This is only one "flavor" of WordPress. Google Cloud offers several other WordPress flavors. Each one a bit different and one of them likely to fit the needs of a customer. Each can be tested to see which is the best fit for the customer's requirements.

Both companies are offering new additions and improvements all the time. Regarding innovation, there is just no comparison between AWS and Google Cloud and these two vendors. AWS by itself far exceeds the year to year change as well as improvement offered by both SAP and Oracle. AWS and Google Cloud spend far less as a percentage of their revenues on sales and marketing. Instead they a far higher percentage of their revenues to development and building infrastructure. You could tell this without even looking at the financial statements of these four companies. Interested in seeing the breath of this innovation as it appears to the user?

Let us review AWS's services.

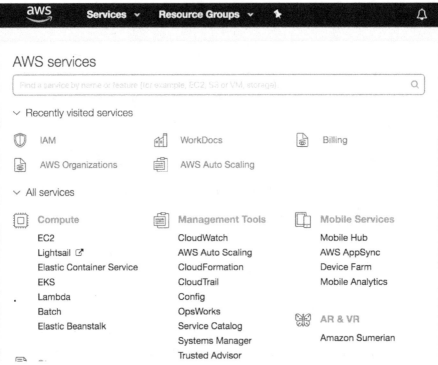

AWS's service catalog shows the amazing breadth of AWS's offerings. This catalog can be searched from this screen, or from Google.

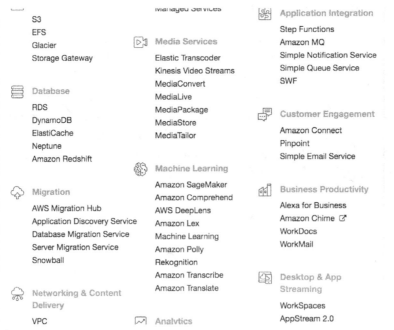

This is the second page.

Database Migration Service	Amazon Lex	WorkDocs
Server Migration Service	Machine Learning	WorkMail
Snowball	Amazon Polly	
	Rekognition	
	Amazon Transcribe	**Desktop & App**
Networking & Content	Amazon Translate	**Streaming**
Delivery		WorkSpaces
VPC	**Analytics**	AppStream 2.0
CloudFront	Athena	
Route 53	EMR	**Internet of Things**
API Gateway	CloudSearch	IoT Core
Direct Connect	Elasticsearch Service	IoT 1-Click
	Kinesis	IoT Device Management
Developer Tools	QuickSight	IoT Analytics
CodeStar	Data Pipeline	Greengrass
CodeCommit	AWS Glue	Amazon FreeRTOS
CodeBuild		IoT Device Defender
CodeDeploy	**Security, Identity &**	
CodePipeline	**Compliance**	**Game Development**
Cloud9	IAM	Amazon GameLift
X-Ray	Cognito	
	Secrets Manager	
	GuardDuty	
	Inspector	

No one can keep up with AWS's services and new service introductions!

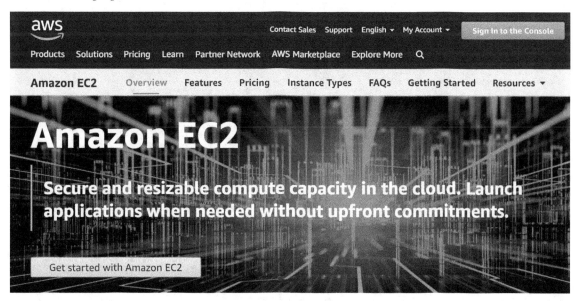

Once a service is found, it can be activated by selecting the "Get Started with...." button. If you are logged in, it opens immediately. If not, all that is required is to sign in to the console.

AWS has so many services it will often lead to information overload.

Welcome to the anxiety of being a developer trying to keep up with all the changes that constantly come from the options that can be deployed in cloud.[56]

---

56   http://turnoff.us/geek/good-night-programmers/

Conclusion

This chapter was designed to illuminate the reader that SAP and Oracle are not really cloud vendors. Eventually they will be, but they will be pulled to the cloud kicking and screaming. And by the time they make it, they will have lost much of their market position.

They are presently somewhere in the third or fourth stage of grief, which is bargaining and depression.

- Stage 1: Anger

- Stage 2: Denial

- Stage 3: Bargaining

- Stage 4: Depression

- Stage 5: Acceptance

At the time of this publication SAP and Oracle are pretending to the world that they are something they are not. And there is certainly plenty of gas (and money) left in the tank in the on-premises model. SAP and Oracle have demonstrated that they will ride the on-premises model until its end, which is really not so much an end per say, but a greatly reduced part of the overall market (mainframes are still with us after all), and that will lead to new entities taking their place. And those new entities will be cloud.

AWS and Google Cloud will be two of them. In the next chapter, we will cover one of the most popular uses of AWS and Google Cloud, which is to move on-premises databases out to these providers.

SAP has an enormous number of basically out of it customers who can't do any independent research and find Deloitte or Infosys to be "good sources of information." SAP can milk that account base for many years. Most likely SAP is studying IBM very intently. IBM is a poster child for how to manage a long-term decline. The growth is finished, but there is plenty of money still to be extracted from the installed base.

Chapter 2: Moving From Oracle to Open Source Databases with AWS and Google Cloud

Oracle representatives like discussing Oracle's market share in the database market. They love talking about the different things the Oracle database can do, and how it has many advanced features.

What they don't like discussing is the costs for the Oracle database. That topic nearly always gets deemphasized when conversing on the subject of the Oracle database.

So how expensive is the Oracle database?

The open source project MariaDB created a series of cost estimates for MariaDB versus Oracle as well as a TCO. Before we dive into it, let us explain the background and views Brightwork Research & Analysis on TCO studies.

- *Who is Performing the Study?*: We also don't think the **vendor or a consulting company** for that matter are the right entities to be performing TCO estimates. When an analyst firm like Forrester is hired to perform the TCO study, they will rig that study to make the entity paying them have the lowest TCO.

- *Predictable Outcomes*: The TCO studies that we have reviewed have nearly always been financially biased, with predictable outcomes (the entity performing the TCO nearly always bestows the lowest TCO to themselves).

- *The Issue of the Incomplete Nature of TCO Studies*: TCO studies have a long history of being incomplete (the less complete the TCO study is, the lower the TCO which makes vendors and consulting firms positively ecstatic).

We would never accept cost estimates from a vendor without analyzing them. And there is no doubt that MariaDB is pro MariaDB. And there is no doubt that the lead developer for MariaDB, Michael Widenius hates Oracle, and his lack of trust for Oracle is why he forked MariaDB from MySQL after Oracle acquired Sun Microsystems and therefore MariaDB in 2009. MariaDB is both an open source project but also a corporation that promotes

MariaDB (there is both a MariaDB.com and a Maria DB.org – which is the foundation). While private entities have an atrocious record of performing research, the best research comes from non-profit entities. Our university system is primarily non-profit (and the for-profit universities tend to not produce research).[57] MariaDB is not a non-profit, its corporation is for profit, but private and has raised $98 million in capital.[58] The TCO study is published by the corporation.

However, there are a few things we want to cover about the MariaDB costing paper.

- We have reviewed a huge number of TCO estimates for our book on TCO. This MariaDB cost study is one of the best that we have ever reviewed.

- As MariaDB is an open source database, and therefore, we think this comparison while limited in the paper to MariaDB, actually would apply similarly to other open source database projects like MySQL and PostgreSQL, etc..

Now that we have addressed how suspicious we are of TCO studies, and discussed what MariaDB is, let us begin with the basic cost comparison table.

	MariaDB	**Oracle[1]**
Database/Proxy	$7,500	$47,500
Scalability	Included	$23,000
Partitioning	Included	$11,500
Compression	Included	$11,500
Security	Included	$15,000
Firewall	Included	$6,000
Total	$7,500 (Server)	$114,500 (Core)

---

57 One might ask the question if why if Brightwork Research & Analysis is so against profit-oriented research, why is Brightwork Research & Analysis setup as a for profit? It is a good question. We are not large enough to be set up that way. We easily could be, with salaries paid out and no profit taken above that level, but the income received by Brightwork is too variable to do this in a way that makes any sense. Although it might in the future as we think so highly of the non-for-profit model. What we do instead is have a policy to never take income from a vendor or a consulting company to produce content. Neither Gartner, Forrester, IDC or other analyst firms follow this rule. Large media entities such as ComputerWeekly have built their entire business model around taking income from industry sources. We could easily increase our revenues by offering to produce paid placements to industry sources, and we don't. Therefore, we run the company not as a nonprofit, but as a "not profit-maximizing" entity.

58 https://www.crunchbase.com/organization/mariadb-2#section-funding-rounds

Notice how the add-ons from Oracle add up. Oracle sells its database in "pieces." However, the eyes really begin to pop when we review the next table.

MariaDB		Oracle	
Database Servers	3 Active	Database Servers	3 Active
Proxy Servers	2	Processors/Server	2
Total Servers	5 ($7,500/Server)	Cores/Processor	16
		Total Cores	96
		Core Factor	0.5
		Adjusted Cores	48 ($114,500/Core)
Total	$37,500	Total	$5,496,000

This is what companies are paying in order to use Oracle? Amazing.

MariaDB (AWS)		Oracle (Oracle)		Oracle (AWS)	
Database Servers	3 Active	Database Servers	2 Active 1 Standby (R)	Database Servers	1 Active 2 Standby (R)
Proxy Servers	2	Cores/Server	32	vCPU/Server	64
Total Servers	5	Total Cores	96	Total vCPU	192
				HT Adjustment	0.5
				Total Cores	96
Total	$37,500	Total	$2,592,000	Total	$9,888,000

This is one of the most interesting graphics in the TCO study. This graphic shows the price drastically increasing when the Oracle DB is run on AWS (under this scenario). Notice again that MariaDB stays low on AWS.

In its conclusion of the study, MariaDB goes on to state the following:

> *"After three years, running on three on-premise servers, each with two, 16-core processors:*
>
> *The total cost of Oracle is 80x higher than MariaDB*
>
> *The annual cost of Oracle is 30x higher than MariaDB*
>
> *Organizations can save $9 million after three years by choosing MariaDB*
>
> *Organizations can save $1.1 million annually by replacing Oracle."*

These type of numbers make one wonder. Companies are locked-in to Oracle in some cases, but in other cases, they aren't, and they are still using the Oracle DB.

We will cover the effort in transitioning from Oracle, which is not minor, but it was important to place these costs at the beginning of this chapter to highlight how substantial the cost is to run Oracle. One cannot stop at "migration costs are expensive" without acknowledging the current giant running balance of staying on Oracle.

The Price of CockroachDB Versus Amazon Aurora

One might think that this type of comparison is only an issue for commercial databases like Oracle versus open source. However, the following is a comparison of CockroachDB versus Amazon Aurora. These are both designed from the ground up for the cloud.[59] Aurora was designed by Amazon to have up to 15 read replicas across different availability zones, and the backups are continuous and designed for 99.999999999 percent durability and backed up to S3. Aurora is a distributed database that divides the data into 10 GB segments which are spread across the database cluster that is across availability zones.[60] [61] However, a customer can use the similar CockroachDB on AWS if they find that option more appealing. CockroachDB provides the following comparison between their database an Aurora.

---

59   What makes a cloud designed database different than a monolithic database that is ported to the cloud is explained well in the following quotation. *"What do I mean by using the inherent benefits of the cloud? It's simple really: cloud-native databases can leverage the ability to quickly schedule resources within a facility, but also across facilities, cloud service providers, and even continents. This can allow them to provide scale, unmatched resilience, low-latency global operation, and data sovereignty compliance. Monolithic databases remain useful pieces of technology, but because they require scaling up just one master node, they are evolutionary dead ends. They are the products of a smaller, less-connected era, and their shortcomings risk becoming liabilities for your business as it evolves."* - https://www.cockroachlabs.com/blog/database-evolution/

60   https://d1.awsstatic.com/whitepapers/getting-started-with-amazon-aurora.pdf

61   The 99.999999999% durability value comes from the S3 bucket as described as follows: *"The file gateway uses Amazon S3 buckets to provide storage for each mount point (share) that is created on an individual gateway. When you use Amazon S3 buckets, mount points provide limitless capacity, 99.999999999% durability on objects stored, and a consumption-based pricing model."* - https://d1.awsstatic.com/whitepapers/aws-storage-gateway-file-gateway-for-hybrid-architectures.pdf

TPC-C at 1,000 Warehouses

Database	CockroachDB 2.0	Amazon Aurora RDS MySQL
Throughput	12,475 tpmC	12,582 tpmC
3-Year Cost *Detailed below*	$49,670	$260,670 – $540,6051*
$/tpmC	$3.98	$20.72 – $42.97*
Hardware	3x Google Compute Engine n1- highcpu-16 with attached Local SSDs	2x r3.8XL (One read replica with automatic failover)

CockroachDB thinks that it offers a better value than Aurora. CockroachDB touts its throughput in the following quotation.

> *"CockroachDB has over 99% of Aurora's throughput, with only 10 to 20% of the cost. We think it's safe to say that on the TPC-C 1k warehouse benchmark, CockroachDB is a much more attractive option."[62]*

Claims are a dime a dozen in the software industry.

So is this claim true?

To determine the validity of this comparison, one needs to review the assumptions in the paper as the paper states that CockroachDB and Amazon RDS.

> *"use very different operation models."*

In the past it was difficult to verify vendor claims regarding how they compared to other options. However, with the cloud, it is **now quite** straightforward to perform such tests.

In fact, in the paper CockroachDB states the following:

> *"We don't want you to simply take our word on our performance. We want you to try it out for yourself."*

---

62   CockroachDB vs Amazon Aurora Price Comparison, Cockroach Labs, Sean Loiselle

That is not a phrase that is uttered very frequently by on premises vendors like SAP or Oracle! In fact, we have never heard it uttered. The concept on SAP and Oracle projects is to listen to your sales rep (or consulting partner).

To figure out the best option, companies will need to move away from the on-premises model of buying by demos and projections, into dynamic testing cloud services and cloud services in conjunction with one another. This means, of course, increasing the size of the portion of their IT staff that performs testing.

Adding testing capabilities can be achieved by moving some of the work that is currently being conducted to manage databases to fully managed databases at AWS or Google Cloud. That leaves some staff available to be reassigned.

In the long run, it means more time spent testing and validating and less time managing solutions that were purchased under inaccurate assumptions and that are not good fits for the requirements. This may sounds great hypothetically, however, this is no simple thing, particularly if there is an embedded pattern of doing the opposite. Ill-fitting solutions produce a vast overhang in IT departments. They are everywhere. In line with the cloud service availability, we continually promote scientific testing at our clients. It is an uphill fight. This is because we frequently get feedback that it is the preference to stay away from testing. Testing "takes too long." It is "too much effort." That sentiment has to change to determine what services can be leveraged.

The Common Problems with the On Premises Database Management Model

The current model of on-premises database management does a poor job of scaling and is also inefficient in that it duplicates labor in many locations. Under this "distributed model" each company maintains many databases.[63] This is because it relies upon many databases must be maintained in a less capable manner than providers like AWS or Google Cloud who can apply economies of scale to database management. As just one example, the average database server in a data center in an on-premises environment has a 5 to 10% utilization.[64] The ability to get that utilization far higher (on the IaaS's provider's server) is just one of many areas of improvements in efficiency. That is before the application of higher levels of database specialization are taken into account.

---

63   According to Forrester the average DBA maintains 40 databases. - https://go.forrester.com/blogs/10-09-30-how_many_dbas_do_you_need_support_databases/

64   https://www.cio.com/article/3237114/database/counting-database-costs-inflexible-databases-are-unaffordable-databases.html

Considering Oracle's Database Assumptions

For many years now, Oracle, with little competition, has dictated how the relational database will be, how much maintenance it will require, and how many people will be needed to be on staff to support it. When companies pay 22%+ to Oracle this covers opening tickets with Oracle and having those tickets worked; this does **not** include the cost of the database administrators (DBAs) or other overhead. To even get the Oracle database to run correctly, quite a bit more DBA time and effort is necessary than in any widely used RDBMS. Oracle is widely considered to be one of the most difficult databases to get to run properly. Therefore, the actual cost of maintaining Oracle DBs is the 22%+ added to the implementation, attached to the internal resources and DBAs that support the Oracle DBAs.

Oracle's sales strategy is to continue to add functionality to justify the high price of the Oracle DB. However, the fact is that while some companies can leverage the upper-level functionality of the Oracle DB, the vast majority do not. Moreover, this is why most Oracle customers are still using one of 11 versions of the Oracle DB rather than 12 or 18 (Oracle changed its versioning and "jumped" from 12 to 18, so the follow-on to 12 is not 13.) Seeing the reduced value of Oracle's support, a vast number of Oracle customers have dropped support and are unconcerned with the latest version of the Oracle database and either self-support or use a third party support entity.

The observation of one our authors, Mark Dalton, gathered from his experience at his company AutoDeploy is that the primary motivation for customers to move to the cloud databases is to leave behind Oracle's inflationary TCO. Mark has observed the following features of those companies that migrate to AWS.

- All of the migrations of our customers run on fully managed AWS RDS services (MariaDB, PostgreSQL, or MySQL). The ones who keep running 9i or 11i **no longer pay Oracle for support**. They've been running unsupported for years.

- They stop paying for features they don't need and support they see little value from.

- The performance is neither better nor worse than before.

- The cost savings are quite large, with a median saving of 80% of annual IT OPEX spend.

While all of this has been happening, open source relational databases, notably PostgreSQL have for the most part caught up with the Oracle DB. This would be more widely publicized, but the open source projects don't have the money to promote this type of information the way that SAP or Oracle of course do. This, as we have pointed out previously,, is the flaw in the commercial software model, money means the ability to promote solutions over open source alternatives.

The truth is that the vast majority of applications, PostgreSQL can substitute very well for Oracle, and while Oracle would like to propose that PostgreSQL is not as "enterprise ready" as Oracle. The existence of so many PostgreSQL instances that handle such large volumes so well makes it difficult for Oracle to make this argument reasonably. New databases like Aurora, developed by AWS for the cloud (rather than being developed on premises and then ported to the cloud) have been designed to leverage what cloud hardware resources rather than on-premises hardware resources. This gives them an advantage against the Oracle database that was adapted to run on the cloud from it is on-premises history.

343 systems in ranking, August 2018

Rank			DBMS	Database Model	Score		
Aug 2018	Jul 2018	Aug 2017			Aug 2018	Jul 2018	Aug 2017
1.	1.	1.	Oracle	Relational DBMS	1312.02	+34.24	-55.85
2.	2.	2.	MySQL	Relational DBMS	1206.81	+10.74	-133.49
3.	3.	3.	Microsoft SQL Server	Relational DBMS	1072.65	+19.24	-152.82
4.	4.	4.	PostgreSQL	Relational DBMS	417.50	+11.69	+47.74
5.	5.	5.	MongoDB	Document store	350.98	+0.65	+20.48
6.	6.	6.	DB2	Relational DBMS	181.84	-4.36	-15.62
7.	7.	↑9.	Redis	Key-value store	138.58	-1.34	+16.68
8.	8.	↑10.	Elasticsearch	Search engine	138.12	+1.90	+20.47
9.	9.	↓7.	Microsoft Access	Relational DBMS	129.10	-3.48	+2.07
10.	10.	↓8.	Cassandra	Wide column store	119.58	-1.48	-7.14

DB-Engines ranks database popularity. Its method is not perfect, but is more of an indicator. This is because the exact prevalence of each database is not knowable. DB-Engines track the rise of PostgreSQL. Of the top four databases, which are all of a similar design, PostgreSQL is the only one with year over year growth. The overall relational database market is not growing anywhere near PostgreSQL's year over year 47%+ growth. Some of this growth has come at the expense of some of the databases above the list. MySQL (owned by Oracle, but open source), SQL Server and PostgreSQL (also open source) are far lower in price than Oracle, and for the vast majority of applications can do everything that the Oracle DB can do. Moreover, all of them are easier to use and easier to optimizer as well as lower in maintenance than Oracle. DB2, an IBM database which goes after a similar market to Oracle is also declining in popularity, but from a much lower base.

PostgreSQL, as with other databases ranging from MariaDB to Aurora to CockroachDB are all far easier to administer than Oracle. AWS knows this quite well, and this is in part what lead AWS to introduce the RDS (which stands for Relational Database Service), but could just as easily be called Managed Relational Database Service) offering. That is the database software itself that is easier to administer. However, AWS adds onto this by making RDS multitenant and then makes the entire service centrally managed.

The AWS RDS has the following characteristics:

- In RDS, the particular database is called the database engine.

- The DB instance is the building block of RDS, what AWS calls the isolated database environment in the cloud.

- There is a many to one relationship between the DB instances and the RDS license, which allows up to 40 DB instances per RDS license.

- The DB instance has a computational and memory capability as determined by the DB instance class, which falls into the categories of Standard DB, Memory Optimized DB, and Burstable Performance DB.

- The DB instance can create any number of customer-created databases.[65]

Multitenancy, VPC and the RDS

A major advantage of RDS is that it is multitenant. Multitenancy functionality is quite advanced and allows many user's data to be kept in the same RDS. This is how the RDS gains such high degrees of economies of scale, and how it reduces maintenance overhead. This is why the cloud is so much more than hosting or "private cloud." It means creating large-scale economies from managing many customers on one instance of software. In this case a database.

RDS has a default security. However, unless one is using a legacy database, the RDS service is protected with a VPC or virtual private cloud is used to segment the customer's DB instance from other DB instances, even though the customers share or are multitenant on the RDS.[66]

- *VPC as a Sub-cloud*: A VPC is a Virtual Private Cloud which is a sub-cloud, a private cloud within a public cloud. AWS and Google Cloud are public clouds.

- *Mini Private Clouds*: The VPC capability means that they can segment the public cloud into mini-private clouds.

- *Data Isolation*: While the RDS or Cloud SQL database instance is public, the VPC means the VPC isolates the customer data.

---

65 https://docs.aws.amazon.com/AmazonRDS/latest/UserGuide/Welcome.html
66 https://docs.aws.amazon.com/AmazonRDS/latest/UserGuide/USER_VPC.WorkingWithRDS InstanceinaVPC.html

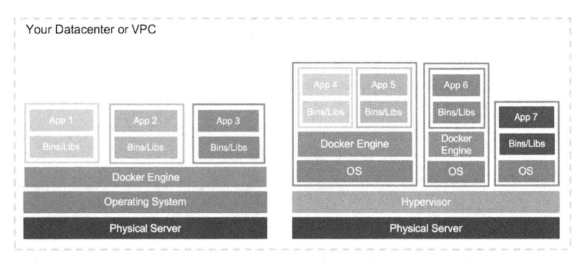

The VPC creates a virtual network within AWS for each customer. The metaphor of a "network" applies because it is as if it is a network in one's own on premises data center.[67] In the graphic above, containers are shown within either a datacenter or a VPC, implying that the two are logically the same.[68]

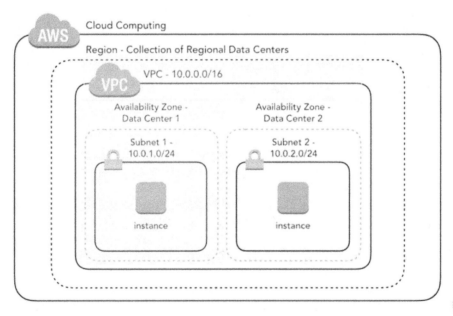

In this more detailed graphic notice again the VPC "contains" two different Availability Zones.[69]

67 https://d1.awsstatic.com/enterprise-marketing/SAP/SAP_on_AWS_Implementation_Guide.pdf
68 https://goto.docker.com/rs/929-FJL-178/images/Docker-for-Virtualization-Admin-eBook.pdf
69 https://www.lynda.com/Amazon-Web-Services-tutorials/Scaling-serverless-vs-server-based-applications/697727/747621-4.html

The VPC provides a high degree of control related to things like selecting IP address ranges, configuring routing, and other security features. As each DB instance has a various amount of compute resources allocated to it, with so many customers in the same VPC protected database, the administration overhead declines significantly.

The combination of lower overhead database software combined with multitenancy and central administration takes RDS into an area where Oracle cannot compete. This is because Oracle is not offering what AWS is offering. Oracle has a cloud DaaS service, but it is nothing at all like AWS or Google Cloud's offering.

If customers chose to perform a homogeneous migration from their Oracle on-premises database to the RDS (or bring up a new Oracle RDS), then that customer still gets two of the three benefits listed above.

The relational database management service or RDS and Cloud SQL offering are one of AWS's and Google Cloud's most popular services. Through this managed service, AWS and Google can concentrate database resources to manage enormous numbers of customer's data centrally. In a new development in the history of databases. In either the on-premises model or in the hosted model (say with an IBM or CSC data center) each customer installs data into a database that they purchase that only contains their data. Then multiple database administrators employed at the customer manage those single customer database instances. The fundamental inefficiency of single-tenancy **is a primary root of the inefficiency of the on-premises database modality.** AWS RDS and Google Cloud SQL are not merely offering that same design but hosted with them. Instead, RDS and Cloud SQL are multitenant. This means that each customer has their data in one database. However, the data can be protected by a VPC, but it still (through some amazing technological developments that were previously unthinkable) resides in one database.

Therefore, while it seems like the customer data is all together in the database, the VPC per customer means it is isolated. This is why Oracle and SAP's pronouncements about "private cloud" are silly. Private cloud is Oracle and SAP's way of cloud washing hosting, which is a method of moving a server from on-premises to the vendor's premises. It's not cloud. One can obtain privacy from an efficiency public cloud **by using a VPC.**[70]

---

70   We don't want to give the impression that VPC is a switch that flipped. There are a large number of options when it comes to the VPC setup. *"AWS Managed VPN, AWS Direct Connect, AWS Direct Connect Plus VPN, AWS VPN CloudHub, Software VPN, Transit VPC, VPC Peering, Software VPN, Software to AWS Managed VPN, AWS Managed VPN, AWS Direct Connect, AWS PrivateLink, Software Remote Access VPN"* - https://docs.aws.amazon.com/aws-technical-content/latest/aws-vpc-connectivity-options/aws-vpc-connectivity-options.pdf#introduction

This design provides large economies of scale in database management. Also, it means that Oracle cannot compete with AWS or Google Cloud on both price and functionality. Oracle offers a sophisticated database, but their ability to manage their database in a cloud environment is vastly inferior to AWS or to Google Cloud. This level of detail is rarely explored in public articles that cover this area. The distinctions in this area are generally lost on all but those that work in a hands-on capacity in the area.

Oracle prefers if the entire discussion around infrastructure to be focused on the database rather than viewing the database as part of an **overall infrastructure capability**. And open source or databases that are closed source but accessible with little license overhead (like those offered by AWS and Google Cloud) are part of what allows for infrastructure flexibility. Increasingly in the AWS and Google Cloud world, Oracle licensing and auditing is a liability.

This is explained in the following quotation from Enterprise CIO.

> *"Why is using an open-source database particularly good for new projects? First, relational databases are not as differentiated as database vendors want everyone to believe. There are many databases that are secure, scalable, and well-supported in the industry. Second, because open-source databases are by definition not hampered by arcane licensing rules, companies can put them to work with lower license and support fees — or retire them — with little financial consequence. This speeds decision making, promotes application development, and encourages a nimble environment."*[71]

If a company has their data in an open source database like PostgreSQL or MariaDB or even Aurora (which is not open source but lacks Oracle's auditing department), they are at a distinct disadvantage concerning what they can do with both their databases and also their applications.

As bad as Oracle's "advice" to companies has been, Oracle at least has respected, although highly self-centered, knowledge of databases. SAP's advice to their customers has been far worse, and far more self-centered, but branching into assertions that are technically false. For years SAP has been telling customers that they need to perform multiple types of

---

71   https://www.enterprise-cio.com/news/2017/mar/29/three-strategies-reduce-your-database-total-cost-ownership/

database processing **from a single database**.[72] The fact that this is incorrect has not stopped either SAP or their partner network for saying it is true. SAP consulting partners waste no time, in fact, repeating anything SAP says, and on SAP topics the Internet primarily serves as an echo chamber where SAP, SAP consulting firms and media entities paid by SAP publish articles that say the exact same things. That is whatever SAP says. Overall the amount of independent information on SAP is vanishingly small.

We have covered in detail how SAP's proposals about HANA have ended up being proven incorrect in article ranging from What is HANA's Actual Performance?, A Study into HANA's TCO,[73] to How Accurate Was Bloor Research on Oracle In Memory?[74]

Werner Vogels on Leveraging Multiple Database Types

While SAP has proposed using a single database type (the one database type SAP wants customers to focus on, which is HANA), and finds its most willing customers in those that know the least about databases, AWS offers their customers the choice of leveraging many different database types.

In an excellent article by Werner Vogels who is the CTO of AWS explains this.

> *"A common question that I get is why do we offer so many database products? The answer for me is simple: Developers want their applications to be well architected and scale effectively. To do this, they need to be able to use multiple databases and data models within the same application."*

Notice the last part of this paragraph, where Werner Vogels describes using..

> *"multiple databases and data models within the same application."*

Wait, let us back up. What was that?

We all know that applications have a single database right? How does a single application use multiple databases?

---

72 The single database approach is differentiated from the microservice design as described in the following quote. *"Decentralized data management enhances application design by allowing the best data store for the job to be used. This also removes the arduous task of a shared database upgrade, which could be weekends-worth of downtime and work, if all goes well. Since each service team owns its own data, its decision making becomes more independent. The teams can be self-composed and follow their own development paradigm."* - https://d1.awsstatic.com/whitepapers/DevOps/running-containerized-microservices-on-aws.pdf

73 http://www.brightworkr.com/saphana/2016/10/14/actual-hana-performance/

74 http://www.brightworkr.com/saphana/2017/08/01/accurate-bloor-research-oracle-memory/

What is Werner talking about?

Well, it turns out Werner is describing software development that is different than the monolithic environment for which the majority of those reading this book most likely are most familiar with.

Werner goes on to say..

> *"Developers are now building highly distributed applications using a multitude of purpose-built databases."*

That is the application that we think of is one way of developing, but this is giving way to distributed applications that can access **multiple databases.**

It is an unusual way of thinking about applications. Particularly for those of us who came up under the monolithic model (which is most of people that work in IT). It means rethinking much of what has been part of the standard model in IT for many years.

The Limitations of the Relational Database

Werner goes on to describe the limitations of the relational database.

> *"For decades because the only database choice was a relational database, no matter the shape or function of the data in the application, the data was modeled as relational. Is a relational database purpose-built for a denormalized schema and to enforce referential integrity in the database? Absolutely, but the key point here is that not all application data models or use cases match the relational model."*

We have seen in the rapid growth of databases like MongoDB and Hadoop that specialize in either unstructured data or data with lower levels of normalization. However this brings up the question of why these different database types have begun to proliferate.

The proliferation is in part covered by Werner when he describes how Amazon ran into the limitations of using the relational database.

> *"We found that about 70 percent of our operations were key-value lookups, where only a primary key was used, and a single row would be returned. With no need for referential integrity and transactions, we realized these access patterns could be better served by a different type of database (emphasis added). This ultimately*

led to DynamoDB, a nonrelational database service built to scale out beyond the limits of relational databases."[75]

Let us consider that AWS has a very fast growing relational database service in RDS. However, they also have fast-growing non-relational databases like DynamoDB, as well as many other database types. AWS is offering a menu of databases, each targeted towards specific applications. So how many database types are there? Werner has an answer for this as well.

The Different Database Types According to Werner

Below we have provided a synopsis of the different database types, their intended usage, and the database that reflects them by Werner.

- *Relational*: Web and Mobile Applications, Enterprise Applications, Online Gaming (e.g., MySQL)

- *Key Value*: Gaming, Ad Tech, IoT (DynamoDB)

- *Document*: When data is to be presented as a JSON document (MongoDB)

- *Graph*: For applications that work with highly connected datasets (Amazon Neptune)

- *In Memory*: Financial Services, Ecommerce, Web, Mobile Applications (Elasticache)

- *Search*: Real-time visualizations and analytics generated by indexing, aggregating, and searching semi-structured logs and metrics. (Elastisearch Service)

Werner sees applications leveraging multiple database types. But SAP and Oracle do not see it that way. And as pointed out by AWS's documentation, databases are often selected based upon factors that are not part of a thorough examination of the requirements.

"Although a workload's database approach (RDBMS, NoSQL) has significant impact on performance efficiency, it is often an area that is chosen according to organizational defaults rather than through a data-driven approach. As with storage, it is critical to consider the access patterns of your workload, and also to

---

75   *"Because DynamoDB does not support a standard query language like SQL, and because there is no concept of a table join, constructing ad-hoc queries is not as efficient as it is with RDBMS. Running such queries with DynamoDB is possible, but requires the use of Amazon EMR and Hive." - https://d1.awsstatic.com/whitepapers/migration-best-practices-rdbms-to-dynamodb.pdf*

consider if other non-database solutions could solve the problem more efficiently (such as a using a search engine or data warehouse)."[76]

This means that IT departments will need to spend more time matching the database processing type to the database.

The Multi-Application Nature of Solutions Distributed by AWS

The multi-application nature of solutions is explained as follows by Werner.

> *"Though to a customer, the Expedia website looks like a single application, behind the scenes Expedia.com is composed of many components, each with a specific function. By breaking an application such as Expedia.com into multiple components that have specific jobs (such as microservices, containers, and AWS Lambda functions), developers can be more productive by increasing scale and performance, reducing operations, increasing deployment agility, and enabling different components to evolve independently. When building applications, developers can pair each use case with the database that best suits the need."*

However, what are packaged solutions offering? Monolithic applications that are the exact opposite of this.

SAP is a perfect example of a monolithic application provider. SAP wants customers to use a single database. Furthermore, they want customers to use "their" single database as in HANA. Which according to SAP can do all the processing as well as all the different database types described by Werner above.

When SAP talks to their customers they propose that they have the best of everything. The best applications. The best coding language (ABAP), the best middleware (PO/PI/SAP Cloud Platform Integration). And of course the world's greatest database in HANA, that can outperform any database in any type of database processing.

It's a great story.

The only problem with the story is that HANA can't perform anywhere near where SAP says it can. And not only is HANA not a universal database that performs all types of processing the best, no database works the way described by SAP.

---

76 http://d0.awsstatic.com/whitepapers/architecture/AWS_Well-Architected_Framework.pdf

The AWS Customers Using Multibase Offerings

AWS states the following customers are using these various database types in conjunction with one another to support one overall application.

- *Airbnb*: DynamoDB, ElastiCache, MySQL

- *Capital One*: RDS, Redshift, DynamoDB

- *Expedia*: Aurora, Redshift, ElastiCache, Aurora MySQL

- *Zynga*: DynamoDB, ElastiCache, Aurora

- *Johnson and Johnson*: RDS, DynamoDB, Redshift

The traditional design, with monolithic applications supported by (usually RDBSM) a single database is called the monolithic database approach or architecture, which is a particular approach to software development.

Microservices Architecture

With monolithic, tightly coupled applications, all changes must be pushed at once, making continuous deployment impossible.

Traditional SOA allows you to make changes to individual pieces. But each piece must be carefully altered to fit into the overall design.

With a .microservices architecture, developers create, maintain and improve new services independently, linking info through a shared data API.

A microservice design breaks up the code base into microservices, each with their own database. This is how multibase development is working in many companies.[77]

Werner clearly sees this as a multibase strategy with a strong future. He goes on to say.

---

77 This is one of the best graphics we have seen that explains microservices, and it is from Microtica. http://www.microtica.com/2016/10/discovering-microservices/

> *"Purpose-built databases for key-value, document, graph, in-memory, and search uses cases can help you optimize for functionality, performance, and scale and—more importantly—your customers' experience. Build on."*

Now the question becomes,

> *"Where do SAP and Oracle stand on leveraging the multibase approach?"*

It turns out there is a problem for SAP and Oracle in this regard.

The Problem that SAP and Oracle Cloud Face Leveraging a Multibase Approach

Something conveniently left out of SAP and Oracle's descriptions of their cloud is how it is primarily focused on SAP and Oracle products. With SAP and Oracle, (and this is a critical distinction) the cloud is viewed as merely a pathway to lead to SAP and Oracle's products. SAP allows you to bring up services on AWS, Google Cloud or Azure, but they are to support SAP products. Both SAP and Oracle dabble in connecting to non-SAP and non-Oracle, but only to co-opt an area so **they can access markets.**

AWS and Google Cloud are quite different. Notice the variety of databases available at Google Cloud.

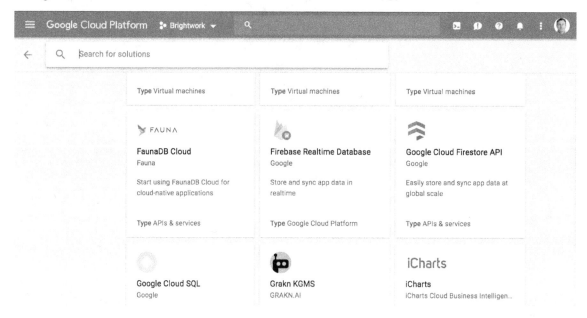

There are over 94 databases out at Google Cloud, and far more out at AWS. These databases can be brought up and tested very quickly. Selecting one of the databases brings up the configuration screen. it is a fantastic thing. The number of database and database type services is continually increasing with AWS and Google Cloud. AWS and Google Cloud do not demonstrate a pattern of redirecting customers to use their internally developed products instead of open source products.

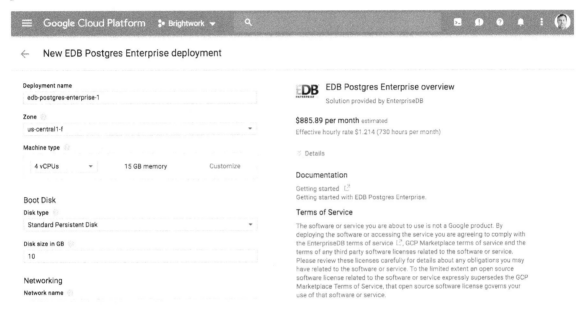

Right after this is launched, one can bring up a different database type, (say NoSQL or Graphic) and immediately begin testing. Under the on-premises model, this would not be possible. Instead of testing, the company would go through a sales process, and a commitment would be made, often from inaccurate information provided by sales reps. The customer would be stuck with (and feel the need to defend) whatever purchase had been made.

Leveraging the Multibase Design and The Pendulum Swinging from Packaged Software

We have entered a period of multibase capabilities, and AWS and Google Cloud are the leaders in offering these options. This is transforming how databases are utilized. Moreover, the more open source databases are accessed, the worse commercial databases look by contrast. Furthermore, the use of multibase databases dovetails with a rise of custom development that leverages not only different databases, but **also different languages**, all to support one application. That is while it may look like one application to the user it is multiple applications or microservices.

- Packaged solutions ruled the day for decades. Each one of these packaged solutions was built around a single database, normally the RDBMS, which meant getting everything from one database type.

- After the 1980s, custom coded solutions were for "losers." (This is no joke, those that did not purchase packaged solutions were subjected to critiques.) Many companies bought ERP systems because they were told by financially biased parties that anyone with a brain needed and ERP system.

- According to SAP, all systems that were not SAP were classified as "legacy" as we covered in the article How SAP Misused the Term Legacy.[78] And all legacy systems were to be replaced by "fantastic ERP" systems that would make your dreams come true.

And who agreed to all of this? This is a topic we will cover further on in the book.

Migrating from RDBMS to NoSQL with DynamoDB

Earlier in the book we covered migration of RDBMS to RDBMS. However, it is now understood that the RDBMS was selected in many cases when it was not the best database type.

This is explained in the following quotation.

> *"Even though RDBMS have provided database users with the best mix of simplicity, robustness, flexibility, performance, scalability, and compatibility, their performance in each of these areas **is not necessarily better than that of an alternate solution pursuing one of these benefits in isolation.(emphasis added)***
>
> *For an increasing number of applications, one of these benefits is becoming more and more critical; and while still considered a niche, it is rapidly becoming mainstream, so much so that for an increasing number of database users this requirement is beginning to eclipse others in importance. That benefit is scalability. As more and more applications are launched in environments that have massive workloads, such as web services, their scalability requirements can, first of all, change very quickly and, secondly, grow very large. The first scenario can be difficult to manage if you*

---

78 http://www.brightworkr.com/sap/2017/04/sap-used-term-legacy/

have a relational database sitting on a single in-house server. For example, if your load triples overnight, how quickly can you upgrade your hardware? The second scenario can be too difficult to manage with a relational database in general.[79]

This means that some of the migrations from RDBMS should be to other database types, and in many cases to NoSQL but also other. This could be considered a re-platforming of the database.

- Six of the top ten databases are RDBMSs (Oracle, MySQL, SQL Server, PostgreSQL, DB2, Access). They average a year on year change in popularity as measured by DB Engines of -43%. And that is propped up by PostgreSQL with a +46% year over year change. And the total negative year over year change is far more negative than this.

- If you take the top 20 RDBMSs, taken as a total group, they are significantly negative year over year growth.

- Four of the top ten databases are non-RDBMSs (MongoDB, Redis, Elastisearch, Cassandra). They have a year over year change of +19%.

Changes are afoot in the database market. The only RDBMSs with any significant growth are open source RDBMSs like PostgreSQL and MariaDB. And non-RDBMSs, which are primarily open source, are growing faster than the RDBMS category. This means that increasingly, RDBMSs are being broken apart and re-platformed with some of that data moving to non-RDBMSs.

A NoSQL/key value store database like DynamoDB does not setup its tables the same was as an RDBMS.[80] A key value database stores data with a simple key value.

---

79   https://readwrite.com/2009/02/12/is-the-relational-database-doomed/

80   The top key value store databases listed in order by popularity include Redis, DynamoDb, Memcache, Azure Cosmos, Hazelcast and Encache. Interestingly while Oracle often brings up Oracle NoSQL, Oracle NoSQL is only the 12th most widely used key value store database according to DB-Engines. While Oracle's RDBMS is far more popular than PostgreSQL, in NoSQL, Oracle NoSQL is only 2% as widely used as Redis and 4.4% as widely used. What this means is as soon as one moves away from the RDBMS, Oracle's dominance disappears. - https://db-engines.com/en/ranking/key-value+store

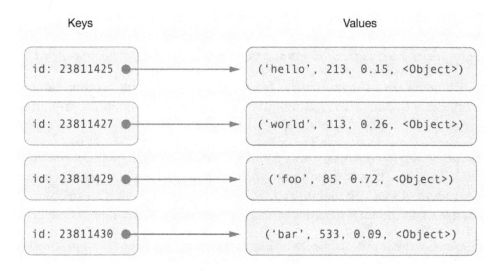

Key value databases function by assigning a unique ID or key to each combination. Notice in the graphic above, each ID number applies to a different combination of values to the right.[81]

Key value databases look very odd to people familiar with the relational model. Interestingly, there is a simple allegory to help explain the benefits of the key value database.

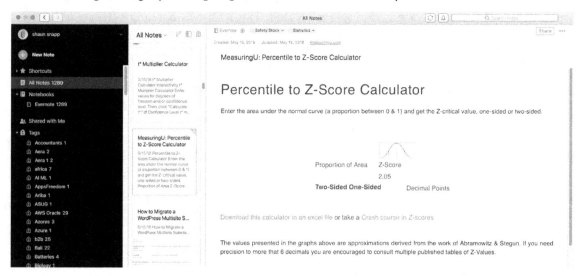

Like a lot of people I use Evernote to organize articles and notes. In terms of how the entries are organized for the articles it is relational in that a tag can be applied to each article. This particular article belongs to both the Safety Stock tag and the Statistics tag.

---

81   https://www.dataquest.io/m/234/guided-project%3A-implementing-a-key-value-database

However, one of the most effective methods of note taking is described in the book How to Take Smart Notes, which has associated software that supports the method.[82] Notice that the software looks remarkably similar to a key value database.

In this software called Archive, each note is only designated by a number, which is in a sequence. However, a key value data management system like this can be integrated with a relational note system through the introduction of hyperlinks. Notice I have a hyperlink out to an Evernote shareable link. This demonstrates in a simple way how a relational system (although not a relational database) can be used in conjunction with a serialized system.

- A key value database allows one to store complex data in single file.

- Two perfect use cases for the key value database are to retrieve the comments by user for a certain post, or the browsing history for a specific cookie for a specific site which are examples of serialization data, or to store the state of application..

However the disadvantage of the key value store is that the schema is undefined. This means that SQL can't be used to query the data and you need to write code to do that. This is a problem on every project that use key value databases, because reports require big efforts. However, for reports one can use an additional database with SQL capabilities.

> *"Because DynamoDB does not support a standard query language like SQL, and because there is no concept of a table join, constructing ad-hoc queries is not as*

---

82   https://www.amazon.com/How-Take-Smart-Notes-Nonfiction-ebook/dp/B06WVYW33Y

efficient as it is with RDBMS. Running such queries with DynamoDB is possible, but requires the use of Amazon EMR and Hive."[83]

DynamoDB offers flexible data modeling, higher performance and scalability along with operational simplicity.[84]

SQL	NoSQL
Optimized for Storage	Optimized for Compute
Ad Hoc Queries	Instantiated Views
Scale Vertically	Scale Horizontally
Good for OLAP	Good for OLTP at Scale

NoSQL differs from SQL in advantages and disadvantages. As explained by Rick Houlihan, "all databases contain relationships, it just depends upon the type of relationships."[85] *Furthermore NoSQL is a misleading term, as NoSQL databases **often use SQL**. The preferred description of NoSQL is now the elongated "Not Only SQL."*

DynamoDB is a "serverless" database does not use a static schema, or a static connection between the tables with related fields. DynamoDB scales better than an RDBMS, it scales far better horizontally (so to multiple nodes in different availability zones) and is very good at handling a large number of concurrent requests, with mobile applications being the perfect use case.[86]

The major disadvantage being that joins of columns from two separate tables.

DynamoDB is perfect for low response times, proposed by AWS as being single digit millisecond responses.

83 https://d1.awsstatic.com/whitepapers/migration-best-practices-rdbms-to-dynamodb.pdf
84 http://basho.com/resources/key-value-databases/
85 https://www.youtube.com/watch?v=xV-As-sYKyg
86 https://d1.awsstatic.com/whitepapers/migration-best-practices-rdbms-to-dynamodb.pdf

Example: *Analysis of Streaming Social Media Data*

Lambda is triggered

KINESIS   **DYNAMODB**

Social media stream is loaded into Kinesis in real-time.

Lambda runs code that generates hashtag trend data and stores it in DynamoDB

Social media trend data immediately available for business users to query

DynamoDB is shown alongside with Lambda (in the middle) as DynamoDB is "serverless."[87]

The migration from RDBMS to DynamoDB is considered by AWS to have the following steps.

1. Migrate tables being used by workloads involving non-relational data make excellent choices for migration to DynamoDB.

2. Setup the backup process for both the RDBMS and DynamoDB (with potentially running the databases in parallel for a time).

3. Understand the composition of the source data.

4. Understand the cost and performance of running a workload on DynamoDB.

5. Denormalization of the RDBMS data.

6. Testing (Functional, Non-Functional, User Acceptance)

---

87 https://aws.amazon.com/dynamodb/

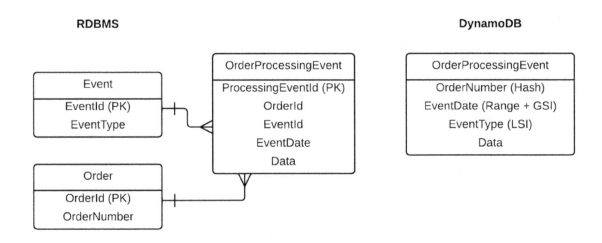

Notice how much the schema changes from being stored in the RDBMS to DynamoDB.[88]

So many options are becoming available, the re-platforming of databases brings up all manner of discussion and testing points. For example, SAP and Oracle have proposed using in-memory database designs where the RDBMS contains a column store. However, there are so many options on AWS that can beat this design in performance and cost and flexibility. One is the use of Elasticache. Another is the use of Redis (an in-memory store on with column-oriented design). Elasticache can be used with anything (database or not database) to speed performance, and Elasticache can be used with along with Redis (in fact Elasticache can speed just about anything).

The options for accessing different components and then combining those components in beneficial ways available currently is like never before. And we owe this to the cloud service providers as well as to the open source communities.

Who knows when these developments would have taken place if it had been left to the on-premises vendors?

Migration to MongoDB

And the benefits of migrating SQL to NoSQL apply to other popular NoSQL databases like MongoDB, which is a document oriented database.

---

88   https://d1.awsstatic.com/whitepapers/migration-best-practices-rdbms-to-dynamodb.pdf

"When I joined MongoDB, about 5 per cent of all projects were relational migrations - now it's 30 per cent as companies look to transform. Cost can be a factor, but more often it's development speed and running at scale. It's not unusual to see developer productivity up 3 to 5x after switching [from an RDBMS], coupling MongoDB with a shift to cloud, microservices, and agile/devops."[89] – **Mat Keep, Director of Product Marketing**

A Coming Rise in Custom Development?

Now as distributed applications are accessing multiple databases, are we entering a period where the pendulum switches to custom coding again? Under the SAP or Oracle paradigm, you accepted the databases that were "approved" by SAP and Oracle. All competition was driven out of the process. Oracle applications worked with the Oracle database. For the longest time, SAP worked with Oracle database, and only a handful of other closed source databases. But even this limited competition was not good enough for SAP. SAP finally decided to introduce HANA to push the Oracle database out of "their" accounts.[90] SAP now thinks that all SAP applications should sit on an SAP HANA database.

While Oracle and SAP are trying to convince their customers to use only one type of database, AWS and Google Cloud are offering a kaleidoscope of different database options. Werner Vogels describes a combination of components that are **selected and stitched together**. Most of these databases are open source. Moreover, one can choose from a wide variety offered by AWS or a smaller number offered by Google Cloud.

The entire approach by AWS and Google Cloud regarding the multibase is inherently contradictory to monolithic packaged applications, because the packaged application uses one database, and works in a particular and defined way. We will cover this topic including containers and microservices later in the book.

But for now, and to keep with the continuity of the chapter, let us move onto the benefit that AWS and Google Cloud provide for deployment speed.

---

89   https://www.theregister.co.uk/2018/05/31/rise_of_the_open_source_data_strategies/
90   In SAP's worldview, they own the entire account, lock, stock and barrel. Sales to other vendors in an SAP customer are seen as deviations from the accepted norm and are aggressively dissuaded by SAP sales reps and by SAP consulting companies. The use of 100% SAP components, SAP applications, databases, middleware is the approved solution from SAP. We will review several SAP marketing graphics that also propose large solution architectures which contain large 100% SAP solutions.

AWS and Google Cloud For Speeding New Development

A significant distinction between AWS and Google Cloud versus Oracle and SAP is the speed at which AWS and Google Cloud can develop and market new offerings. Basically, they can conceive of it, test it, and then add it as an offering to the AWS and Google Cloud site. The on-premises vendors have to go through a much longer cycle. Then they have to educate salespeople to push concepts. The entire SAP/Oracle model is around lengthy sales cycles, exaggerated claims, and lengthy implementations, with outcomes that don't match the promises made in the sales cycle. AWS and Google are some of the few enterprise participants who seem to communicate and initiate principally through their website. We learn about AWS and Google Cloud through their website, not through calling up sales reps.

How AWS and Google Cloud Educates on Cloud

As a research entity, we/Brightwork Research & Analysis are very focused on documentation. So how do AWS and Google Cloud measure up? Let us review.

- AWS does a great job of explaining what cloud computing is. AWS's documentation is first rate and their presentations very matter of fact and honest as to what they offer.

- Google Cloud also creates excellent documentation, and every service opens to documentation to get into more detail.

- AWS and Google Cloud are also easier to understand and follow because it **lacks the heavy involvement** from marketing. Secondly, another positive aspect is that because neither AWS nor Google are vendors, they have less of an incentive to cover up shortcomings or issues with the software.

The combination of the ability to find out about services online, to test services using AWS and Google Cloud's ready to go infrastructure, the ability to close down services at will, the excellent documentation and training all increases the ability to bring up all the supporting components and to speed development. Furthermore, during development, AWS and Google Cloud allow for the easy sharing of developed items. Once the development is ready for user testing (As we cover at the end of the book in our case study on bringing the Brightwork Explorer application to AWS.), one is able to receive feedback through sharing the application link rapidly. We were able to quickly get our application up and running without worrying about code optimization or hardware sizing, as with the elastic capabilities of AWS and Google Cloud, we knew we could increase our capacity at any time. Under AWS and Google Cloud, the entire development process is made more efficient. In fact, at this point, we can't see developing without leveraging either AWS or Google Cloud. It is a new day for software development.

Conclusion

In this chapter the reader should have attained an appreciation for how SAP and Oracle as well as their massive ecosystems are incentivized to fight the progress offered by the cloud. There are changes brewing in software development, and they are being in part enabled by both AWS and Google Cloud, as well as other providers and a variety of database types that can be easily accessed and are open source enabling a high degree of experimentation. AWS and Google Cloud are focal points where many of these trends come together. AWS and Google Cloud are both part of this trend and at the same time enabling it. For companies that have SAP or Oracle to look to SAP or Oracle for answers on these trends, is looking in the wrong place. And to continue without considering what all these development mean, and how they can be leveraged is pure folly.

We will now move into an explanation of AWS RDS. However, we wanted to make sure that we highlighted that migrating to AWS or Google Cloud is about **much more** than merely migrating monolithic applications and relational databases to the cloud. It means opening up environments to many alternatives that neither SAP nor Oracle is interested in its customers to know much about.

AWS and Google Cloud have so many options to choose from that we can't cover every different database, much less the combination of various databases in this book. However, the principle of the multibase approach and the idea that multiple different database types can be combined and leveraged within on "application" is critical to the long-term ability to leverage of AWS and Google Cloud.

Chapter 3: Database Migration, The AWS RDS and Google Cloud SQL

Migrating databases and applications to AWS or Google Cloud has numerous benefits that have already changed how IT is managed at a wide array of companies.

These benefits include the following:

1. Reducing fixed costs

2. Gaining economies of scale

3. The ability to test services and to learn new things

4. Increased flexibility

5. Reducing lock-in

6. Gaining access to new solutions

7. Gaining access to more open source solutions

8. Improved visibility to spend, and leveraging the strong innovation from AWS and Google Cloud.

The list of improvements in quite extensive. Amazon RDS manages the work involved in setting up a relational database. This is from provisioning the infrastructure capacity you request to installing the database software. Once your database is up and running, Amazon RDS automates everyday administrative tasks such as performing backups and patching the software that powers your database. With optional multi-availability zone deployments, Amazon RDS also manages synchronous data replication across Availability Zones with automatic failover. Using RDS is only one of the options for migrating an RDBMS to AWS. The other option is to use EC2.

AWS describes the advantages and disadvantages of EC2 vs RDS thusly.

> *"Choosing Between Amazon RDS and Amazon EC2 for Your Oracle Database Both Amazon RDS and Amazon EC2 offer different advantages for running Oracle Database. Amazon RDS is easier to set up, manage, and maintain than running Oracle Database in Amazon EC2, and lets you focus on other tasks rather than the day-to-day administration of Oracle Database. Alternatively, running Oracle Database in Amazon EC2 gives you more control, flexibility, and choice. Depending on your application and your requirements, you might prefer one over the other. Many AWS customers use a combination of Amazon RDS and Amazon EC2 for their Oracle Database workloads"[91]*

However, the RDS is a fully managed database, and it also provides significant economies of scale as AWS manages so many databases inside of each RDS instance. But as AWS observes, RDS is not right for every usage, and universality of application is not the impression we intend to provide in this chapter.

On the topic of innovation, one thing that catches everyone off guards has been that AWS, in particular, has been and will be adding so many features and capabilities. A challenge with AWS is the rate of innovation is high-speed compared to most customers, so there's a significant learning curve involved, and that learning curve keeps extending out to new things as soon as one "thing" is mastered. Many of us in technology have been told that we have to be dedicated to continual learning. However, AWS pushes the envelope of what is possible for a company to absorb.

As observed by AWS in their AWS Migration Whitepaper, the best way to migrate is incrementally. A major reason for this is simply the learning curve to figure out AWS and how to best leverage the AWS services.[92]

Massive and Immediately Scalability

Unlike on-premises databases, AWS offers virtually unlimited scalability both regarding database size, but also regarding the computational resources that the database consumes. One can have a large database with fewer computational resources (and less cost) or a smaller database with more computational resources. All of this depends upon the application's particular need.

---

91 https://docs.aws.amazon.com/aws-technical-content/latest/oracle-database-aws-best-practices/oracle-database-aws-best-practices.pdf?icmpid=link_from_whitepapers_page

92 https://s3-ap-southeast-1.amazonaws.com/mktg-apac/Cloud+Migration+to+AWS+Campaign/AWS+ebook+Migrating+to+AWS.pdf

Getting Started with Backups

One easy way to get started with AWS or Google Cloud is by backing up data to either one. Every company needs a remote backup, so this can get the process started and begin scaling up in familiarity. This is explained by AWS in the following quotation.

> *"Organizations are looking for ways to reduce their physical data center infrastructure. A great way to start is by moving secondary or tertiary workloads, such as long-term file retention and backup and recovery operations, to the cloud. In addition, organizations want to take advantage of the elasticity of cloud architectures and features to access and use their data in new on-demand ways that a traditional data center infrastructure can't support."[93]*

Long term storage can go with AWS Glacier or Google Cloud Nearline.

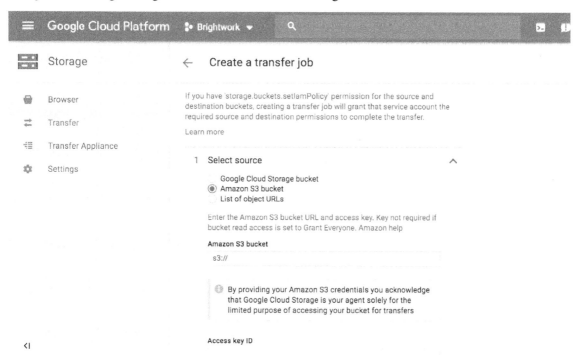

As we discussed earlier, one has a lot of flexibility when using both AWS an Google Cloud. Here we can begin by backing up our data on AWS, and if we choose, to switch to Google Cloud.

---

93   https://d1.awsstatic.com/whitepapers/aws-storage-gateway-file-gateway-for-hybrid-architectures.pdf

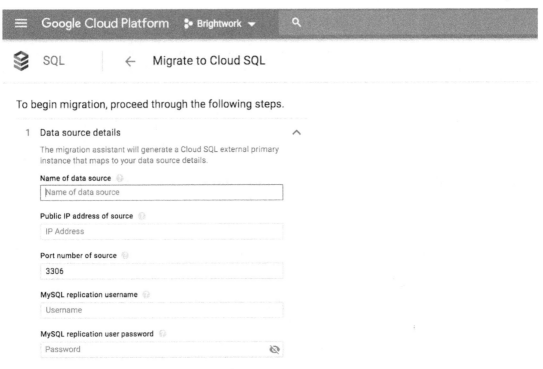

Right after creation, data can be set up for migration.

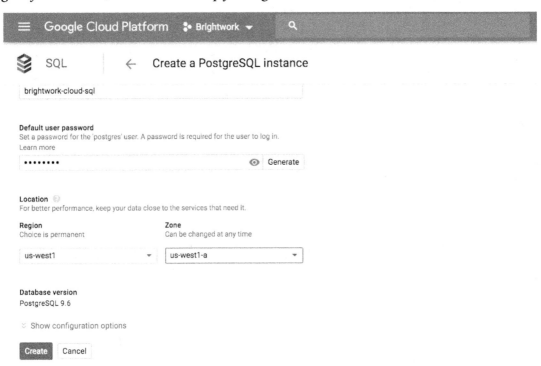

After backing up data, a second natural progression is to migrate some databases from on on-premises SQL or AWS RDS. PostgreSQL is a particular favorite of ours. Companies that migrated from the Oracle DB to PostgreSQL often never look back.

We are in a golden age of resource management. One can bring up instances, test them, and bring them down in ways that would have been unthinkable in the past.

Moving Past Stage One of Using AWS and Google Cloud

Backups and database migration are just the starting points for getting one's feet wet with AWS and Google Cloud. Rather a testing-based migration of what makes sense to AWS, starting with the low hanging fruit, and moving up to the more advanced items. We also identify what has been low hanging fruit from our exposure to AWS and Google Cloud, and recommend starting places. It is so easy to start small with AWS and Google Cloud that the testing approach is the natural default position. The overall testing approach and low cost and low-risk capability to perform testing are one of the areas that strongly differentiates AWS and Google Cloud from SAP and Oracle. This shortens the time by which feedback is received. This changes the overall decision-making process in IT organizations, and it means that the IT organizations can rely less upon projections and sales information and more on trying out the various offerings from AWS instead of having to project.

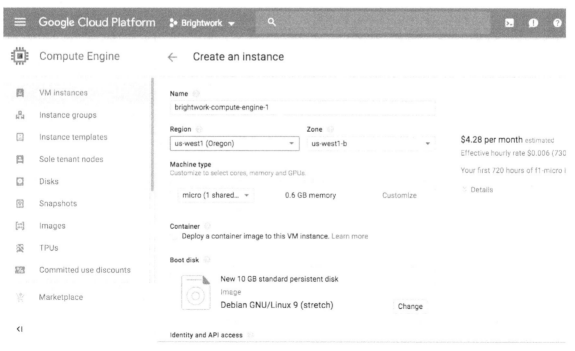

Virtual machines are a primary building block of the cloud. Notice we can set up even a micro virtual machine to create a small test environment.[94]

Migrating databases to AWS will be a breath of fresh air for SAP and Oracle customers. While SAP and Oracle base their business on lock-in, which perpetuates a mentality where old investments need to be protected (as they cannot easily be switched off), SAP and Oracle want customers to buy specific things.

AWS RDS is offered for the following databases.

1. *Aurora*: This is the only database in this list created/owned by AWS (and not open source), shares many similarities with MySQL, and known for high scalability and native high availability)

2. *MySQL*: The original open source database continues to have high popularity, but due to being undermined by Oracle, is losing to other open source projects like MariaDB that have forked off of MySQL.

3. Oracle: (Oracle offers support for both 12 and 11, as so many Oracle customers are still on 11)[95]

4. *MariaDB*: MySQL "2.0" with a list of increasingly impressive features, MariaDB is used by both Wikipedia and Google (internally).

5. SQL Server: Microsoft's database is declining, but gets high marks for ease of use and is one of the top four databases in general use.

6. *PostgreSQL*: The performance heavyweight in the relational open source market. PostgreSQL is a problem for Oracle, because it undercuts their performance argument. The number of use cases which require Oracle over PostgreSQL shrinks ever year.

---

94 On the topic of VMs from House of Brick (a consulting firm known for straight shooting advice on Oracle) *"I personally appreciate the simplicity, scalability, and robustness of a single Oracle instance running on a standard Linux VM hosted on a VMware cluster. Vertical scaling of VMs running Oracle database software is effortless when more CPU or memory is required. The HA(high availability) features of VMware are excellent and proven. Human resources are readily available in the marketplace to support this stack. This proven solution positions your organization to pivot to the cloud provider of your choice in the future."* - http://houseofbrick.com/oracle-database-appliance-the-good-the-bad-and-the-ugly/

95 https://docs.aws.amazon.com/AmazonRDS/latest/UserGuide/CHAP_Oracle.html

	Price Per Hour (East Ohio AZ) (Standard)		
Instance Type	PostgreSQL	Oracle	Ratio
db.t2.micro	$0.02	$0.07	3.89
db.t2.small	$0.04	$0.14	3.89
db.t2.medium	$0.07	$0.28	3.84
db.t2.large	$0.15	$0.57	3.93
db.m4.large	$0.18	$0.82	4.52
db.m4.xlarge	$0.37	$1.65	4.51
db.m4.2xlarge	$0.73	$3.29	4.51
db.m4.4xlarge	$1.46	$6.58	4.50
			4.20

Of the different RBBMS databases offered by RDS, Oracle is by far the most expensive. The graphic above compared the instances that were available for both PostgreSQL and for the Oracle database. On average Oracle costs over 4 times as much to run per hour on AWS as did PostgreSQL.[96] This analysis was performed against the Standard Edition 1 of Oracle. Standard Edition 2 was roughly another 8% more than Standard Edition 1.

One of the topics is whether AWS charges more for products that it developed rather than open source options. Therefore, we decided to compare Aurora versus PostgreSQL.

---

96 This comparison was a point in time, and naturally pricing will change. This analysis can be recreated at any time in the future by reviewing AWS's current pricing. The following links are where we found the pricing we included in the comparison matrix above https://aws.amazon.com/rds/postgresql/pricing/, https://aws.amazon.com/rds/oracle/pricing/

	Price Per Hour (East Ohio AZ) (Standard)		
Instance Type	**Aurora**	**PostgreSQL**	**Ratio**
db.r4.large	$0.29	$0.25	0.86
db.r4.xlarge	$0.58	$0.50	0.86
db.r4.2xlarge	$1.16	$1.00	0.86
db.r4.4xlarge	$2.32	$2.00	0.86
db.r4.8xlarge	$4.64	$4.00	0.86
db.r4.16xlarge	$9.28	$8.00	0.86
			0.86

It turns out that AWS does charge more for PostgreSQL than for Aurora, or for homegrown database versus an open source database. And the difference is around (14/86) or 16.6% more. Therefore, this in part answers the question of how much incentive AWS has to push their databases over other alternatives. The answer from a financial perspective is "not much."

AWS RDS is free for customers to try and provides 35 different instance configurations ranging from 2 CPUs to 128 CPUs. This includes from low network bandwidth to 20 MBPS. Moreover, of course, scalability allows one to switch between the different configurations. This type of flexibility never existed before AWS introduced the RDS, and as usual, AWS is the first to introduce such things.

The Oracle Autonomous Database

While we have focused on open source databases, AWS supports Oracle. Oracle to Oracle is the easiest migration. However, moving on from the Oracle database is where the more extended savings can be found as AWS offers managed database service.

This means that AWS now performs much of the work ordinarily performed by the DBA. Oracle had no practical answer for this, so they came up with an impractical one. They decided to develop a fallacious concept called the **autonomous database**.

With the automated database Oracle proposed the following:

- Total automation of all database tasks would be possible because of machine learning and artificial intelligence (Apparently it had been working in secret on these topics for decades but never discussed with anyone).

- Oracle's machine learning and artificial intelligence would make one of the highest overhead and convert it to not only a low maintenance database but a maintenance free database. Oracle states that the automated database will **instantly sense** when the Oracle DB must be patched or upgraded and will perform the upgrade automatically.[97]

We analyzed the autonomous database in the Brightwork article How Real is the Oracle Autonomous Database?[98] It was evident that Oracle's autonomous database was/is fake. The reason for its introduction was to try to forestall the movement to AWS. Without AWS, the "autonomous database" is never launched by Oracle.

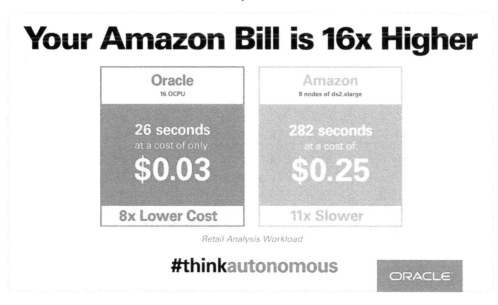

Oracle made a big push on its supposed autonomous database, but the story about this database fell apart as soon as the details were explained. Oracle increased the price of its

---

97   The problem is that even if it were true, upgrading Oracle has some technical as well as monetary implications. Therefore, this automated AI routine would also need to be able to read the account balance of the customer, as well as the customer's mind to determine if the customer wants to upgrade. Many companies don't want to upgrade Oracle, because of the financial implication. Other things described by Oracle about the autonomous database also don't add up.

98   http://www.brightworkr.com/saphana/2018/04/18/how-real-is-the-oracles-autonomous-database/

database on AWS before this announcement of the autonomous database. AWS has an excellent reputation for database performance, the proposal of Oracle on both performance and cost is not believable. Secondly, the vast majority of customers will not want to use Oracle Cloud, which is what is required to run the "autonomous database."

As was just shown several pages previously, our independent comparison showed that the Oracle database costs more than four times as much to run on AWS versus PostgreSQL. However, Oracle stated it will run databases at 1/8th of the cost of AWS? The following is explained by Dan Woods (#2).

> *"In January (of 2017), Oracle changed the fine print on some of its license terms, essentially doubling the cost of running Oracle software on AWS and Azure, while leaving the cost of running on the Oracle Cloud unchanged.*
>
> *While the impact of this is obvious, making it cheaper to run the same Oracle footprint on Oracle's cloud compared to AWS and Azure, it is not at all clear that Oracle is going to benefit in any significant way from making it more expensive to run on other clouds. Here's a look at why Oracle may have done this and the likely impact.*
>
> *So then will this price change actually cause more people to use the Oracle cloud? For that to happen, someone would have to switch their entire cloud deployment from AWS or Azure to the Oracle cloud for the sake of the increased cost of one part of the infrastructure. Given that Oracle isn't in the mix in most of the cloud deployments I've heard of, and that its cloud is far behind both AWS and Azure in terms of features, adoption, and ecosystem, it is likely that it would cost a huge amount more to move to the Oracle cloud than to stay with AWS or Azure, so no, this policy change isn't going to cause a rush of Oracle cloud sales.*
>
> *So is Oracle in effect giving up on competing with AWS and Azure databases on feature, function and price? Is the doubling of prices of its software the only way that Oracle can make more dough on the fastest growing clouds? Whatever this policy change is intended to be, it certainly isn't a show of strength by Oracle. It seems more like a show of weakness and an attempt to grab a sliver of revenue that may be out there for a short while."[99]*

Dan's comments were published in Forbes in Mar 23, 2017. But this price change makes it easier to make the case that Oracle is more lower in cost on Oracle Cloud than on AWS or Azure.

---

99 https://www.forbes.com/sites/danwoods/2017/03/23/does-oracles-aws-pricing-increase-make-strategic-sense/#71968e067ab7

The Oracle autonomous database is comprised of the following items:

1. Oracle database 18c enterprise edition (with all database options and management packs included)

2. Oracle Exadata X7-2 is the deployment platform. Oracle autonomous database runs on Oracle Exadata X7-2. The X7-2 systems only dedicate OCPUs and a single PDB (Pluggable Database) to each cloud client. The memory, flash cache, and other resources on an Exadata system are not dedicated. Oracle will decide how many other clients share the PDB resources available within a single Exadata machine. Clients with strict SLAs for production workloads won't accept this multi-tenant (noisy neighbor) configuration even if they were located in the same city block as the Oracle DC. The Oracle cloud automated database and database operations components (scripts, best practices, procedures).

Oracle offers two configuration choices for autonomous database: enterprise and mission critical. The 99.995% availability is only true for the mission critical configurations which costs 2X the monthly subscription fee. This increased cost is based on the requirement of a standby database which doubles infrastructure and storage resources.

The Exadata X7-2 systems only dedicate OCPUs and a single PDB (Pluggable Database) to each cloud client. The memory, flash cache, and other resources on an Exadata system *are not dedicated*. Oracle will decide how many other clients share the PDB resources available within a single Exadata machine. Clients with strict service level agreements for their production workloads have to ask themselves if this type multitenant configuration is acceptable. This is the sequence we predict with the autonomous database.

1. The new "autonomous" database will run fine on small data sets, but when you get in the terabyte range, it will become a severe problem.

2. The reason that the autonomous database will perform poorly is that it will take forever (and it does) to run statistics.

3. It will be necessary to get a good Oracle DBA (a dying breed) to perform a diagnosis of what is wrong.

4. This DBA will determine the statistics job is the problem because it takes too long to gather statistics on terabytes of data.

5. After the DBA does his handy work, the machine learning algorithm will make poor decisions on database tuning because the database statistics used by the Oracle cost-

based optimizer are out of date. The statistics will be out of date because it takes too long to run them and the DBA made a workaround.

6. The performance will become a serious problem.

7. When asked why the statistics are out of date, they will find out the DBA began exporting and importing statistics to improve performance.

8. They will blame the DBA and fire him.

9. The customer will complain.

10. Oracle will go back to square one.

11. A new statistics machine learning package patch will come out, and the cycle will repeat itself.

Where do our predictions come from? From experience that one of the authors, Ahmed Azmi has obtained from years of working with Oracle. And there is another problem with the autonomous database. Oracle's claim is that the autonomous database uses machine learning to automatically detect anomalies in usage patterns. This means it has to have access to sufficient customer data to train a customer-specific threat model that can protect each specific customer. Furthermore, there is a question as to how to preset a rule to distinguish between a spike caused by an attack from a spike caused by seasonality.

There are common scenarios which show that using the Oracle database from the Oracle Cloud versus AWS is a bad decision. Oracle offers a well-regarded if overpriced and high overhead database. Although how high the overhead is for the Oracle database is often understated.

> *"Even in areas where Oracle likes to trumpet the richness of functionality it offers, like Oracle HA, the reality is that much of the "richness" is actually external to the database itself. You "have to add a ton of stuff outside of the database [to make it work] for replication, failover, monitoring, etc," Keep says. Of course, this being Oracle, each of these add-ons is sold separately, resulting in a fat price tag and a seriously complex system to manage. Even worse for Oracle, the only way for a developer to get access to such Oracle extras is on the Oracle cloud, which basically no one wants to use."[100]*

But the Oracle Cloud is a completely different matter. It is so insubstantial, that there no reason to use it. And the autonomous database only "works" if it is run in the Oracle

---

100 https://www.theregister.co.uk/2018/05/31/rise_of_the_open_source_data_strategies/

Cloud. This of course makes whether the database is autonomous impossible to verify. If it were actually autonomous, it could be run either on premises or in the Oracle Cloud, but obviously it can't.

Many companies that have the Oracle database have to stay with it.

And common reasons are the following:

- Fear of migrating and the potential risk of downtime.

- Stored procedures writing for the Oracle DB.

- Contract lock in

- Compatibility issues with applications.

And as noted by Silvia Doomra.

> *"If you're using a packaged software application whose vendor does not certify on PostgreSQL, migrating is probably a non-starter."[101]*

The Approach of Beginning with Homogeneous Migration Followed by Heterogeneous Migration

- When the source and target database are the same, this is referred to as a "homogeneous" conversion.

- When the databases are different, this is referred to as a "heterogeneous" migration.

Homogeneous migrations are often the starting point for migration. This is because it allows the customer used to the AWS or Google Cloud environment. Then as the customer learns more, they can then migrate the Oracle RDS to PostgreSQL, MariaDB, or other.

We see the progression as follows.

1. *The Heterogeneous Migration*: The on-premises Oracle application is migrated to Oracle for RDS and a VM or container for the application is created for the application software. The heterogeneous migration is tested, and when it passes testing, the AWS instance becomes production, and the on premises instance can be decommissioned.

---

101 https://aws.amazon.com/blogs/database/challenges-when-migrating-from-oracle-to-postgresql-and-how-to-overcome-them/

2. *The Homogeneous Migration*: A copy is made of the VM or container for the application. The Oracle RDS is then migrated to a new (for example) PostgreSQL RDS. The VM or container application is connected to the PostgreSQL RDS. The new instance is tested, and when all tests are passed, the Oracle RDS and the first VM or container are shut down. The PostgreSQL and VM/container copy become the production instance.

When moving away from Oracle databases, it is then necessary to perform a "heterogeneous" conversion, which is more complicated. A database like PostgreSQL usually does an excellent job of managing the same workloads as Oracle 11 or 12 or 18. In fact, for any Oracle database version, there is are quite good open source databases that can do virtually anything Oracle can do. Moreover they can do it with far less overhead.

This is covered in the following quotation from Gartner.

> *"Today, there are about 300 database options available, including open-source and cloud alternatives such as MongoDB, PostgreSQL and Amazon. The database market has been commoditized. According to Gartner,* open-source databases have now reached parity with traditional databases in terms of functionality, tools and available resources — all with a lower TCO."*[102] [103]

This movement from commercial databases to open source databases is a growing trend and one we see speeding up in the future. And we are not the only ones, Seeking Alpha agrees.

> *"We see the $29.6b commercial database market contracting 20-30% by 2021, and do not believe Oracle (NYSE:ORCL) can transition its revenue streams (from legacy commercial database to cloud-based subscription offerings) fast enough to offset the decline of this market, which represents a major legacy core of its revenue."*[104]

Many Oracle instances can be migrated to PostgreSQL or MariaDB, etc.. as they do not use Oracle DB's more advanced functions. There are several items that must be addressed which include the following steps:

---

[102] https://www.riministreet.com/Documents/Collateral/Rimini-Street-eBook-10-Telltale-Signs-Change-Database-Strategy.pdf

[103] We ordinarily don't quote Gartner, and in particular we don't think Gartner knows enough about databases to be an authority on this topic. They have produced some appalling research on databases in the past, one example of which we covered in the article Can Anyone Make Sense of the ODMS Magic Quadrant? We have a particular problem with the work of Gartner database analyst Donald Feinberg. However, apparently someone told Gartner that the above statement is true, so they repeated it. It happens to be correct.

[104] https://seekingalpha.com/article/4044813-death-commercial-database-oracles-dilemma

1. Modify Incompatible SQL
2. Schema Conversion
3. Data Replication
4. Migrating Code (Converting PL SQL Stored Procedures)

Something important to consider is that no database is exactly like another database. Therefore moving from Oracle will mean changes.

This is explained very well by this anonymous quote.

> *"The thing is, you don't switch from Oracle (say, Exadata boxes) to something comparable as there is nothing directly comparable. What companies do is rethink their approach to BI, reporting and such and move to SaaS solutions, while simplifying greatly."*[105]

Moving from anyone one is familiar with comes with an adjustment. The question is whether the change is worth it. And for a large percentage of the Oracle databases out there, the answer is a resounding yes.

Let us go into the steps that are required for migration.

Step 1: Modify Incompatible SQL

There are differences in SQL from Oracle SQL to PostgreSQL. However, the modification can be performed, and Oracle SQL is considered one of the least efficient variations on SQL.

- Many consider the language overspecialized.

- Oracle SQL is so complex that it is expensive to operate.

- Oracle SQL is more difficult to troubleshoot and has become decreasingly user-friendly.

- The overhead of Oracle SQL is not leveraged by the majority of companies, so they pay the extra cost, but do not receive the benefit of the additional complexity.

After the SQL modification is performed, one gets the benefit of cleaner SQL. In most cases, **most of the effort** in migration is SQL modification.

---

105 https://developers.slashdot.org/story/18/05/27/1925236/oracles-aggressive-sales-tactics-are-backfiring-with-customers

Step 2: Schema Conversion

This is where the schema (the tables and the relationships) from the Oracle database is moved over to PostgreSQL (in this example).

Invariably objects are built up in any database that is no longer used. So part of the process of conversion is only migrating what is necessary. AWS offers a schema conversion tool that provides a wide variety of conversions.[106]

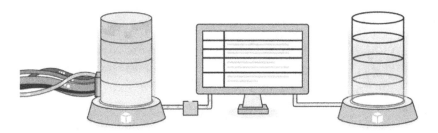

This graphic is from AWS's RDS migration page.

The list is included below:

Source Database	Target Database on Amazon RDS
Oracle Database	Amazon Aurora, MySQL, PostgreSQL, MariaDB
Amazon Aurora, MySQL, PostgreSQL, MariaDB	Amazon Redshift
Oracle Data Warehouse	Amazon Redshift
Microsoft SQL Server	Amazon Aurora, Amazon Redshift, MySQL, PostgreSQL, MariaDB
Teradata	Amazon Redshift
IBM Netezza	Amazon Redshift
Greenplum	Amazon Redshift
HPE Vertica	Amazon Redshift
MySQL and MariaDB	PostgreSQL
PostgreSQL	Amazon Aurora, MySQL, MariaDB
Amazon Aurora	PostgreSQL
IBM DB2 LUW	Amazon Aurora, MySQL, PostgreSQL

---

106 https://aws.amazon.com/dms/#sct

Step 3: Data Replication

This is where data is copied from the schema in the source to the schema in the target.

For both AWS RDS and Google Cloud SQL, the source database can be replicated to one or more regional databases.

Step 4: Migrating Code (Converting PL SQL Stored Procedures)

Stored procedures were for a long time promoted by Oracle to improve performance. Something called PL-SQL manages Oracle's stored procedures. (procedural language SQL).[107] However, this reduced database portability and enabled lock-in.

Since SAP created HANA, they began promoting stored procedures for the same reason that Oracle did, to increase lock-in. However, SAP has been pushing aggressively to recast all of its reverse engineering of other databases, which Brightwork Research & Analysis covered in the article Did SAP Just Reinvent the Wheel with HANA?[108] Therefore, SAP decided to call their stored procedures "code pushdown." Brightwork Research & Analysis covered in the article How Accurate are SAP's Statements on Code Pushdown?[109]

PL-SQL in Oracle can be converted to PL/pgSQ in part automatically, but some of the conversion will be manual.

Database Bloat

The fact is that a very large number of Oracle databases are just not doing that much that is particularly interesting or advanced. That is they are doing things other open source DBs could very quickly do at far lower expense. Yet many of these companies have Oracle DBAs managing them inefficiently on premises and at high cost.

This is referred to as database cost bloat.

---

107 A bit about stored procedures can be found in Oracle's documentation. *"You already know how to interact with the database using SQL, but it is not sufficient for building enterprise applications. PL/SQL is a third generation language that has the expected procedural and namespace constructs, and its tight integration with SQL makes it possible to build complex and powerful applications. Because PL/SQL is executed in the database, you can include SQL statements in your code without having to establish a separate connection."* - https://docs.oracle.com/cd/B28359_01/appdev.111/b28843/tdddg_procedures.htm

108 http://www.brightworkr.com/saphana/2018/03/01/sap-simply-reinvent-wheel-hana/

109 http://www.brightworkr.com/saphana/2018/02/27/accurate-saps-arguments-code-pushdown-cdss/

Database bloat pulls resources away from other things IT departments, perpetually short on budget for value-added items. Oracle supported and reinforced this entire inefficient approach; and Oracle is only now reacting to efficiencies imposed from the outside -- in this case AWS, Google Cloud and Azure. Without this change being brought from the outside, Oracle which makes enormous amounts of money from the status quo would prefer to keep things as they are as their database is a cash machine.

AWS and Google Cloud can cut the Oracle bill in two critical ways, one is the database license and the second is the support. For databases that support applications without open source database certification, Oracle to Oracle migration makes a lot of sense. It means turning an internally managed database into a managed service database. If the open source database can be used, then really large savings and efficiencies are possible. Companies that use Oracle should focus on this because a company can't migrate a chunk of their databases away from Oracle DB by using Oracle for IaaS/PaaS.

How Does Oracle View the Cloud?

Oracle has a curious view on the future of the cloud and Oracle's place in it. Mark Hurd, the CEO of Oracle has stated that **Oracle gets 3x in revenue for every customer that moves from on-premises to cloud**. That is where Oracle's head is at regarding the cloud. Customers need to prepare to pay Oracle much more, for the exact same thing.

Oracle's support has a 93%+ margin. Why should customers pay such a support margin if the open source databases are so well documented and one can have a managed database (either Oracle or open source) from AWS or Google Cloud? That is as long as the application support for open source is there and or if an older version of Oracle can be leveraged (allowing support to be dropped)? There is a great deal of money being wasted with the Oracle database and database support. We are not proposing that all Oracle DB's can be ripped out, we fully appreciate the case by case nature of the question, but the more Oracle databases a customer has, the more liability it creates. This is a liability in the form of dealing with Oracle account managers visit, audits, lots of DBAs consuming resources without scaling, and many other negative implications. One can minimize those liabilities by migrating some Oracle DBs to AWS or Google Cloud, and other Oracle DBs to non-Oracle using managed DBs on AWS or Google Cloud.

Properly Leveraging AWS RDS

We listed the significant steps to using RDS, but there are others. The RDS environment is different from an on-premises environment, and we do not intend to gloss over the differences. For example, some things can be leveraged for backup that doesn't exist in an on-premises environment. One of these is Lambda, the usage of which is described in the following quotation from House of Brick.

"The House of Brick best practice for proper backup retention is to use manual snapshots to store snapshots of the database in S3 on a monthly and annual basis. Using an encrypted S3 bucket is important for ensuring the security of the backup data. Because running these backups manually would be tedious and error prone, using a scheduled Lambda function is highly recommended for this purpose. The following example python 2.7 code illustrates à Lambda function that can be used for monthly snapshots for the instance OracleRDStest1 in the US-EAST-1 region.

```
import botocore
import datetime
import re
import logging
import boto3
region='us-east-1'
rds_instances = ['OracleRDStest1']
def lambda_handler(event, context):
    source = boto3.client('rds', region_name=region)
    for instance in rds_instances:
        try:
            timestamplabel = str(datetime.datetime.now().strftime('%Y-%m-%d-%H-%-M-%S')) + "monthly-snap"
            snapshot = "{0}-{1}-{2}".format("mysnapshot", instance,timestamplabel)
            response = source.create_db_snapshot(DBSnapshotIdentifier=snapshot,
            DBInstanceIdentifier=instance)
            print(response)
        except botocore.exceptions.ClientError as e:
            raise Exception("Could not create snapshot: %s" % e)
```

> *Once appropriate retention is established, backup reliability and availability also needs to be considered. It is possible for an entire AWS region to become unavailable, which has happened in the past. Keeping the backups in a S3 bucket in the same region as the RDS instance creates the potential nightmare scenario of simultaneously losing access to the database and all database backups. To combat this, House of Brick recommends mirroring the monthly, annual, and most recent daily backup to an encrypted S3 bucket in another region and on a different AWS account. The latter point is key, as it offers protection of the backup data from technical failure, human error, and malicious intruders. If the protected bucket is properly configured to allow versioned read/write access on a cross-account basis to the production account hosting the RDS instance, then the production account can never damage or delete retained backups, even if the production account is compromised to the root account level."[110]*

This quotation was included to emphasize that once in AWS or Google Cloud there are things to leverage that are new, and different ways of doing things. One does not manage an on premises environment the same way that one manages a cloud environment.

Let us take a moment to discuss the AWS and Google Cloud managed database.

Understanding the AWS and Google Cloud Managed Database Services

This is a relatively new service which has profound implications for changing how databases are administered.

The AWS managed database service is described by Brian Hostetter.

> *"Right, even if you run Oracle in AWS, you don't have to deal with capacity planning, patching, high availability, backups. RDS takes away the undifferentiated heavy lifting and allows your DBA's to tune and work on better ways of querying, that is much more valuable than backing up LUN's like on prem."*

The TCO reductions for databases are quite impressive, with the most significant impact being in labor and M&S ongoing fees. There is also the agility of immediate access and the ability to dynamically scale up and down, so companies don't have to spend on unused capacity. This removes the time and expense of performing the database planning.

---

110 http://houseofbrick.com/oracle-rds-best-practices-for-backup/

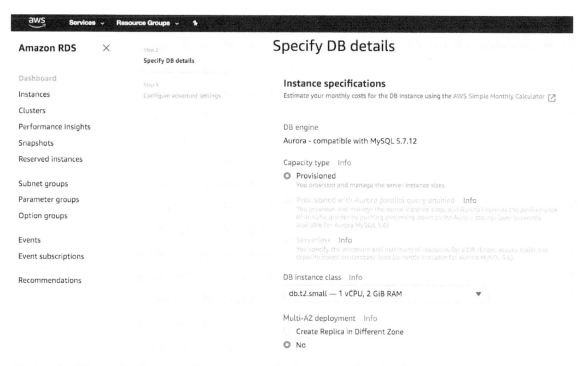

Notice the "Serverless" option for Aurora, which auto scales the database.

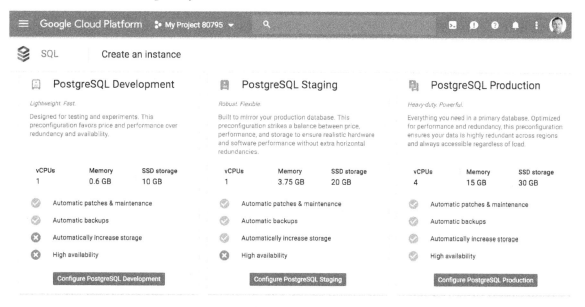

The development instance of PostreSQL on Cloud SQL does not scale. But the Staging and Production options do scale, but only for storage, not for the virtual CPUs. The vCPUs are set per category.

Under the on-premises model, everything had to be planned out, and companies invariably made forecast errors, which resulted in under or over capacity.

- If there's a usage increase due to seasonality or promotions, the customer can easily scale without the huge cost or RAC hardware, software, and implementation cost.

- Scaling is built into RDS and Google Cloud SQL not only across data centers, but also AZs and regions.

A natural question arises.

Why didn't Oracle offer the managed database service to customers long ago? The reason is that Oracle has not been innovating in the ways that AWS and Google Cloud have been innovating. First, Oracle lacks AWS and Google Cloud's cloud capabilities. Second, AWS and Google Cloud do not have on premises-based partners they have to worry about alienating. AWS can apply their technology advantage without protecting the status quo because AWS and Google do **not have anything invested** in the status quo.

Furthermore, Oracle has another problem, and this is related to AWS and Google's pricing strategy. AWS and Google's strategy is to cut prices and to keep cutting prices. Last year, AWS had a significant round of price cuts across its services. In some cases, up to 21%. It was their 62nd price cut to that date. Oracle has no history of cutting prices. Quite the opposite in fact.

Customers see this, and they want to participate. Labor has an 85% deflation in the cloud. The fully loaded cost of a single Oracle DBA is $120,000/year. The complete hardware and software infrastructure admin labor is redundant when the service is fully managed by automation. There is a reduction of 22% on software maintenance and the 10% reduction in hardware maintenance. Even the support reduction alone will pay for many of the migrations to AWS and Google Cloud.

The following quote highlights this.

> *"In terms of database administration, RDS has allowed us to forget about things like backups, capacity management, and patch management. Our projections are that we will pay about one quarter of what we were paying in our private infrastructure." - **Todd Hofert, Director of Infrastructure Operations, Trimble.***

As well as this one.

> *"While license fee savings from open source hit 100 per cent, open-source databases also yield significant savings in hardware costs. All in, companies can expect to*

save 70 per cent by shifting from Oracle to a database like MongoDB (even once you account for the cost of migration, re-skilling DBAs, etc.) On the AWS platform, the list price for running Oracle (RDS) is $25.68 per hour. Running PostgreSQL or MySQL (RDS) is 1/8th to 1/10th that cost.

As big as those savings are, however, the bigger cost differential derives from developer and DBA productivity.

For DBAs skilled with Oracle's database, they can often manage up to 25 database servers, on average. That same DBA can manage a million database servers on Amazon's RDS, thanks to the benefits of automation. Talk about scale."[111]

Conclusion

AWS's RDS is one of their most popular services. It is extremely successful, however, in our view, it is still underutilized. There are so many opportunities for either homogeneous or heterogeneous migration. A big part of more companies taking advantage of AWS is merely understanding and getting comfortable with using AWS. AWS provides explanations for how to manage the migration, provides a migration service as well as the ability to put customers in contact with partners that will support database migration. Database migration is one of the early steps that open up many other options for companies that they do not have if they keep their databases on premises.

SAP and Oracle have no answer for the managed database service, and Oracle's autonomous database, which we believe is fake, is an example of this. AWS and Google Cloud have such an advantage here because SAP and Oracle have so little experience managing databases for customers. Managing databases has never been a part of SAP and Oracle's business model.

Now that we have covered the database migration topic, with its associated cost improvements, now let us switch gears and move to another benefit of AWS and Google Cloud. This is how AWS and Google Cloud can speed the development of software.

---

111 https://www.theregister.co.uk/2018/05/31/rise_of_the_open_source_data_strategies/

Chapter 4: Complications of Migrating SAP to the Cloud

This book is very much in favor of utilizing AWS and Google Cloud, but we are careful not to sugar coat the process of leveraging these providers. This means taking a realistic look at what it means to migrate SAP applications and SAP's database to the cloud.

To begin, SAP's history has been not only on premises but more often bare metal rather than virtual machines.

This is explained by Ravi Padmanabhan of Velocity Cloud.

> *"The SAP application requires dedicated virtual machines not necessarily dedicated hosts - hence these hyperscalers provide lots of flexibility on how we deploy virtual machines. Depending on how you decide to utilize EC2 / GCE there are lot of economies that can be gained by customers who transform their SAP infrastructure to them."*[112]

Any EC2 instance can run a non-production SAP application, however for production SAP applications, it is necessary to use an SAP certified EC2 instance.

---

112 We include the Wikipedia definition of hyperscale to better interpret the quotation. *"In computing, hyperscale is the ability of an architecture to scale appropriately as increased demand is added to the system. This typically involves the ability to seamlessly provision and add compute, memory, networking, and storage resources to a given node or set of nodes that make up a larger computing, distributed computing, or grid computing environment. Hyperscale computing is necessary in order to build a robust and scalable cloud, big data, map reduce, or distributed storage system and is often associated with the infrastructure required to run large distributed sites such as Facebook[1], Google[2], Microsoft[3], Amazon[4][5], or Oracle[6]. Companies like Ericsson and Intel provide hyperscale infrastructure kits for IT service providers.[7]"* - https://en.wikipedia.org/wiki/Hyperscale
https://d1.awsstatic.com/enterprise-marketing/SAP/SAP_on_AWS_Implementation_Guide.pdf

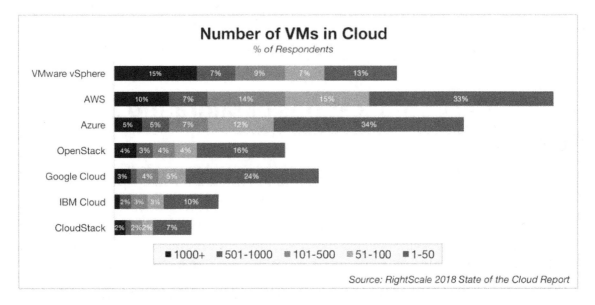

Where is SAP Cloud in terms of the number of VMs run in the cloud? As usual, the top three cloud IaaS entities are again AWS, Azure and Google Cloud. If customers are to initiate a VM, it will most likely be by using AWS, Azure or Google Cloud.

However, a dedicated virtual machine is significantly different than are a shared virtual machine. For one they cost more. This is simply a disadvantage when trying to migrate to AWS or Google Cloud.

When it comes to using databases, there are restrictions in using some of AWS's most popular offerings.

> *"Regarding Dynamo DB - yes this is not a certified database for the SAP core applications except for use as an extension on Hybris. The No SQL technology is not certified since the SAP application is traditional application as opposed to a Cloud Native hence they stay focused with certified databases on Oracle, SQL, ASE and HANA. There is enough flexibility for customers with the certified databases that I don't see lack of Dynamo DB as a disadvantage. On RDS, this does not work well for SAP but is ok for Oracle applications. The reason is due to the nature of the database management structure within SAP - since this is primarily BASIS driven, using a web service like RDS does not make a lot of sense due to the database management capabilities that are inherent within the application itself. Regardless, RDS really is only a different way to purchase database licensing and management services - again I don't see this as an inhibitor for SAP customers adopting hyperscale."*

Therefore these realities can seem at odds with the expectations of SAP to AWS migration.

> *"AWS manages the physical infrastructure up to the virtualization layer. The operating system and any SAP applications and databases running above the virtualization layer are managed by the customer. If a managed service is required, AWS has a network of partners that offer SAP consulting and managed services on AWS."[113]*

Deploying SAP Databases on AWS

One can always migrate SAP to bare metal, but bare metal is merely hosting – it is moving the server from the customer location to AWS, it is not cloud. The benefits come when migration takes place to a cloud, which means virtualization. Recall from our earlier explanation of what makes cloud, the benefits of cloud do not extend to simple hosting. If you take a look at AWS products assortment, only one, AWS EC2 would be relevant for SAP's on-premises products. SAP has made many cloud acquisitions such as SuccessFactors and Ariba that do not have these limitations. However, for SAP's internally developed products, and where SAP receives most of its revenue (ECC, BW, HANA, APO, etc.), this limitation applies. Bare metal servers are necessary for SAP application servers. To use anything else you have to be able to integrate it with SAP ERP, but SAP PI/PO, SAP's middleware application is far from being able to do that.

The relatively smooth migration to the cloud could be only on HANA database. However, HANA does not support clustering. Clustering is set up to provide load balancing and for fault tolerance.

AWS has a nice definition of clustering.

> *"An Amazon Aurora DB cluster consists of one or more DB instances and a cluster volume that manages the data for those DB instances. An Aurora cluster volume is a virtual database storage volume that spans multiple Availability Zones, with each Availability Zone having a copy of the DB cluster data. Two types of DB instances make up an Aurora DB cluster."[114]*

Therefore it is a combination of databases that are managed by one instance of a database server.

---

113 https://aws.amazon.com/sap/faq/
114 https://docs.aws.amazon.com/AmazonRDS/latest/AuroraUserGuide/Aurora.Overview.html

Big companies will have an issue replacing the Oracle database with HANA in significant scale. This is because it is unsafe to use a single database instance and backup with replication will never replace real cluster.

HANA is the most prominent item offered by SAP on AWS. However, it should be remembered that HANA is only used at a **tiny** percentage of SAP customers. Most SAP customers still use Oracle, DB2 or SQL Server. This is explained numerically in the following quote from the book SAP Nation 2.0.

> *"SAP says over 7,000 customers are using HANA, which means the majority of its nearly 300,000 customers are still persisting with databases from Oracle, Microsoft, IBM, and SAP's own Sybase and MaxDB. In periodic updates, SAP shows the state of support for Oracle's database version 10g, 11g, 12c, its engineering systems and related products. That diversity will continue for years, as customers will not jettison the elaborate systems management and talent infrastructures they have built around those databases."*

HANA only seems so prominent because of SAP's marketing. This can be seen by DB-Engines, which is a website which tracks database popularity.

Marketed extremely heavily, HANA has not grown in popularity a database since the beginning of 2017.[115]

Furthermore, customers that bought and implemented HANA in almost all cases did so on premises. And they bought a huge hardware footprint to use it, which is something we cover

---

115 https://db-engines.com/en/ranking_trend/system/SAP+HANA

in the article The Secret to Not Talking About the Cost of HANA.[116] What is the likelihood that they are now a market to migrate to AWS? Not high.

And part of the reason for HANA being featured so prominently on AWS is quite obviously because SAP is trying to get more adoptions of HANA. That is not because many customers will be migrating HANA to AWS.

Another significant item offered on AWS from SAP is the Adaptive Server Enterprise or the renamed Sybase DB. However, the renamed Sybase DB is not a fixture at many SAP customers. This is usually that case that SAP does not migrate customers from acquisitions into core SAP. Therefore Adaptive Server Enterprise/Sybase DB will factor even less so in SAP customer migrations than HANA.

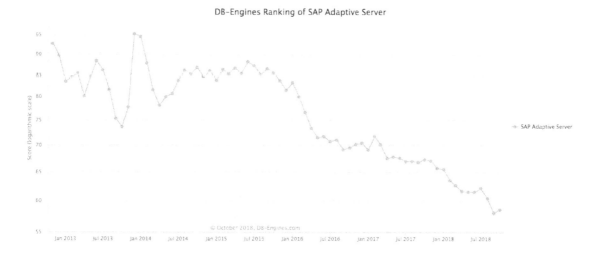

Sybase DB/SAP Adaptive Server is one of the most rapidly declining databases. Although, notice that the base is 55, not zero, therefore the rate of this decline is exaggerated by roughly a factor of 2x in this graphic.

With HANA and the Adaptive Server Enterprise being the two most prominently featured products on AWS, it means that two most prominently featured SAP products on AWS will have very limited usage by SAP customers.

---

116 http://www.brightworkr.com/saphana/2016/12/11/secret-not-talking-cost-sap-hana/

Evaluating SAP's Previous Proposals on Cloud and SAP Infrastructure

One of the things that tend to be glossed over is the number of promises that SAP has made regarding infrastructure that has not come true, as well as what the new SAP cloud components mean for Basis, which is the infrastructure layer in SAP.

To get this perspective we needed to find an SAP Basis resource to explain SAP's infrastructure history. The following quotation is from Cemal Doganay who has worked in SAP Basis since 1998. This quotation describes the impact of moving from the on-premises SAP infrastructure to SAP's cloud.

> *"I remember the fact that every new product was welcomed with new hopes and pushing us to install ASAP from 6.40 Web Application Server, MDM, XI, MDM, APO etc. At the end, none of the initial problems were efficiently resolved but they resulted in the requirement for new products and new interfaces.*
>
> *That still goes on.*
>
> *I finally experienced my first SAP Cloud Project. It is a project that will migrate a legacy system and its interfaces to S/4 HANA . That sounds very exciting. The infrastructure is a private cloud which is called HEC (HANA Enterprise Cloud) which I call "Restricted Hosting."*
>
> - *Interestingly, there is no operating system access. I found ways to run couple of operating system command. But that was the extent of it.*
>
> - *In order to configure HANA Monitoring for example, we needed to open an HEC ticket to provide some rights to the database user.*
>
> - *Therefore, we are limited to using the SAP GUI and and HANA Studio which is again limited.*
>
> *Since the project began, I feel that what a SAP Basis Administrator does in the SAP cloud environment is to stick to Solution Manager and its capabilities plus user management. It seems that for the SAP Basis Administrator On Cloud lies in Solution manager Administration plus User management. Yet, even in the Solution Manager in the monitoring area, it is highly advised to concentrate on business related monitoring rather than technical side because HEC (they say) already monitor required items.*

According to, what is called, 'HEC Catalog', we are not allowed to do other things. For example, Upgrades, SPS Updates, SAP Stop/Start actions. We are told we should plan Start/Stop times one week before even in Development Systems. Otherwise, probably they will charge extra.

Some items like applying OSS Notes (SAP's support note system) can be performed by SAP or by the customer. Of course, it should be billed separately if SAP does that.

What I observe in this short time is that Fiori involvement in a project will bring more maintenance headache because security efforts should be doubled. If a backend user is created that should be also created on Fiori server and proper authorizations should be assigned. So, it looks more and more as if the SAP Administration On Cloud becomes Solution Manager + user management."

Hopefully this provides a more realistic feel of the realities faced by SAP infrastructure as the cloud encroaches into on premises SAP environments.

Conclusions

SAP has unique challenges when leveraging AWS or Google Cloud. Customers have no qualification to "hack" the SAP with their integration bus and there only a few developers who know both SAP inwards and Cloud inwards. And of course, SAP will newer provide an adequate API to SAP.

SAP's databases are a poor fit for the cloud. HANA is almost always run on premises unless an inexpensive or free version is used for testing or development on AWS.

- SAP has spent the past few years getting customers that purchased HANA to buy outsized servers.

- SAP's Adaptive Server Enterprise is a database in steep decline and is a database companies are migrating from, rather than focusing on migrating to the cloud.

- HANA and Adaptive Server Enterprise are the two easiest SAP products to use in AWS. But after that, everything is more difficult to migrate to AWS. In this way, they are misleading. SAP is touting the ease of placing its databases on AWS but leaving out the complications of what happens after that.

In our next chapter we will move on to discussing how AWS compares against SAP and Oracle Cloud.

Chapter 5: SAP and Oracle Versus AWS and Google Cloud Pricing

Let us begin with the topic of license and pricing complexity. AWS and Google Cloud offer good pricing transparency and the ability even to adjust consumption to adjust the resulting cost. Both SAP and Oracle pricing and licensing is so complicated, it is impossible to be in conformance with all of the licensing rules.

Section I		Oracle Database			Prices in USA (Dollar)
	Named User Plus	Software Update License & Support	Processor License	Software Update License & Support
Database Products				
Oracle Database				
Standard Edition 2	350	77.00	17,500	3,850.00
Enterprise Edition	950	209.00	47,500	10,450.00
Personal Edition	460	101.20	-	-
Mobile Server	-	-	23,000	5,060.00
NoSQL Database Enterprise Edition	200	44	10,000	2,200.00
Enterprise Edition Options:				
Multitenant	350	77.00	17,500	3,850.00
Real Application Clusters	460	101.20	23,000	5,060.00
Real Application Clusters One Node	200	44.00	10,000	2,200.00
Active Data Guard	230	50.60	11,500	2,530.00
Partitioning	230	50.60	11,500	2,530.00
Real Application Testing	230	50.60	11,500	2,530.00
Advanced Compression	230	50.60	11,500	2,530.00
Advanced Security	300	66.00	15,000	3,300.00
Label Security	230	50.60	11,500	2,530.00
Database Vault	230	50.60	11,500	2,530.00
OLAP	460	101.20	23,000	5,060.00
Advanced Analytics	460	101.20	23,000	5,060.00
Spatial and Graph	350	77.00	17,500	3,850.00
TimesTen Application-Tier Database Cache	460	101.20	23,000	5,060.00
Database In-Memory	460	101.20	23,000	5,060.00
Retail Data Model	800	176.00	40,000	8,800.00
Communications Data Model	1,500	330.00	50,000	11,000.00
Airlines Data Model	800	176.00	40,000	8,800.00
Utilities Data Model	800	176.00	40,000	8,800.00
Database Enterprise Management				
Diagnostics Pack	150	33.00	7,500	1,650.00
Tuning Pack	100	22.00	5,000	1,100.00
Database Lifecycle Management Pack	240	52.80	12,000	2,640.00
Data Masking and Subsetting Pack	230	50.60	11,500	2,530.00
Cloud Management Pack for Oracle Database	150	33.00	7,500	1,650.00

Unlike SAP, Oracle's price list is "published," but it's both very complicated to calculate and does not include discounts. So even if the calculation is performed from the price list, that does not tell you the price a company will pay.[117] Rounds of negotiation on Oracle pricing include Oracle

---

117 https://www.oracle.com/assets/applications-price-list-070574.pdf

pricing resources because the pricing is too complicated for the sales rep to calculate on their own. As can be seen in many screenshots in this books, pricing is estimated in both AWS and Google Cloud before the service is activated. As the changes are made to the service, the prices are updated. This is leveraging the web and online calculation to make pricing easier. Oracle, decides to keep its pricing in a complicated format to calculate, and even if calculated correctly, the actual price can never be known without contacting a sales rep from Oracle.

And there is a very good reason for all of this pricing opacity, as the following quotation attests.

> *"The main benefit of NoSQL is they are usually open source and either completely free, or relatively low cost since some support is usually purchased. Most people don't realize how expensive Oracle and DB2 are, often costing a license fee of $1 million per server, plus $200,000 per year for ongoing support after that. Most enterprise applications need more than one server for fault tolerance, staging, QA, testing, development, etc (although licensing costs for non-production installations are often less than the production server)." - **From Mark A commenting on the article The Death of the Commercial Database Oracle's Dilemma."**[118]*

This tells anyone quite a bit about the emphasis these various entities place upon pricing transparency. Also, there are many odd things with Oracle. Unlike SAP, Oracle's price list is "published," but it's both very complicated to calculate and does not include discounts. So even if the calculation is performed from the price list, that does not tell you the price a company will pay. Rounds of negotiation on Oracle pricing include Oracle pricing resources because the pricing is too complicated for the sales rep to calculate on their own.

How Transparent is AWS and Google Cloud Pricing?

As can be seen in many screenshots in this books, pricing is estimated in both AWS and Google Cloud before the service is activated. As the changes are made to the service, the prices are updated. This is leveraging the web and online calculation to make pricing easier. Oracle, decides to keep its pricing in a complicated format to calculate, and Oracle is continuously trying to get the most sales dollars out of their customers. There is no sales culture of selling customers what they need. This is covered in the following quotation.

> *"With Oracle, a significant determinant of total cost of ownership is the choice of software edition and the various options and packs selected. Oracle sales will often push Enterprise Edition without any analysis of actual requirements. Prior*

---

118 http://www.brightworkr.com/saphana/2017/07/08/accurate-seeking-alpha-relative-decline-sql/

to SE2…customers can actually run enterprise-class workloads with Standard Edition."[119]

While we have distinguished SAP and Oracle versus AWS and Google Cloud, we would be remiss if we did not point out that AWS and Google's pricing is not identically clear. Most users consider Google to have more understandable and traceable pricing than AWS. The overall pricing model of Google Cloud is more straightforward. But this is in good part also because AWS releases so many services when compared to Google Cloud.

Why The Price Paid for Oracle is Often Unknowable

Something left out of the analysis is whether the actual overall costs of SAP or Oracle knowable by customers. Oracle will often carry on about something they have that is better than an open source alternative. However, what is left out, is that the open source database alternative does not come with Oracle's sales and licensing rules. However, since when is anything discussed without consideration for the cost? Let us take the example of an automobile. No doubt the Lamborghini Countach is a fine automobile. How many people reading this book own one?

Oracle would like cost and liability, the cost of dealing with Oracle and Oracle audits and the restrictions with what companies can do with Oracle licenses to not to be part of the discussion. SAP similarly does not want to discuss the indirect access liabilities that come with their HANA database. Yet no other database comes with this level of liability.

---

119 http://houseofbrick.com/wp-content/uploads/2016/08/2016_HoB_RDBMS_Licensing-White-Paper.pdf

What is not to like about the Countach?[120] Are we going to talk about price at some point? What does an oil change run on a Countach? Just the oil is $80 per quart. Furthermore it uses 18 quarts, making for a $1,440 price oil change – but that is just for the oil. Labor is extra.

People who think the Countach is expensive will need to get ready for a shock when preparing to pay the bill for Oracle's database; add on the costs of the time spent negotiating with Oracle, reading circuitous Oracle contracts, hardening the database against audits, in addition to the overhead of maintaining an Oracle database. By comparison, the Countach is an absolute bargain. Furthermore, the comparison is entirely appropriate as many other sports cars can do most of what the Countach can do, but with far less overhead.

With Oracle's highly complex terms and conditions, what often looks like **one price at one point**, becomes a different price down the road. For example, the enterprise edition version of the database can quickly become prohibitively expensive. Oracle does something strange in that it prices its database by the number of processors or cores. There the number of cores (processors) contracted variants on discounts for scale. Virtual machines implications that also impact the pricing, which we will be discussing shortly.

---

120 https://blog.dupontregistry.com/lamborghini/lamborghini-countach-specs-price-photos-review/

"It's Time for Your Audit Sir"

Oracle is the best known user of audits in enterprise software. And while Oracle proposes legitimate reasons for audits, in reality Oracle uses audits in the most dishonest way imaginable. Oracle uses audits to control customers and drive them to things that Oracle would like them to purchase.[121]

Oracle's attempts to legitimize their audits are undermined by the fact that no other software vendor uses audits in such an extreme fashion as Oracle. No other vendor places triggers in their software that are deliberately designed to be exploited during an audit. Oracle resources endorsing Oracle's audits illustrate the fundamental corruption of the person attempting to defend such manipulative and abusive practices. An obvious question becomes apparent. If virtually all other vendors that charge far more reasonable prices for their software do not need to perform such audits, why does Oracle claim the right to do so?

So how to Oracle audits work in reality?

One strategy they use is to boobie trap the installation. A typical audit scenario we have seen is that Oracle delivers software with essentially all functionality, default, enabled. The actual bill of material is not relevant. They put the onus on the customer to deactivate the functionality to tie out to the bill. However, **few customers** do this. Also, **few Oracle consulting firms advise their customers to do this**. As with the SAP consulting partners market, this is one of the many things that leads us to question who much Oracle consulting partner market looks out for their customers versus looking out for themselves (and for Oracle).

Oracle knows when to audit the customer, as they placed the trap in the installation in the first place. When the audit hits the customer Oracle will tell the customer something along the lines of the following.

> *"Look here this is what you procured yet you have transportation turned on, have you used this module?"*

---

121 House of Brick offers the following advice as to compliance with Oracle on audits. *"During these audits, Oracle may ask for a lot of information, only some of which they are likely entitled to receive according to the contract. When considering these requests, you should ask yourself, "Is the requested information actually related to my use of the Oracle programs?" Again, an experienced, qualified third party can help you understand what is and what is not appropriate to share. Oracle is entitled to know where you are using its software. But that does not entitle Oracle to probe into other areas of your IT environment where Oracle software is not in use. We have seen that oversharing of information with Oracle may lead to inflated claims of non-compliance. It may also lead to additional unnecessary efforts to eliminate those claims."* - http://houseofbrick.com/navigating-oracle-audits/

The customer often has no idea. Then the audit starts!

Oracle's audits attack the entire stack. That is from apps, middleware, to the database. Oracle then comes up with a number which **conveniently** matches/exceeds a sales rep cloud quota. Then the horse trading starts, and they state something along the following.

> *"Your cost is 500k for all this illegal use of software. We're also going to have to charge you interest based on time of use and this is going to get ugly."*

So a deal is cut.

> *"Buy 500k Oracle Cloud ANYTHING and we'll make this problem go away."*

And then...

> *"Sign this non-disclosure and everything is fine."*

Let us review the sequence of events.

1. *Set the Audit Land Mine*: The problem, in this case, is a landmine that is preset by Oracle to go off when the audit is conducted.

2. *Complicit Oracle Consulting Partners*: Oracle consulting partners are complicit by not informing the customer as to the preset landmine. Any Oracle consulting partner that would advise their customer about the landmines in the implementation would put their partnership with Oracle on tenuous ground. This is why companies that have a history of helping customers with these types of issues, like House of Brick, are not Oracle partners.

3. *The Audit*: Oracle then audits the account, knowing precisely what they will find as they set the landmine.

4. *The Determination of the Audit Bill*: The Oracle sales rep works backward from their quota to determine the audit charge.

The solution is then for the customer to buy more software. The customer ends up paying exorbitant compensation to Oracle. The IT department is then motivated to use somehow the software they "purchased" to cover up for what happened.

However, when the sale of the item is reported to Wall Street, it is reported as if it is voluntary. Oracle does not set aside a part of its quarterly analyst calls to state that "40% of our cloud sales were coerced through audits of other products." There is a lawsuit filed against Oracle for misrepresenting audit lead cloud purchases as a consequence of authentic demand at customers which will be covered in more detail later in the book.

How Big of a Deal are Oracle Audits?

One should consider the seriousness of an Oracle audit concerning what it means for the work effort on the part of the customer. Oracle's strategy is to drown the customer in paperwork to overwhelm their ability to respond to the audit. When Mars sued Oracle over their audit, Mars claimed that they were required to provide over 233,089 documents over a year period to Oracle.

Mars asserted Oracle lied the reasons it requested information.

> "Oracle demanded information to which it is not contractually entitled regarding servers that do not run Oracle software and Mars personnel who do not use Oracle software," Mars' complaint read. "Oracle made these demands under false pretenses under false premises that non-use of software nonetheless somehow constitutes licensable use of software for which Mars owes Oracle."[122]

As is usually the case, this information is only available because it came out in a lawsuit. Non litigated audits (which is nearly all of them) stay private. However, why would so many documents be requested by Oracle?

According to Dave Welsh of House of Brick Technologies, this case in 2015 was the first litigation of Oracle on VMware. Oracle did not like this case to be discussed because it shed light on something they would prefer to do in the shadows which is Oracle's pricing with respect to virtual machines. Dave Welsh proposes that Oracle settled out of court so quickly with Mars because Oracle **did not want its claims around Oracle on VMware tested in court**. This is because they want to continue to bring these same audits with the same set of assertions against other customers, as his following quote attests.

> "I'm sorry that it appears Oracle opted not to appear in court. I'm also not the least bit surprised. In my opinion, Oracle appears interested in trying to see if it can get any more money out of any of its Oracle on VMware customers. It also appears to want to do that without a court's evaluation."[123]

And Arthur Beeman, who was the lead counsel for Mars made the following statement regarding the outcome of the case.

> "That filing…represented such a threat to Oracle's practices as it related to the licensing that there was an agreement to immediately stay the matter… and then

122 https://www.infoworld.com/article/3024957/software-licensing/what-does-an-oracle-audit-look-like-this-one-certainly-wasnt-pretty.html
123 http://houseofbrick.com/mars-vs-oracle/

eventually there was a settlement and it was dismissed with prejudice less than two months after the filing."[124]

These are not uncommon experiences. AutoDeploy has experienced the audit scenario above with every one of their customers. It's a feature of their sales process, not a bug.

This is corroborated by the lawsuit brought by the City of Sunrise Florida Firefighter Fund that was brought up earlier in the book. The Firefighter Fund is suing Oracle for not disclosing that a portion of its cloud revenue reported as voluntary was anything but. This was, as asserted by the Firefighter Fund, because Oracle has been using audits to coerce customers into buying cloud products, and not telling investors. All while Oracle has made it appear as if the cloud business has been customers coming to Oracle asking to purchase cloud offerings.[125]

Oracle also misleads customers in its documentation as to what the rules are about auditing, which is covered in the following quotation.

> *"Another area that causes confusion with many Oracle customers is the policy documents that Oracle publishes. Most of these documents (Partitioning Policy, Licensing Oracle Software in the Cloud Computing Environment, Licensing Data Recovery Guide, etc.) are not referenced by the agreement and are thus not binding in your contract with Oracle. The Partitioning Policy document is frequently cited by Oracle to customers running on VMware. Just remember that this document does not contain binding policy. There are some non-contractual documents, however, such as the Licensing Oracle Software in the Cloud Computing Environment (Cloud Environment) policy from Oracle, that are fundamentally different. In this particular document, **Oracle is granting additional privileges beyond the contract, rather than restricting them.(emphasis added)**"[126]*

SAP and Oracle must have been separated at birth!

This is because we found this exact issue with SAP when they released what was supposedly an announcement to ameliorate the concerns of their customers regarding something called indirect access.[127] In a nearly identical pattern to that displayed by Oracle regarding audits,

---

124 http://houseofbrick.com/oops-they-did-it-again-debunking-oracles-claims-of-needing-to-license-prospective-events-in-the-cloud/

125 http://www.brightworkr.com/saaseconomy/2018/08/13/oracle-sued-for-making-false-claims-about-cloud-growth/

126 http://nocoug.org/Journal/NoCOUG_Journal_201708.pdf#page=4

127 We cover the distinction between legitimate indirect access and illegitimate in the article How to Best Understand Type 1 Versus Type 2 Indirect Access. - http://www.brightworkr.com/sap/2017/04/type-one-versus-type-two-indirect-access/

SAP pretended in their announcement to soften their position on indirect access, but instead which served to claim more restrictive indirect access rules on customers. Brightwork Research & Analysis covered this topic in detail in the article SAP's Recycled Indirect Access Damage Control for 2018.[128]

As a brief interlude, SAP has perhaps unsurprisingly been using indirect access to force cloud purchases as is covered in the following quotation from the book SAP Nation 2.0.

> *"Other customers report "gun to the head" behavior. In a spin-off situation, SAP demanded a hefty assignment fee, but offered an alternate multiyear contract on its cloud products, which the customer did not need. In another such situation, SAP threatened to invoke its "indirect access" clause (a tactic many customers report)- again, the customer was offered a cloud subscription as an alternative."[129]*

Oracle also declares that they may change their license agreements at any time.

> *"Reliance on such documents may be risky, however, as Oracle expressly points out in the Licensing Oracle Software in the Cloud Computing Environment policy that it is non-binding and subject to change at any time. However, to the extent that Oracle is knowingly publishing extra-contractual documents on which its customers rely by making large investments, an argument can be made that Oracle should be estopped or prevented from changing course down the road, especially if such a change would cause injury to Oracle customers. Whether a court would accept this argument, or find that the customer proceeded at their own risk, is an open question."- **Pamela Fulmer***

How the Total Costs are Hidden from SAP & Oracle Customers

A big part of the on premises software model is that costs are hidden. It is a curiosity to participate in sales support and to see executives spend so much time focusing on the initial purchase cost when the initial purchase cost is such a small percentage of the overall TCO of any on-premises application or database.

With SAP and Oracle, costs are always hidden to the degree possible.

As with other on-premises purchases, the costs are absorbed as part of the overall IT budget. Costs don't ever seem to decrease with SAP or Oracle. SAP and Oracle customers typically

---

128 http://www.brightworkr.com/indirectaccess/2018/04/10/saps-recycled-indirect-access-damage-control-for-2018/
129 https://www.amazon.com/SAP-Nation-2-0-empire-disarray-ebook/dp/B013F5BKJQ

have their IT budgets overconsumed by SAP and Oracle, and this leaves areas unaddressed because SAP and Oracle don't offer everything necessary to run a company, or at the very least to run it well.

SAP and Oracle's focus focus on continually increasing costs is something that is the opposite of what is found when using AWS or Google Cloud when costs are far more transparent, and the overall costs are far lower. This is combined with the ability to close down services that are not used, significantly reducing the overhang of previous applications that did not work out, and issue which so consumes financial resources on SAP and Oracle customers.

SAP or Oracle offers a wide variety of discounts, with higher discounts, provided the more a customer purchases. However, these byzantine and arbitrary discounts (and which makes Oracle so tricky to price) only impact the initial purchase price, it does nothing to change the rest of the TCO of the products purchased. The discussion on SAP and Oracle negotiations is highly centered around how the sales rep can reduce the initial cost if the customer buys more.

For example, if we take support, at one time both SAP and Oracle charged 15% per year for support. Then Oracle increased its support cost to 20%, and SAP quickly followed suit to match them. Currently, SAP and Oracle customers pay 22%+ support. And this is for support that is primarily outsourced to third world countries. Oracle performs more audits of its customers than any other vendor, and SAP uses indirect access to bring multi-million dollar claims against (some of) its customers.

All of this happened as both SAP and Oracle's costs for providing that support declined significantly as both vendors migrated support from developed countries to primarily India, and both companies report in their financial statements that support revenue is between an 85% and 93% margin business. All of the increases in support occurred while SAP and Oracle's support costs **decreased** quite significantly. This support profit margin is so high that we looked for other areas where profit margins were similarly high, and we found one, which Brightwork Research & Analysis chronicled in the article How do SAP and Oracle's Support Profit Margins Compare to Pablo Escobar.[130]

One might ask the question, why do Oracle and SAP have support margins that are so similar to a business which trafficked cocaine? Oracle and SAP prefer to spend on acquisitions rather than shoring up (and reducing the costs to their customers) of their support.

What is odd about SAP and Oracle's continually escalating consumption of the IT budget is that IT is supposed to become more efficient with more significant investments. However, the scale returns from SAP and Oracle are not there. SAP and Oracle ceaselessly promise

---

130 http://www.brightworkr.com/sap/2018/08/how-do-sap-and-oracles-support-profit-margins-compare-to-pablo-escobar/

new products that will reduce TCO, a promise that is never fulfilled. Moreover, this is not exclusive to SAP and Oracle. It is also, at least in part, a function of the job shop or one-off nature of on-premises software. For an on-premises enterprise software purchase, the license costs are on average only 10% of the overall TCO of the application. Most of the costs end up being long-term maintenance.

Cloud service providers vendors like AWS provide a managed service, and this means that the costs are not hidden as they are with on-premises. It means that while not all the costs are fully allocated to the AWS bill, a far higher percentage of them are allocated to the AWS bill.

Seeking Alpha provides a good synopsis of what drives companies to AWS and by extension Google Cloud.

> *"I think it is probably important to understand why customers choose AWS and why they choose cloud services at all. I will expand on this a bit but simply put, AWS is simply cheaper, simpler and more reliable than any other way most users can get the same amount of computing.*
>
> *Cheaper, simpler and more reliable works for almost everyone. The current Gartner Magic Quadrant report shows AWS with one of the largest leads that I have ever seen in that series. The No. 2 in the report MSFT is said to have almost the same completeness of vision but far less executing competence."*[131]

AWS describes its pricing thusly:

> *"AWS offers on-demand, pay-as-you-go, and reservation-based payment models, enabling you to obtain the best return on your investment for each specific use case. AWS services do not have complex dependencies or licensing requirements, so you can get exactly what you need to build innovative, cost effective solutions using the latest technology.*
>
> *"AWS services are priced independently and transparently, so you can choose and pay for exactly what you need and no more. No minimum commitments or long-term contracts are required unless you choose to save money through a reservation model. By paying for services on an as-needed basis, you can redirect your focus to innovation and invention, reducing procurement complexity and enabling your business to be fully elastic." - **AWS Pricing**[132]*

---

131 Something we needed to note was that Microsoft pays Gartner far more than does AWS. And vendor payments influence Gartner. If they didn't Gartner would not receive one third of its overall revenues from vendors. We cover Gartner in depth in the book Gartner and the Magic Quadrant. http://www. brightworkr.com/scmfocuspress/it-decision-making-books/gartner-and-the-magic-quadrant/

132 https://d0.awsstatic.com/whitepapers/aws_pricing_overview.pdf

Normally we don't simply provide a quotation from a provider without commenting, or correcting the quotation. However, in this case, it is difficult to take issue with anything in this AWS quotation.

Secondly, AWS offers all of these things but is growing rapidly in functionality. This is known by anyone who works with AWS, but it is also pointed out by Seeking Alpha.

> *"Amazon says it added no fewer than 516 features to AWS last year. I have no idea what all these features are and even if I did I doubt that it would materially advance my evaluation of the forward momentum of AWS.*

> *But the point is that AWS market share lead means that it can amortize development costs over a significantly large base of revenues making more attractive and affordable for the company to add features."*

The point is that no one, not even those that work at AWS can keep up with even a fraction of the services, and services tweaks that AWS introduces.

AWS and Google intentionally lower prices to lure customers to their platform. That's is one way they sustain 49% growth year over year. AWS and Google could charge more. Instead, they purposefully cut prices every year (more often than that...we typically get price cuts every month). They can do this because, at their scale, the large discounts they get on hardware. Companies like Oracle, on the other hand, **are accustomed to far higher margins**. This margin is the problem for Oracle and the opportunity for the likes of AWS and Google. It is not possible, for Oracle to compete on price and scale to even 25% of the total revenue from the cloud.

AWS and Google Cloud Define Elastic

The emphasis of AWS and Google Cloud is "elastic." This means that the services offered by AWS and Google Cloud can be easily scaled. AWS also has auto scaling which is covered in the AWS document AWS Auto Scaling.[133] Autoscaling is free to use (it's just a matter of configuration).

Autoscaling currently applies to the following AWS offerings:

- Amazon EC2 Auto Scaling groups
- Aurora DB clusters

---

133 https://docs.aws.amazon.com/autoscaling/plans/userguide/as-plans-ug.pdf

- DynamoDB global secondary indexes

- DynamoDB tables

- ECS services

- Spot Fleet requests

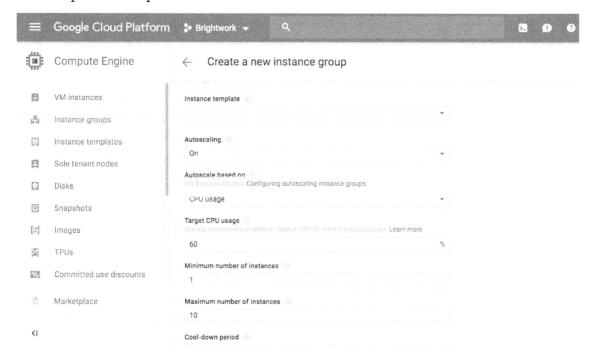

Under the Compute Engine in Google Cloud, notice the second option is "Autoscaling." Any service can be scaled manually, but also scaling can be automated. The downside? If a large load hits the system, the pricing may catch customers off guard. That is why it is important to keep an eye on the running costs.

AWS continually reinforces the idea that because it is so easy to scale up, that customers should start small.

> *"No minimum commitments or long-term contracts are required unless you choose to save money through a reservation model. By paying for services on an as-needed basis, you can redirect your focus to innovation and invention, reducing procurement complexity and enabling your business to be fully elastic."*

And when any "serverless" service is enabled, the autoscaling is automatic.

Stuffing the Account with Licenses

Everything described up to this point regarding AWS and Google Cloud is the opposite of SAP and Oracle. AWS and Google Cloud are offering flexibility to customers while for decades SAP and Oracle have provided lock-in. SAP and Oracle rely upon "highly motivated" salespeople to meet their quota. This is a problem not only with SAP and Oracle but with the on-premises sales model as well – SAP and Oracle are merely two of the most aggressive at manipulating this model. Even the autoscaling feature described in the previous section is considered a novelty with SAP and Oracle. However, characteristics like this provide freedom for the customer. It is based upon an entirely different sales principle than the status quo. SAP and Oracle try to get as much of their applications and databases into the customer regardless of its utility. It is quite common to find both SAP and Oracle customers "stuffed" with applications that they barely use or that are shelfware. License consultants help companies negotiate what to do with shelf ware licenses with SAP and Oracle.

One sales rep whom we know for SAP had so stuffed their customer base with applications (and made so much money) that knowing they would have little ability to push more software into their customers, they **quit SAP** the following year and took the year off!

A natural question would be why did this degree of stuffing make sense for the sales rep?

Here is why.

Stuffing customers filled with product triggered a number of compensation accelerators that allow for more compensation to the sales rep that if they had spread those sales over multiple years. SAP and Oracle create these incentives to which the sales reps respond. It has nothing to do with what is sustainable or good for the customer, but what is in line with the short-term objectives of the Oracle executives.

One extreme example of this stuffing is Fusion (or now various Oracle Cloud components, Oracle ERP Cloud, Oracle Procurement Cloud, etc...) for Oracle. Oracle Cloud is where many customers own licenses they don't use. SAP has their own ERP system that is used primarily as shelfware at customers that own a license. Moreover, that is S/4HANA for SAP, which has since its introduction had only around **17% of those that hold a license recorded by SAP as having implemented the application**. With the actual number of customers live far lower than this, as we covered in the Study of S/4HANA Implementations.[134] This is for a product that should have been free to existing customers of the ERP system (called ECC) as we covered in the article Why S/4HANA Should be Free.[135]

---

134 http://www.brightworkr.com/softwaredecisions/2017/09/27/s4hana-implementation-study-complete/
135 http://www.brightworkr.com/saphana/2016/09/03/sap-s4-hana-free/

AWS and Google Cloud's approach is much more similar to a utility than to a finished good purchase. In some cases, AWS and Google Cloud's billing increments have become ridiculously (from the context of traditional IT mindsets) small. This includes per second billing for EC2 (and there is billing below the second now) and for Google Cloud's services. For instance, AWS's "serverless" Lambda allows code to be run without any servers to be provisioned, which means that only the compute time is charged. That by itself is quite amazing. The other side of "on tap" billing is the reservation, whereby AWS allocates capacity in return for the customer purchasing the allocation.

As one example, all of DynamoDB's pricing is published.

| Menu | aws | Contact Sales | Products | More ▾ | | English ▾ | My Account ▾ | Sign In t |

Amazon DynamoDB   Overview   Features   Pricing   Getting Started   Migrations   Resources

same Availability Zone. Though standard Amazon EC2 regional data transfer charges of $0.01 per GB in/out app transferring data between an Amazon EC2 instance and a DAX node in different Availability Zones of the same / Region, you are charged only for the data transfer into or out of the Amazon EC2 instance. There is no DAX data charge for traffic into or out of the DAX node itself.

Region: US East (Ohio) ⇕

Instance Type	vCPU	Memory (GiB)	Pricing
t2.small	1	1.55	$0.04 per Hour
t2.medium	2	3.22	$0.08 per Hour
r4.large	2	15.25	$0.34 per Hour
r4.xlarge	4	30.5	$0.537 per Hour

Notice the per hour pricing for DynamoDB.

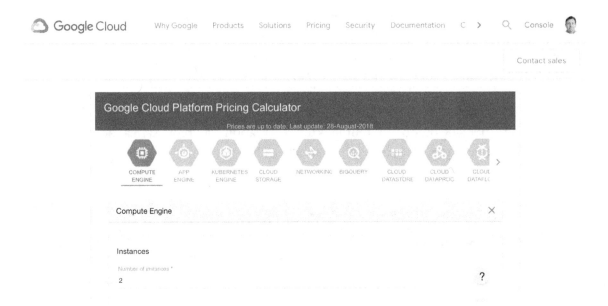

Google Cloud pricing can be calculated in their pricing calculator to create a forecast before the service is brought up. The first step is choosing the right item to be priced. The number of questions asked by the calculation form is extensive. We counted 32 questions for the Computer Engine calculation. Each calculator differs in the questions based upon the item. The Network selection has only nine questions.

Finally, SAP and Oracle talk to customers regarding matching AWS on price, Oracle has stated that running the Oracle Cloud will cost less than AWS. However, this is a ridiculous position to hold for companies that have been coming in consistently so high in price and TCO for their customers since they started doing business. One reason neither Oracle nor SAP can compete with AWS or Google Cloud on price is that they aren't multitenant. In the cloud, economies of scale come, in significant part, from multi-tenancy (we will discuss SAP and Oracle's lack of cloud infrastructure investments further on in the book). Second, SAP does not even have a virtual private server or VPC capabilities, so it could not offer multitenancy also if they had multitenant capabilities. Moreover, of course, neither SAP nor Oracle provides a managed database service.

Furthermore, SAP and Oracle tell a very different story to investors than they do to their customers. Both companies propose that moving to the cloud will **allow them to maintain or even increase their margins**.

This is evidenced in part by the following quotation from the head of SAP.

*"In terms of the March 2020 targets, yes, we absolutely believe that the SaaS/PaaS business, will the biggest net accelerator on cloud gross margins as we exit 2017. They have a huge catch-up to do. But if you think about the fact that at the moment we are essentially operating duplicate infrastructures across the main ones of our SaaS/Paas assets, especially SuccessFactors, that of course is a massive cost burden that will basically go entirely away once all of the customers are migrated by the end of this year. Hence we are still confident that we will achieve the gross margin progression marching towards around about 80% that we have in mind for SaaS/ Pass by 2020." - **Bill McDermott**[136]*

Once again, none of this is a problem with AWS or Google Cloud. AWS and Google Cloud do not have two sets of stories, one where they tell investors they intend to increase margins using the cloud and another story for customers where they state they will reduce costs.

Are Oracle and SAP a bit conflicted as to whether offering cloud services will decrease prices for customers or increase margins for Oracle and SAP? Yes, yes they are.

AWS has been very upfront with their investors that they intend to reduce costs through both scale and automation. Google tends to be a more quiet company regarding these types of topics, but also has a consistent message.

---

136 http://www.brightworkr.com/sap/2017/05/sap-mislead-analysts-q1-2017-earnings-call/

Pay-as-you-go

Google Cloud Platform takes pay-as-you-go pricing to the extreme, with industry leading innovations like per-second billing and automatic discounts with sustained usage. Custom Machine Types can save you up to 50% by matching the machine you want for your workload, eliminating over-provisioning to fit a vendor's rate card. Other providers force you to pay by the hour for a job you only run for minutes or force you to buy 32 GB when you only need 20 GB, which adds unnecessary costs to your bill. Pay-as-you-go pricing amounts to real savings.

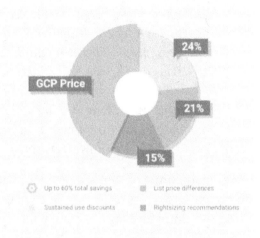

This is the type of thing you will not see on SAP or Oracle's website. A pay as you go explanation. SAP and Oracle view it as in their self-interests to both get as much money as possible un front, and to make pricing as difficult as possible to understand.

Conclusion

SAP and Oracle customers looking to leverage AWS and Google Cloud will find an entirely different orientation in these companies. SAP and Oracle could not be more different than AWS and Google Cloud. While nothing can be done with SAP and Oracle without a high degree of interaction with sales reps, discussions on licensing, investigations into audits and indirect access, AWS and Google Cloud provide access over the Internet to all of their services in an instantaneously usable form. The only thing necessary is a credit card. Oracle and SAP licensing management has its own consulting specialty firms. Upon audits, it is recommended to engage outside legal specialists in software audits. These licensing complexities and many others burn a significant amount of effort that could be put into better uses.

With not only SAP and Oracle, but on-premises software vendors in general, the full costs of purchasing decisions are hidden within the overall IT budget. The billing in AWS and Google Cloud is not the TCO of the services, as there continue to be internal costs associated with using the services and to hiring AWS and consulting partners for assistance. However, the total costs are at least more observable when using cloud service providers. The outcome of more cloud services being used (versus more on-premises purchases) is that the total costs become easier to track.

One of the essential features of cloud services is one of the lesser discussed. This feature is the ability to pause to shut down services, which vastly increases the ability to test services, and co-test services with other services. The ability to quickly and efficiently bring down services is such a massive shift in flexibility that it is difficult to overstate the impact.

The on-premises software model is predicated upon high levels of commitment to purchase decisions that for the most part cannot be rolled back. This is why there is so much IT investment waste at SAP and Oracle customers. There is also a fear in admitting the waste as it career limiting.

Now let us move on to comparing the various clouds mentioned so far in this book.

Chapter 6: AWS and Google Cloud Versus SAP Cloud and Oracle Cloud

SAP has been trying to jump on the cloud bandwagon for year now. For some time, they tried to correlate the cloud with their HANA database in the minds of customers. They did this with what amounted to little more than wordplay and inaccurate product naming. They released the "SAP HANA Platform." This inclusion of the word "HANA" into the name never made any sense a HANA has nothing inherently to do with the cloud. One of the authors, Shaun Snapp, engaged in repeated discussions with SAP consultants on this exact point with multiple SAP consultants who were intent on obscuring the line between HANA, SAP HANA Platform, and HANA Studio. The idea was to try to mislead the listener with the idea that HANA was an amalgamation of these components, and therefore HANA was not simply a database but "so much more."

Shaun began to observe such a premeditated pattern in these discussions that in response and in order to explain the pattern to others he wrote the article How to Deflect That You Were Wrong About HANA.[137]

The outcome?

SAP eventually removed the word HANA from the service and renamed it to the SAP Cloud Platform and finally to just the SAP Cloud. This change to the name made it more difficult for people to conflate/confuse HANA with the HANA Cloud Platform. This was a good thing for the market as there was far more confusion when SAP kept placing HANA in the naming of things that had nothing at all to do with HANA.

However, one has to wonder, why did SAP consultants engage in such extensive misdirection in any case? It appears the only purpose was to obscure the truth. Moreover, these are consultants advising clients! Which means SAP customers need to think about to whom they are taking advice. Many SAP consultants are people don't care to know that a database is separate from a development environment or an IaaS, or are just repeating anything

---

137 http://www.brightworkr.com/saphana/2016/10/16/deflect-wrong-hana/

whether it contains any truth. That is the problem with analyzing statements that are false. One never knows if the individuals themselves knows they are false. SAP puts a lot of information out into the market, and much of it is repeated verbatim without thought.

SAP's Faux Cloud and SAP's Faux Containers

SAP has what amounts to a faux cloud that is used by very few companies. This is evident by the simple act of using the SAP Cloud. When using the SAP Cloud, and it is the norm to run into one problem after another. The overall experience promotes the idea that SAP has created the SAP Cloud to create the impression that one exists, rather than creating a cloud product that is designed to be used by anyone. The overall product is the subject of great underinvestment, and it seems that SAP has other priorities.

SAP Cloud is still essential for SAP, but not for customers, and not for SAP employees. The SAP Cloud is critical because it helps SAP cloudwash for Wall Street. The essential part of SAP Cloud is that Bill McDermott, Rob Enslin, and other top executives need to cash out options. Moreover, they need to maintain the facade of the cloud for Wall Street to do this as Wall Street assigns a higher multiple to companies that look like they are moving to the cloud. Much of this comes from a general misunderstanding about the cloud on the part of Wall Street, but that is what they believe. Therefore even if no customers use the SAP Cloud, it helps maintain the illusion that SAP desires.

However, all of this is nothing new. At SAP's TechEd conference, every year SAP makes new announcements where SAP co-opts some cloud standard or approach. Cloud standards and approaches that will never be used in SAP. This is to make the faithful think SAP is becoming more cloud.

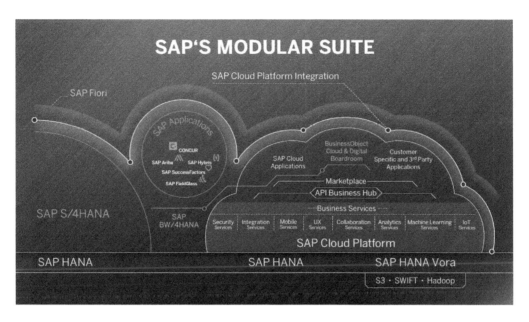

This is SAP's vision for its Cloud Platform (now SAP Cloud). This is very standard SAP diagram in that it is egomaniacal. Everything is all SAP. Vora, a rarely used product with little practical reason for existing is in there for some unknown reason. Overall, this diagram could be called "things SAP would like to sell you."[138]

This graphic is from when SAP Cloud was called SAP HANA Cloud Platform. However, notice how SAP has it identified as a iPaaS – which is just a PaaS.

---

138 https://blogs.sap.com/2017/10/04/abap-in-the-cloud-is-this-a-good-thing/

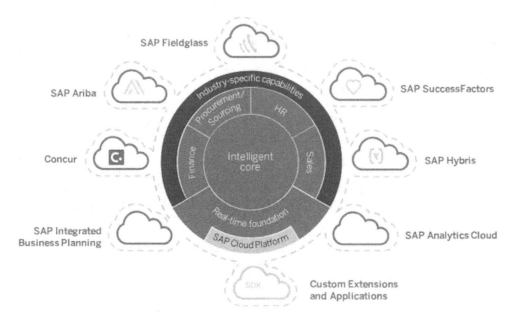

Notice the orange curved box on the bottom. Notice how the SAP Cloud supports everything else. The Intelligence Core is supposed to be S/4HANA Cloud. This is a diagram that shows using SAP for absolutely everything. However, in practice, it makes little sense to use SAP Cloud. It's a beautiful diagram though. You have to credit SAP for making some of the nicest graphics in the industry.

SAP has tried to ape everything that AWS and Google Cloud have been doing, but without a lot of it making much sense. SAP Cloud now supports Kubernetes! Which is extremely odd. This is because SAP does not support containers. Instead, SAP creates monolithic applications, so the embrace of Kubernetes seems pure fantasy – take your pick.

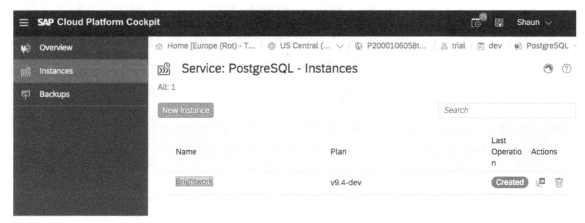

*The SAP Cloud is without any exaggeration, the worst cloud we have ever tested. SAP calls the SAP Cloud a PaaS, but it is a very incomplete PaaS. Some instances can be brought up, but that is the extent of the SAP Cloud with any efficiency. The user interface is Fiori, and is slow, with every change between screens being roughly between 3.5 and 6 seconds, but went all the way up to 8 seconds on some screens. Every time we switch to a new screen, we have another wait time. It's a wait time you don't find in non-Fiori applications. We covered the problems with Fiori's performance in the article **Why is the SAP Fiori Cloud So Slow?** Which was testing S/4HANA Cloud, and the performance again a problem as Fiori is the UI for the SAP Cloud.[139]*

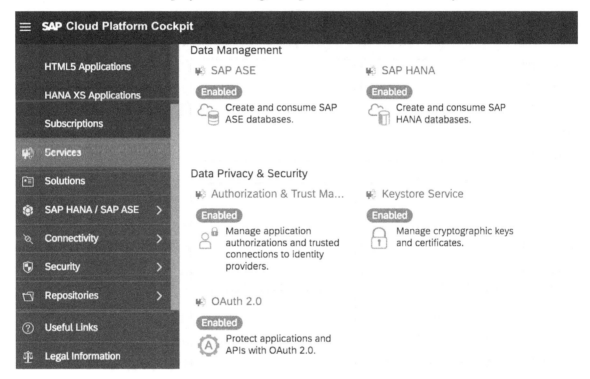

Services can be brought up in the SAP cloud, but it is problematic to do so. The experience leads one to want to leave the SAP Cloud to work in a real cloud offering rather than this facia cloud. Everything in SAP Cloud is clumsy and time-consuming to use, and we received numerous errors in bringing up basic services. It is nothing like the experience of working with AWS and Google Cloud.

---

139 Curiously after being extremely slow for S/4HANA Cloud, when we retested the cloud ERP system in October 2018, its performance had markedly improved. So there is hope for SAP Cloud's performance, if only SAP will allocate the resources and time to speeding its performance. The question is, does SAP want to?

What SAP calls a PaaS is just an IaaS "facilitator," but a very limited IaaS or IaaS passthrough which allows one to access true IaaS's. Moreover, we will get into why that is a serious problem in a moment. But sufficed to say, developing within the SAP Cloud is pointless.

Why Does SAP Cloud Not Yet Support HTTP 2.0?

One of the very bizarre aspects of SAP Cloud, that is another indicator as to SAP's lack of investment is the fact that SAP Cloud does not as of this publication support HTTP 2.0. AWS, GCP, and Azure all support HTTP 2.0. The newer protocol (released 2015) supports multiplexed requests across a single connection. Instead of buffering requests and responses, it handles them in streaming fashion. HTTP 2.0 reduces latency and increases performance.

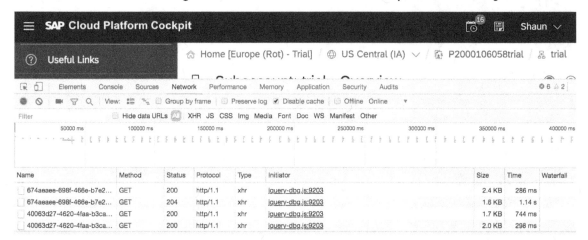

The SAP Cloud network analysis shows HTTP 1.0. (See under protocol column).

The Google Cloud network analysis shows HTTP 2.0. (See under protocol column).

HTTP 2.0's multiplexing and concurrency, dependency streaming, header compression, and server push can decrease web resource load time compared to HTTP 1.1. Furthermore, HTTP 1.1 is more secure than HTTP 2.0. This means if SAP Cloud is connected to AWS, the connection from SAP Cloud to AWS reduces the security of AWS.

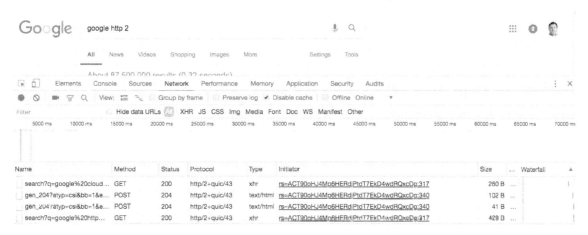

Notice that even Google Search, which only transmits search information between a local computer and Google also has HTTP 2.0.

Security Reduction with PaaS?

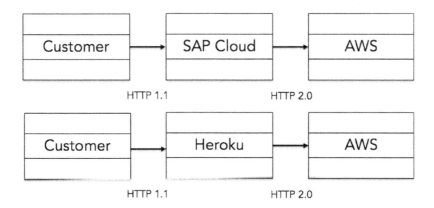

Not only SAP Cloud, but also Heroku (a PaaS) reduce the security of the overall design as they both communicate to AWS or to Google Cloud using HTTP 1.1.

SAP could add HTTP 1.1 very easily, but they have not seen fit to do so. The reason is likely that SAP Cloud is little used. So there is not much point. In a discussion on this topic SAP resource proposed that SAP Cloud acquired protocols from an acquisition of PLAT.ONE. This is a deceptive statement that was designed to trick anyone listening. First, you don't need to acquire a company to "use HTTP2.0." HTTP 2.0 is an open standard developed by the ITEF. This would be like saying you acquired the ability to "use HTML" from a vendor you purchased. People are behaving as if SAP Cloud is real and just "missing a few things." SAP Cloud is not functional. This leaves SAP resources in the position of having to make excuses for it, and in many cases making false statements about SAP Cloud.

But the HTTP 1.1 issue versus 2.0 is a small issue in the overall scheme of things.

This is correctly pointed out by Denis Myagkov:

> *"The HTTP version is not the problem. It actually depends on the server settings. Today most common approach is to hide all micro-services behind a 'reverse proxy' like Nginx. To add HTTP/2 support to Nginx I just need to add 5 letters.*
>
> *The real problem is that SAP cloud has no tool comparable to AWS VPC.*
>
> *A Virtual Private Cloud (VPC) lets you provision logically isolated resources in a virtual network that you define. You have complete control over your virtual networking environment, including selection of your own IP address range, creation of subnets, and configuration of route tables and network gateways.*
>
> *For example, you can create a public-facing subnet for your web servers that has access to the Internet, and place your backend systems such as databases or application servers in a private-facing subnet with no Internet access. You can leverage multiple layers of security, including security groups and network access control lists, to help control access to your instances in each subnet.*
>
> *More importantly, you can create a Hardware Virtual Private Network (VPN) connection between your corporate data center and your VPC to leverage public cloud as an extension of your corporate data center.*
>
> *SAP Cloud has no concept of a VPC. This makes it impossible to deploy production-grade enterprise workloads on SAP Cloud and by extension, refactoring any non-trivial ABAP code to run on SAP Cloud. Without VPC, for instance, there's no way to apply IAM (Identity Access Management) policy to the endpoints of your own cloud estate. This is both a security and an operations nightmare.*

And this problem is HUGE! This by itself makes SAP Cloud useless for anything more intricate than 'Hello World' application. There also no analogs of AWS IAM, however in AWS permission management is a core component. So in SAP Cloud any junior developer will be able to devastate all solution in production."

To list the limitations with the SAP Cloud would be a chapter on its own. However, a lack of VPC capabilities is not the end of the missing items. SAP Cloud lacks either a load balancer and reverse proxy in addition to VPC. As soon as there is no VPC, the security argument is lost. Is this a solution that is ready for anyone to use? The lack of documentation or usability of the SAP Cloud are indicators that the SAP Cloud sees minimal usage.

We were on a project where the SAP Cloud was being used by an SAP consulting partner. Using AWS or Google Cloud or Azure was not even discussed.

Why?

Because the consulting partner only recommended using SAP solutions. There was not any discussion of any competition. It was the SAP Cloud just because of the relationship between the consulting partner and SAP. We see this all the time, where the interests of the client are entirely secondary to choosing whatever SAP happens to offer.

In addition to massive limitations, things not working, and incredible latency in using the SAP Cloud, it also comes with significant liabilities. One liability is that the SAP Cloud Platform is, unlike AWS or Google Cloud, **not** an open environment. However, you can't tell this from reading what SAP has to say about the SAP Cloud. Those reading this book probably have had the SAP Cloud/SAP Cloud Platform promoted to them at some point. There are essential features of this SAP offering.

Observe how SAP tries to propose the converse in this quote.

"SAP Cloud Platform is an open platform-as-a-service (PaaS) that delivers in-memory capabilities, core platform services, and unique microservices for building and extending intelligent, mobile-enabled cloud applications. The platform is designed to accelerate digital transformation by helping you quickly, easily, and economically develop the exact application you need – without investing in on-premise infrastructure. Based on open standards, SAP Cloud Platform offers complete flexibility and control (emphasis added) over your choice of clouds, frameworks, and applications."[140]

---

140 https://cloudplatform.sap.com/index.html

First, by the nature of their business models, SAP and Oracle do not create open cloud offerings. Therefore, this claim is of a highly dubious nature. SAP and Oracle can't market their clouds effectively without embellishing their closed nature with open terminology.

Now while it may be true that the SAP Cloud "can" be connected to non-SAP assets, that rest assured that SAP will do everything it can to direct customers to use more SAP if they use the SAP Cloud. For instance, for some time SAP has been proposing that the SAP Cloud improve SAP's integration capabilities.

> *"Easily exchange data in real-time with SAP Cloud Platform Integration. Integrate processes and data between cloud apps, 3rd party applications and on-premises solutions with this open, flexible, on-demand integration system running as a core service on SAP Cloud Platform."[141]*

How is this accomplished? Other questions naturally come to mind:

1. *Better Than Other Integration?:* Why is this better than using another integration application? SAP has been guilty of making many previous exaggerated claims about its "platforms" that end up not being easier to use than competing offerings.

2. *On Demand Integration?:* What does *"on-demand integration mean"*? Any integration harness or application is on-demand for the people that use it.

3. *Runs as a Core Service?:* What does it mean that it runs as a core service as part of the SAP Cloud Platform? Isn't it part of the SAP Cloud Platform anyway?

SAP goes on to say the following about the SAP Cloud and integration's key benefits:

> *"Access a deep catalog of integration flows.*
>
> *Integrate both processes and data through unified technology engineered for the cloud.*
>
> *Get an integration service that is secure, reliable and delivered and managed by SAP in SAP's secure data centers across the globe.*
>
> *Lower TCO with an affordable, pay-as-you-go subscription model and minimal up-front."*

Does SAP have any independent studies that can demonstrate that the SAP HANA Cloud Platform lowers TCO, or is this just a sales statement that has nothing to back it up? That is, of course, a rhetorical statement. We know SAP doesn't. SAP usually does not provide

---

141 https://www.sap.com/products/hana-cloud-integration.html

evidence of TCO claims. One of the few times they did, when they paid Forrester to estimate HANA's lower TCO claim, the study was unusable.[142]

SAP goes onto say more:

> *"With SAP Cloud Platform Smart Data Integration, you can replicate, virtualize and transform data from multiple sources and store it in your SAP HANA instance on SAP Cloud Platform. Smart data integration offers pre-built adapters to common data sources plus an adapter SDK that lets you get data from any source for a 360-degree view of your business. Thanks to a cloud-first architecture your data is securely transferred from on-premises applications to the cloud without putting your business at risk."*

How about the SAP Cloud Platform Smart Data Integration item? SAP capitalizes this as if it is a product, not a process within a product. On the Cloud Platform's pricing sheet SAP Cloud Platform Integration is what pushes the customer into the $4,600 to $17,000 per month version of the SAP Cloud. However, we have seen very little use of this component or discussion of the component. SAP does not have a history of having developed a useful integration product, with their on-premises offering, SAP PO/PI becoming less popular with customers as time passes. Therefore it is no "slam dunk" that the SAP Cloud Platform Integration will become a desirable component to use. In fact, the probabilities are firmly against that ever happening. We cover this in more detail in the article How Accurate is SAP on SAP HANA Cloud Integration?[143]

Also, most SAP customers don't have HANA and looking at the low growth rate of HANA, most never will. So what if the customer does not want HANA, can they use the SAP HANA Cloud Platform to store in Oracle, MongoDB, PostgreSQL, Tibero or another non-SAP database? The fact they can't is a problem. SAP is all in on its databases being used in SAP Cloud. However, SAP's databases are not that widely used.

---

142 http://www.brightworkr.com/saphana/2017/07/09/how-accurate-was-forresters-tco-study-for-sap-hana/
143 http://www.brightworkr.com/sap/2017/06/accurate-sap-hana-cloud-integration/

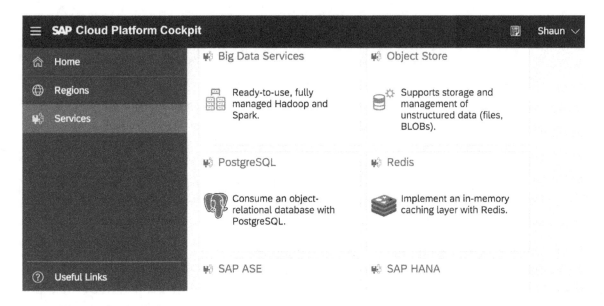

SAP has begun to offer a very limited number of non-SAP database options, including PostgreSQL and Redis.

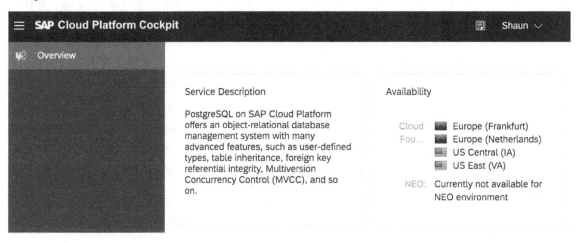

However, when we select PostgreSQL, we find that it is not available for our environment, which is the more limited environment. Why? Because SAP does not offer it themselves, but through AWS, Google Cloud or Azure.

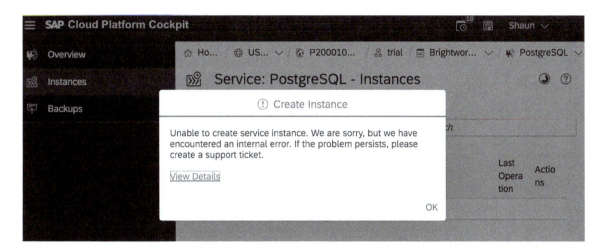

Once we switch into the Cloud Foundry, which has access to AWS, Google Cloud or Azure, we are able to progress a short way in bringing up PostgreSQL, that is until we get this error. These types of errors do not come up when attempting to create a PostgreSQL instance in AWS or Google Cloud directly. This makes us wonder how much PostgreSQL or Redis, that is non SAP databases have been added to SAP Cloud for marketing rather than for real usage purposes.

We analyzed SAP Cloud, trying to figure out how it adds any value. And we think that SAP may have created a new cloud offering, but without telling anyone.

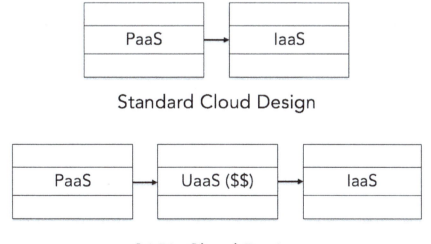

We categorize SAP Cloud not as a PaaS or as an IaaS, but as a UaaS, or what we have coined Upcharge as a Service. The UaaS intermediates between the PaaS and IaaS. The solution design is as follows PaaS + UaaS (for upcharging + cloud frustration) + IaaS. It is that essential component that ensures that the entire solution incorporates SAP.

UaaS does two critical things. First. It SAP-washes the overall cloud endeavor. Some customers want SAP involved, just for a certain comfort level, so instead of being some "pirate" operation, it is now standard SAP. Second, the UaaS helps absorb excess budget, the budgetary consumption of which is reduced by the use of the cloud. The reason for this is that the savings from using the cloud will be too jarring for customers without a value-free intermediator that can absorb some of the excesses. This is why SAP recently signed up to buy more AWS.

> *"SAP announced its multi-cloud strategy more than two years ago," a spokesman for the Walldorf, Germany-based software company said in a statement, referring to SAP's plan to maintain a presence on the world's largest public clouds, such as AWS, Microsoft, Google, International Business Machines Corp. and Alibaba Group Holding Ltd.'s cloud. "We believe in the power of collaboration." SAP declined to comment on the Amazon agreement outlined in the memo."[144]*

SAP can't create infrastructure anywhere near the cost or competence of AWS. So the strategy is now to buy from AWS, but then markup AWS. The profits are far higher to simply buy from AWS. SAP needs a significant margin to interest it in doing things. There is not enough margin in the cloud to interest SAP in building its cloud. Therefore SAP Cloud merely is designed to allow SAP to upcharge customers for AWS, Google Cloud and Azure.

What is the position of the consulting partners? Well lets borrow an scene from a famous movie.

- Jack Sparrow: " *Who are you?*"

- Tai Huang: *"Tai Huang. These are my men."*

- Jack Sparrow: *"Where do your allegiances lie? - With the highest bidder."*

- Tai Huang: *"I have a ship."*

- Jack Sparrow: *"That makes you the highest bidder."*

- Jack Sparrow: *"Good man. Weigh anchor, all hands. Prepare to make sail."*

---

144 https://www.bloomberg.com/news/articles/2018-10-09/amazon-is-said-to-win-1-billion-in-cloud-deals-with-sap-symantec

And as with the pirate Tai Huang in the Pirates of the Caribbean: At World's End, the SAP consulting partners recommend whoever is the highest bidder. They will recommend SAP Cloud as they will get a percentage and SAP can afford to pay them a nice percentage because the markup is so high. As soon as they understand that percentage, they will say..

> *"SAP Cloud is necessary, it is standard SAP."*

And this gets into the topic of why SAP is proposing the SAP Cloud in the first place (outside of cloud washing that is). And this means understanding how SAP controls the development of their customers, historically forcing them to use ABAP and proprietary development tools. Furthermore, Hasso Plattner stated for years that he did not even believe that public cloud (which is just cloud, a private cloud is just hosting) was a fit for SAP customers, as this quotation attests.

> *"During a Q&A session, SAP chairman Hasso Plattner dismissed the benefits of multi-tenant delivery of its enterprise application, primarily those that deal with mission-critical functions like supply chain and financials. Plattner recalled a heated debate over the merits of multi-tenancy with Lars Dalgaard of SuccessFactors after it was bought by SAP in 2012. To this date, Plattner's position, though not unique, remains that SAP's biggest customers -- fearing unnecessary business disruption -- would still prefer deploying their applications either in a private cloud setting or as a managed service, all without the intrusion of continuous updates commonly found in other Cloud applications."*[145]

The first problem with this is that hosting has nearly none of the advantages of the cloud. Therefore, in this quotation, Hasso Plattner may as well be railing against the cloud as an overall construct. This is actually how Hasso feels about the cloud, but over the past few years, he has stopped expressing this view publicly. In our view, it's no longer a perspective that will help SAP credibly cloud wash.

The second problem is that SAP has previously stated that one of the primary reasons that it purchased SuccessFactors to gain cloud expertise. Lars Dalgaard was a well-regarded expert in the cloud. When brought into the fold of SAP, he is told that SAP disagrees with the premise of cloud, clashes with Hasso Plattner and leaves the company. Since the SuccessFactors acquisition SAP has been mostly unsuccessful in converting SAP customers that used SAP's ERP HR solution, called HCM to SuccessFactors. SAP fundamentally rejected the view of Lars and other experts on the cloud, which was a company they made a conscious effort to purchase and purchased at a premium. SAP then tries to get SuccessFactors to port to

---

145 https://www.amazon.com/SAP-Nation-2-0-empire-disarray-ebook/dp/B013F5BKJQ

HANA, which the SuccessFactors team tells the rest of SAP they have no interest in doing as they don't see the value and don't want the complications that come with HANA.

What was the purpose of purchasing SuccessFactors if this was going to be the outcome?

The experience with SuccessFactors is repeated with other cloud vendors that SAP acquires.

And SAP's position on cloud is reinforced by first-hand accounts of its investment into cloud as described in the following quotation from the book SAP Nation 2.0.

> *"There is another concern about SAP's S/4 public cloud. The data center in Sankt LeonRot Germany, while close to SAP's impressive Walldorf headquarters, does not itself inspire much confidence. It has been called puny and primitive compared to the data centers of infrastructure as a service providers like Amazon, Microsoft Azure and Rackspace. Indeed competitors like Infor and Unit4 are using infrastructure-as-a-service (using data centers from Amazon and Microsoft respectively) rather than trying to compete with their scale."[146]*

This is why SAP finally opened the SAP Cloud to accessing AWS, Google Cloud and Azure.

We covered this in the article How to Understand SAP's Multicloud Announcement.[147]

While SAP continues to make headlines with various cloud vendor acquisitions solidifying its cloud credentials with Wall Street, the story from behind the scenes is not good.

> *"Even where SAP offers public cloud options-for example with its SuccessFactors and Concur customers-- the individual data centers are undersized and often supported by co-location vendors around the globe. SAP's about 82 million cloud users are fragmented across products and across geographies. Little attempt appears to have been made to date, to consolidate data centers that support them. While compliance requirements dictate regional diversity in such facilities, they are further reminders of Balkanization in the SAP economy."[148]*

This is the exact opposite of how AWS and Google Cloud have built their cloud capabilities. All of this background is going to make it very difficult for SAP to ever compete in the cloud. This is why we recommend for customers that want to use SAP applications, get them placed on AWS and Google Cloud and pass on SAP's cloud offerings.

---

146 https://www.amazon.com/SAP-Nation-2-0-empire-disarray-ebook/dp/B013F5BKJQ
147 http://www.brightworkr.com/sap/2017/05/best-understand-saps-multicloud-announcement/
148 https://www.amazon.com/SAP-Nation-2-0-empire-disarray-ebook/dp/B013F5BKJQ

In our view, Infor and Unit4 have made the obvious decision. Even the largest SaaS vendor now uses AWS Open question to SAP's cloud - is how to upgrade your application. Try to imagine that you have 200 servers, and you need to upgrade 40 of them from version 1.004 to 1.007. Nobody knows how to do that in the SAP Cloud. In AWS you only need to upload new NGNIX configuration 2 times and all will be done and it will takes about 0.002 seconds for two operations.[149]

The Price of SAP Cloud

The SAP Cloud is an uncompetitive mess, and that is before the topic of pricing is brought into the mix. Let us review a direct comparison of pricing between SAP Cloud and AWS.

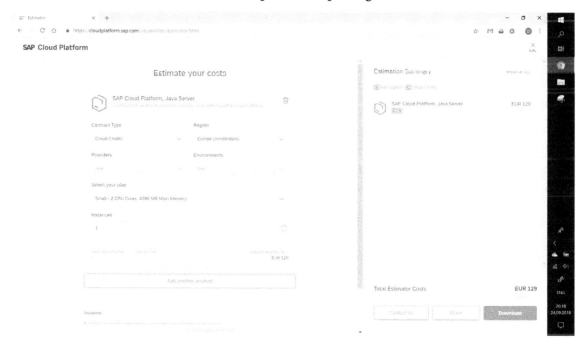

Here is the price for a very small configuration. Notice it comes to €129 Euros is roughly $151 dollars.

149 Denis Myagkov

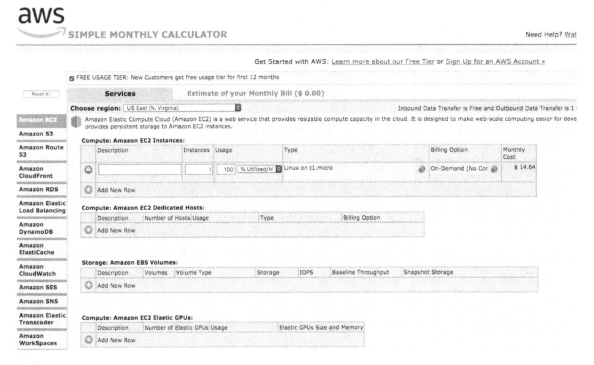

Here is the same configuration on AWS, it comes to $14.64. Now remember, much of what SAP Cloud sells is just access to AWS (or Google Cloud or Azure). And SAP plans to markup that cost by ten times (151/14.46) = 10.44.

Moreover, this is another major problem with SAP Cloud. One can be able to access some AWS, Google Cloud or Azure services, but they will be far more challenging to set up in SAP Cloud, the menu of services are tiny, some that are proposed to be accessible don't work, and the markup applied by SAP is exorbitant.

SAP and ABAP and the Cloud

In order to understand SAP and cloud, it is necessary to dive into the topic of SAP's coding language.

SAP uses an embedded coding language called ABAP. Today ABAP is an inefficient language when compared to modern high-level languages, and there is a healthy debate to be had as to whether ABAP is a true computer language or more of a framework. Interestingly, ABAP was originally designed by SAP as a report generator, as its original German acronym means "generic report preparation processor."

The following explanation of ABAP from Wikipedia is actually quite good, so we have included part of it below.

> *"ABAP is one of the many application-specific fourth-generation languages (4GLs) first developed in the 1980s. It was originally the report language for SAP R/2, a platform that enabled large corporations to build mainframe business applications for materials management and financial and management accounting. ABAP establish integration between independent softwares.*
>
> *ABAP used to be an abbreviation of Allgemeiner Berichts Aufbereitungs Prozessor, German for "generic report preparation processor", but was later renamed to the English Advanced Business Application Programming. ABAP was one of the first languages to include the concept of Logical Databases (LDBs), which provides a high level of abstraction from the basic database level(s),which supports every platform, language and units.*
>
> *The ABAP language was originally used by developers to develop the SAP R/3 platform. It was also intended to be used by SAP customers to enhance SAP applications – customers can develop custom reports and interfaces with ABAP programming. The language was geared towards more technical customers with programming experience. It is extracted from the base computing languages java, c, c++ , python.*
>
> *ABAP remains as the language for creating programs for the client-server R/3 system, which SAP first released in 1992. As computer hardware evolved through the 1990s, more and more of SAP's applications and systems were written in ABAP. By 2001, all but the most basic functions were written in ABAP. In 1999, SAP released an object-oriented extension to ABAP called ABAP Objects, along with R/3 release 4.6."*[150]

SAP was never required to use ABAP, and there was no advantage to using ABAP over other development languages. However, using, and making their customers use ABAP was a premeditated choice in the part of SAP. ABAP allowed SAP to do was to more effectively control accounts because ABAP could only be found on SAP projects. This is one of the great untold stories in SAP. This section will be particularly offensive to ABAP coders. However, ABAP coders and those selling ABAP coding consulting have been misleading customers for decades, and this area is almost never illuminated.

---

150 https://en.wikipedia.org/wiki/ABAP

One primary problem is that SAP states that ABAP is good for everything. Therefore if one declares that ABAP is not good for something, say cloud, then offense will be taken. SAP wants to propose ABAP as a universal language. However, there is no universal language. This is in the same way that Oracle intends to propose a single universal database, but again there is no single universal database. For many years on SAP projects one author, Shaun Snapp was brainwashed. He used to be told this or that is SAP standard. And ABAP needed to be used because it was "standard."

But what about a comparison of pros and cons?

That type of analysis is lacking from SAP projects. To understand ABAP and how the story provided by SAP mutates, it is necessary get a perspective from a person who can write ABAP, but also someone who is independent because one can't write 100% honest things if that person rely on the SAP community for your employment.

The following is from Rolf Paulsen, who is one of the few people with ABAP exposure who provides historical context concerning ABAP. What he has to say about ABAP and cloud is most interesting.

> *"It is simply not possible to port existing (non-trivial) ABAP development into the cloud using the massively restricted ABAP derivate that they made up for "ABAP in the cloud". Test Driven Development, distributed/non-linear development (branching/merging), Continuous Integration and -Deployment, serverless and containerization (to name a few) can be considered as results from the demand to make software development safer and more efficient in spite of increasing change rate.*
>
> *All these topics are mainstream for years in other languages and platforms but don't play a role in ABAP development, no matter on premise or cloud. One major reason out of many major reasons is that the ABAP platform lacks something like a "build and deploy circle" of software. Every code change is done in the same centralized system.*
>
> *The ABAP platform is in no way a competitive for software development.*
>
> *As long as you are developing minor additions to SAP standard that remain stable over time ("fire-and-forget-development") these shortcomings do not play a large role and only on premise they are often outweighted by the ease of integration e.g. with ERP data. But if you are planning to develop software that evolves over time, especially after go-live, the choice of a development platform like ABAP that has never been designed as a development platform from ground up is a choice that*

will eat up high costs for development, setup of development environments, manual testing... compared to other languages and platforms.

Although this view is shared by many people inside and outside SAP who know both sides, this cannot be sold and marketed very well. What is selling better is the vision that ABAP will have a great future in the cloud. IMHO this is likely to become a disservice to many ABAP developers. They are losing time that could be spent learning modern languages, tools and development mindset. They may not get budget and time for training because managers may think that their ABAP knowledge is sufficient to compete in the cloud.

The situation regarding ABAP may be compared to the Java story at SAP several years ago: SAP Netweaver Java came into market with a large amount of marketing hype and fanfare but failed in user acceptance. This is because it could not compete with alternatives like JBoss or WebSphere. Netweaver Java decayed to a platform for XI/PI/PO and Enterprise Portal and was cut off from further technological progress after around 2010.

This mislead customers that ABAP would be superior and Java and other modern development tools and paradigms do not play a role at SAP customers. Years have been wasted without building up knowledge etc. that cannot be made up easily.

We find the same situation today with ABAP in the cloud. Like FORTRAN continues to be for climate simulation, ABAP will remain in its niche as on premise language and maybe language for small "cloud extensions." But it will not be a competitive platform for cloud development. And as is the case around 8 years ago, SAP consultants do not preach that you must not lose more time to learn Java, Python, Jenkins and other stuff.

ABAP in the cloud is a stripped version of ABAP on premise. What does this mean?

There is no way to port on premise ABAP development into the cloud. Every line of ABAP code written today on premise (=99.9999...%) prevents the move of an ERP system into cloud. The opposite for on premise applications e.g. in Java on premise: they can be moved into cloud, containers, and so on. Customers have to decide: shall I start new development in ABAP - with the consequence that not only my ERP system but also my own development will stay on premise forever - or shall I start future proof with another language?"

How would SAP customers gain access to the information provided by Rolf in the quotation above.

Practical Guide to SAP ABAP: Conceptual Design, Development, Debugging Mar 15, 2016
by Thomas Stutenbäumer

Kindle Edition   ☆☆☆☆☆ ▾ 2
$9⁹⁹
Get it **TODAY, Oct 6**

Paperback
$29⁹⁵ ✓prime
In Stock

More Buying Choices
$27.71 (15 used & new offers)

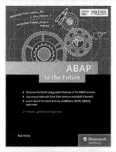

ABAP to the Future: Advanced, Modern ABAP 7.5 (2nd Edition) (SAP PRESS) Oct 20, 2016
by Paul Hardy

Hardcover   ☆☆☆☆☆ ▾ 1
$55⁶⁷ $79.95 ✓prime
FREE Delivery by **Mon, Oct 8**
Only 14 left in stock - order soon.

More Buying Choices
$54.88 (86 used & new offers)

ABAP Development for SAP HANA (2nd Edition) (SAP PRESS) May 31, 2016
by Hermann Gahm and Thorsten Schneider

Hardcover   ☆☆☆☆☆ ▾ 1
$41⁶¹ $79.95 ✓prime
FREE Delivery by **Mon, Oct 8**
More Buying Choices
$31.75 (81 used & new offers)

You can read all of these books on ABAP. You can read all the books on ABAP, and not one of them will explain the quotation above or how SAP uses ABAP to control their customers. This is because these books are written by ABAPers (that would never write such a thing in the first place), and most of them are published by SAP Press – which is essentially SAP's captive publisher. They are in on keeping the story clean. You the reader are the mark, useful to be told a partial story that makes SAP in the words of SAP Press when Shaun Snapp's book was censored "Our job is to make SAP look good!"

The description of this video on YouTube is "During his SAP TechEd keynote, SAP CTO Björn Goerke announced ABAP as the next environment added to the SAP Cloud Platform. A new, modern version optimized for cloud, ABAP" A lot of what SAP does has no other purpose than to make a marketing splash. This ABAP in SAP Cloud is essentially this type of announcement.

SAP is locked into ABAP and has no choice today what language to use in their ERP, SCM, BW due to enormous amount of code that was **generated for 50 years by SAP and by customers.**

Embedded languages was the trend when ABAP was first developed. Even MS Excel has its own embedded language – VBA.

For SAP it solved 3 core challenges:

1. Developers get less ability to write "unsafe" code. Actually, that was done as supposed to. For instance, C++ is the powerful language, but as observed by Denis Myagkov, it provides a whole range of opportunities to shoot your leg off with your own gun.

2. Ability to write platform and operational system independent code. At that time there was whole zoo of different platforms like mainframes and operational systems like FreeBSD and Solaris. Actually ABAP was designed like JAVA.

3. Implement ABAP as DSL – domain specific language. ABAP was inspired by another DSL popular in 1970-1980 – COBOL. In addition ABAP has native seamless integration with many databases (Oracle, Sybase, DB2 and few other).

So, for SAP's solutions ABAP is like a Java Script (JS) for modern browsers. JS also has DSL options like native support of JSON data structures that could be considered like NoSQL Key-Value.

SAP has always promoted the use of ABAP on projects. If any customization was to be performed on an SAP project, SAP insisted to the customer that ABAP be used. Strangely, SAP customers very rarely pushed back on this, which is something that we cover in the article Why SAP Customers Followed SAP's Advice on Coding in ABAP.[151] [152] Customers could have developed in a non-SAP specific language, and then simply integrated into SAP. However, they made a significant error in listening to SAP, because now so many decades of SAP usage, and because SAP (particularly SAP ERP) are so highly customized, an enormous number of customizations are sitting currently in ABAP.

The SAP consulting companies make quite a lot of money on ABAP and therefore are in favor of present and future customers using ABAP. It is important to consider that ABAP is never justified on the basis of any its inherent benefits. Instead, it is used because it is what SAP recommends using. The SAP programming project environment is unsophisticated. While outside of the SAP world different languages are used for their fundamental properties (for instance, selecting Python for mathematics tasks, Scala for more concise code that is Java compatible, Swift for speed, debugging capabilities and compatibility with iOS and the Mac OS), ABAP is selected because SAP says it should be.

---

151 http://www.brightworkr.com/sapdev/2017/11/04/sap-customers-followed-saps-advice-coding/

152 ABAP is an outdated language, however, with so much code written in ABAP and the fact that SAP's applications are monolithic in their design, it becomes very difficult to move away from ABAP. ABAP is not used outside of SAP projects, and it is not competitive with other languages. Because of this, the continued use of ABAP both hurts SAP's development productivity as well as the development productivity of its customers, that must place their customizations in ABAP. This issue is a type of technical debt, and is described in the following quotation. *"Last but not least, monolithic applications make it extremely difficult to adopt new frameworks and languages. For example, let's imagine that you have 2 million lines of code written using the XYZ framework. It would be extremely expensive (in both time and cost) to rewrite the entire application to use the newer ABC framework, even if that framework was considerably better. As a result, there is a huge barrier to adopting new technologies. You are stuck with whatever technology choices you made at the start of the project."* – NGINX lays out the exact problem at SAP. NIGNX is not referring to SAP in this quote, but to a generalized problem. *"To summarize: you have a successful business-critical application that has grown into a monstrous monolith that very few, if any, developers understand. It is written using obsolete, unproductive technology that makes hiring talented developers difficult. The application is difficult to scale and is unreliable. As a result, agile development and delivery of applications is impossible."* - https://www.nginx.com/blog/introduction-to-microservices/ We cover the monolithic design versus microservices in the chapter on Where is SaaS/PaaS/IaaS Going in the Future.

And what SAP says is reinforced by all of the SAP consulting partners as the right thing to follow. What is very rarely observed by SAP resources is that ABAP is not used outside of SAP environments. That should tell anyone everything they need to know about ABAP.

The story laid out above has been the standard for decades in SAP, but recently outside events have caused a change that has impacted ABAP usage. The dominance of ABAP is declining inside SAP, and this is again related to the cloud. Now, instead of opening the ABAP stack for any platform like an on-premise app server, SAP offers to use other languages **but on** SAP Cloud. That is rather than controlling the language they want to control the runtime platform. Essentially, SAP is trying to again control development by allowing a different language in the SAP Cloud, but locking customers into SAP Cloud.

SAP has controlled its projects by force-feeding ABAP into customers, basically taking advantage of their naivete. And this has allowed SAP to control those accounts. But with ABAP incapable in the cloud, SAP needs to maintain control, so they give up the language, but force development into **their** cloud. However, when SAP presents the SAP Cloud to customers, it **does not tell them any of this**. Instead, it tells them that the SAP Cloud is completely open and invites comparisons to AWS. Notice the following quote not from SAP, but from an SAP friendly resources on a LinkedIn comment.

> *"And do not forget that with SCP Cloud Foundry you could take advantage of BYOL (bring your own language); language does not matter anymore! Every developer is welcomed!"*

Notice the implied assumption contained in this statement. The implication is that SAP is now allowing its customers to use the computer languages that they want. But the question should be:

> *"When should that not be the case?"*

Since when does a packaged software vendor have the right to tell a customer what language they should use for coding? Notice that AWS and Google Cloud do not have this type of assumption.

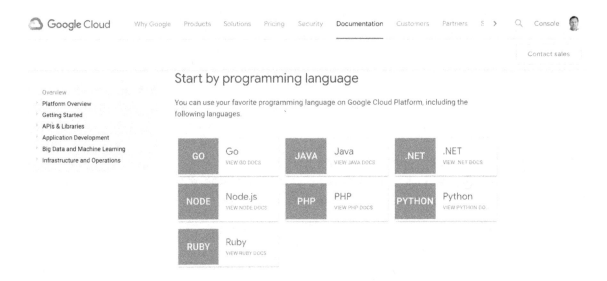

Observe Google Cloud's programming language page. The first language listed is Go, which is a Google created language. However, the rest of the languages listed have nothing to do with Google. They are just popular languages. They are also language used outside of Google Cloud. There is no implication that this is some gift from Google. Google makes itself compatible with a number of languages.

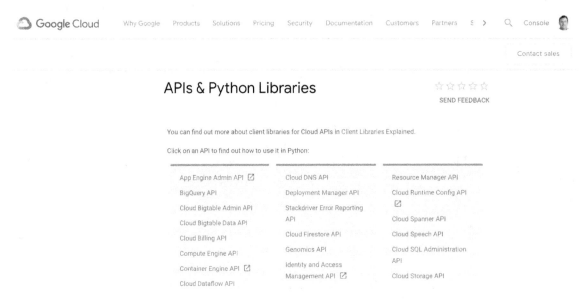

Google Cloud offers a number of APIs for their services. Google explains how to use each of these with Python in this example screenshot. However, Google offers an explanation of how its APIs work for all the languages it offers support for as well.

There is nothing like this on Google Cloud. This is why statements about openness by SAP to non-SAP technologies really fall flat once you peek below the surface. SAP and Oracle come from a mindset of cutting off options and they can't seem to change that mindset for anything but their marketing contentions.

SAP is at a curious crossroads with ABAP.

1. Clients are unable to customize their systems by any other way except with ABAP.

2. SAP itself has stopped ABAP development and shifted focus to its SAP Cloud, Hybris and so on. Where all code is in Java. ABAP was designed as an embedded language for SAP ERP/SCM/BW and proposals that it will be integrated into the cloud are inaccurate.

3. SAP relies upon the lack of programming understanding on the part of people that receive the message of ABAP portability to the cloud to allow it to be a credible statement.

4. SAP's non ABAP code usage is minimal compared to its ABAP code usage.

The Problem with ABAP and Cloud

SAP is facing a brick wall with the cloud. They are so accustomed to dictating the programming language and environment to customers, that they do not like at all the fact that ABAP does not work well for the cloud. Moreover, the cloud is the future. SAP has tried to promote ABAP for the cloud, as Björn Goerke, SAP's Chief Technology Officer, announced the availability of an ABAP development and runtime environment on SAP Cloud Platform in September of 2017 at SAP's TechEd. There are some reasons why this will amount to very little.

1. The Enhancement Framework used in on-premise ABAP is not allowed in the cloud as multiple tenants share the same core code. This means that most existing ABAP-based solutions cannot be ported to the cloud without significant refactoring – if at all. This is probably the first thing that comes to mind when reading about the introduction of ABAP in the cloud.[153]

---

153 Refactoring is the process of restricting existing code. *"Refactoring is usually motivated by noticing a code smell.[2] For example, the method at hand may be very long, or it may be a near duplicate of another nearby method. Once recognized, such problems can be addressed by refactoring the source code, or transforming it into a new form that behaves the same as before but that no longer "smells"."* - https://en.wikipedia.org/wiki/Code_refactoring

2. A common cause of SAP project failure is recreating legacy applications in SAP. People naturally want things to work the same familiar ways. Most ABAP language elements that have been used in on-premise development are no longer allowed in SAP Cloud. Even the most basic data access elements, like tables, are not included as whitelisted objects, which means that an ABAP statement referring to a standard ABAP table will cause a syntax error. You must use a whitelisted API to access any underlying tables. This approach is radically different from ABAP on premise, where you can access almost any ABAP repository element, even if it was never intended for use in custom code.

A lot of what SAP does has no other purpose than to make a marketing splash. This ABAP in SAP Cloud is essentially this type of announcement. If you review the announcement by Bjorn Goerke at TechEd, as soon as he announced ABAP, the crowd erupted in a cheer. Is it practical? Who cares, the important thing is that it sounds good and is trendy. Plus Bjorn made the announcement while wearing a Star Trek shirt. Take that AWS!

SAP Cloud is not much more than a marketing object. A piece of cheese tied to a string, with a rather nasty surprise if you nibble on it. Try using the SAP Cloud, and you will give up very quickly. It is cloud facia, faux cloud, etc...choose your phrasing.

SAP Cloud receives a lot of marketing funding, but on SAP projects it is a non-factor. It does not come up in discussions. SAP is so locked into its previous investments that it can't change. It knows that as soon as it begins to incorporate outside influences, its account control drops. It must also force feed large amounts of billing hours to an army of consultants, or face the reality of no longer being recommended. Everything in SAP's strategy is about defending its on-premises business model from openness, which would dramatically shrink the SAP ecosystem.[154]

SAP has many customers who cannot do any independent research and find Deloitte or Infosys to be "good sources of information." SAP can milk that account base for many years, and the best way to do this is to block out alternatives like AWS and Google Cloud. Allowing these alternatives into "their accounts" opens a crack into a fantastic world that undermines SAP's hard-fought account control. SAP needs, to the degree possible, to impede customers from experimenting with these options. Moreover, SAP's consulting partner ecosystem will help SAP do precisely this.

The Relationship Between Closed Systems and Profit Margins

SAP's system is closed from multiple dimensions, just how closed is normally not discussed in polite company. When SAP consultants speak of the fabulous "SAP ecosystem" and "standard SAP," or "certified SAP solution" there is never the slightest hint to the term "closed" or "sectioned off." The prescription of ABAP to customers is just one manifestation of the closed nature to SAP.

- *High Integration Overhead*: SAP continues to be the most difficult system in which to integrate other applications (in fact SAP ERP only integrates to other SAP applications with significant difficulty).

- *Indirect Access*: SAP uses indirect access to instill fear into companies about connecting non-SAP systems to SAP.

- *Partners Lobbying Against All Non SAP Solutions*: SAP consulting partners as talk down all non-SAP solutions to their clients vastly overstating the TCO impact of integration. This is done entirely because the financial benefits to the consulting partners.

- *Co-option of Open Source Components*: SAP routinely introduces "SAP-ized" versions of open source tools and components.

The list of restrictions and controls in SAP would be its own small book.

All of this is for a fundamental reason. SAP must keep its system closed into order to retain its margins. Accepting open programming would have meant opening SAP, and this is inconsistent with SAP's decades-long strategy. This is because once you don't control the

154 https://www.youtube.com/watch?v=KMlEdOCOMaQ&t=396s

development language, you lose control of what the rules are for interfacing with other systems. That is unless SAP plans to ratchet up indirect access threats even higher. However, SAP knows that if a significant case is brought against SAP for indirect access in the US, they have a very good chance of losing. Teradata has already challenged SAP's use of indirect access in a lawsuit as being in contradiction with US antitrust law. Therefore, like Oracle, SAP prefers to bring claims that cannot stand up in court on an individual or customer by customer basis without having the legality of it tested in each country.[155]

SAP's management knows that it is not feasible to try to bring ABAP into the modern world. Therefore they have moved the control to the cloud. Fiori is another example of SAP's need for control. Fiori provides Smart Widgets, these work together with the particular OData flavor provided by the ABAP backend, e.g., CDS Views. It would be terrific work to provide similar OData services, e.g. on a Java Stack. However, SAP will not do this.

Setting the Trap With Trendy Bait

The main page of the SAP Cloud website has an alphabet soup of trendy items (IoT, Machine Learning, cloud integration services), all things that SAP has little to nothing to do in reality. This is designed to be tantalizing. It is designed to get customers to move and to perform development using the SAP Cloud Platform before they understand the consequences and how they will be limited if they take SAP's bait.

The SAP Cloud Platform has been around for several years now. It was renamed from the SAP HANA Cloud Platform. We previously critiqued the SAP HANA Cloud Platform in the articles Is SAP HANA Cloud Platform Designed for HANA Washing?[156] and Is SAP HANA Cloud Platform Designed for Cloud Washing?[157] Reviewing the new incarnation now, it does not look like much different, except the name has been changed and a few things like "apps" have been integrated.

---

155 SAP did win its case against Diageo. However upon appeal, the case was settled. SAP does not want more cases like that to become headline fodder. The view of one of the authors of this book, Shaun Snapp, is that the judge on the first trial had a weak understanding of how systems are normally connected to each other and Diageo's legal defense was incompetent. Next time Diageo should find representation that has a better understanding of how software works. We covered this in the article The Problem with the Judge's Ruling on the SAP Diageo Case. - http://www.brightworkr.com/sap/2017/05/concerning-parts-judges-ruling-sap-vs-diageo/
156 http://www.brightworkr.com/saphana/2016/08/14/hana-cloud-platform-designed-of-hana-washing/
157 http://www.brightworkr.com/saphana/2016/08/14/hana-cloud-platform-designed-cloud-washing/

SAP's Open Source Lesson 1 :How to Take an Open Source Language and Make it Closed Source

The biggest problem of the SAP Cloud is proprietary Java Development Toolkit. Although it sounds ridiculous and impossible, SAP took a free language, modified it and forced customers to use it in the SAP cloud. (that is Java **was** free, until Oracle (who bought Sun) just recently began charging for Java).[158] [159]

- "SAP Java" also free, but it requires license validation. If could be impossible to go to any other cloud vendor **if SAP changes** the pricing policy.

- SAP has a habit of frequently changing their policies. If they did make this change it would mean that SAP could effectively lock customers in with what was an open source item that they had nothing to do with developing. SAP and Oracle's approach to open source is to infiltrate it (in some cases buy it) and then control it by closing it off. It was the EU regulatory body that required Oracle more or less not do this to MySQL in order to receive approval to purchase it.[160] However, as soon as MySQL was purchased, it was forked to MariaDB. This was done for one very obvious reason. Oracle lacks credibility in the open source community because of its previous behavior with open source projects.

Clues from Decades of SAP Development

SAP's development advice leads to high expense and low development productivity. This is another reason to steer clear from SAP's Cloud as they are trying to take their development approaches to the cloud.

---

158 http://www.oracle.com/technetwork/java/javaseproducts/overview/javasesubscriptionfaq-4891443.html

159 *"Desktop pricing is $2.50 per user per month, or lower with tiered volume discounts. Processor pricing for use on Servers and/or Cloud deployments is $25.00 per month or lower."* In addition to converting a free item to charge item, Oracle also locks in the charge for a year as described by the following quote. *"The standard term is one year."* To be clear, Oracle had nothing to do with Java's development. They acquired Java as part of the Sun acquisition.

160 The US Department of Justice, now firmly in Oracle's pocket and against enforcing any of US antitrust laws, decided to pressure the EU to approve the merger. *"US Department of Justice, at the request of Oracle, pressured the EU to approve the merger unconditionally. The European Commission eventually unconditionally approved Oracle's acquisition of MySQL on 21 January 2010."* – https://en.wikipedia.org/wiki/MySQL Therefore the DOJ now sees it as not only their role to not enforce US laws, but to go to bat for US corporations to prevent other regions from enforcing their antitrust laws.

- Neither Fiori, oData, and other SAP cloud items have very much uptake. Moreover, this is with the ability to push their components to a willing installed base.

- SAP's Netweaver is (in part) an uncompetitive web server/application server, yet is still used by SAP in instead of better alternatives like NGINX or Apache. SAP burns resources and time trying to make its components internally when there are far better components it could use that are made by other companies or are open source projects.

- SAP does not have a successful cloud product that was not acquired and therefore already cloud before it became part of the SAP product catalog. Consequently, their proposed web thought leadership that they claim is unsupported.

Now let us turn our attention to the Oracle Cloud. As with many areas, you will note quite a few similarities.

Issues with Oracle Cloud

We could go through the Oracle Cloud in more detail, however, concerning usability, the use of a brochureware cloud offering that is just like SAP Cloud more designed to serve as "cloud propaganda" rather than be used.

Oracle has made many claims proposing equivalence between Oracle Cloud and AWS that we think is incorrect. Oracle had a study published by Storage Review that promoted the idea of Oracle Cloud having better performance than competing offerings.

> *"There are a wide variety of cloud offerings at this point and even several large cloud offerings with AWS, Google Cloud Platform, and Microsoft Azure at the top of that list. While these cloud service providers offer many great products and services, one thing they typically don't have is performance. When comparing cloud to on-premises, on-prem always beats cloud hands down. Oracle is looking to change this view with its cloud infrastructure offerings."*[161]

Let us go to the last part of this quote.

> *"Oracle is looking to change this view..."*

---

161 https://www.storagereview.com/oracle_cloud_infrastructure_compute_bare_metal_instances_review

What Oracle is really trying to do is compare its bare metal against visualized environments. This is Oracle's "go to" argument against the cloud, to promote the performance benefits of bare metal.

It is not a surprise, and known by everyone that has studied the area, that on-premises bare metal can outperform a virtualized environment. However, it does not follow that performance is not available from the public cloud.

The performance depends upon the resources applied against the load. We have covered how scaled resources can be selected in the cloud, how auto scaling can be enabled, and how "serverless" has autoscaling built in as a natural feature. Therefore the phrasing in this quotation is inaccurate. It is not that performance is lacking in the cloud. It is that virtualized environments require more resources than do bare metal environments. And it also misunderstand the bottleneck faced by databases. This is explained in excellent research paper The Data Center Evolution from Mainframe to Cloud by Nikola Zlatanov.

> *"The mainframe / terminal model was founded on a fundamental scarcity of compute resources. At the time, computers were so large that they required highly specialized rooms, HVAC, operators-the works. If you wanted to use them, you often stood in line, made your case, and were eventually rewarded with some of the scarce and highly valuable cycles via a terminal.*
>
> *We now have so many powerful computers that we are willing to greatly sacrifice raw performance for manageability. You have so much compute out there, it is not about raw performance but simplicity and convenience."*[162]

This is the issue. Oracle is presenting a view where the primary bottleneck is performance, when it isn't.

However, Oracle are not comparing their bare metal service against AWS's bare metal service. Instead, Oracle seeks to compare Oracle bare metal against AWS/GCP/Azure cloud. But why? The comparison should be bare metal vs. bare metal and virtual machine vs. virtual machine. The problem is in this quote above, where Oracle sets the assumption before getting into the testing results. In this quote, public cloud providers like AWS, Google Cloud and Azure are compared against Oracle Cloud. However, Oracle Cloud is a hosting service. Yet, hosting and cloud are discussed as if they are interchangeable terms.

---

162 https://www.researchgate.net/publication/298217471_The_data_center_evolution_from_Mainframe_to_Cloud

Gartner, an entirely profit oriented firm which is extremely "big commercial vendor friendly" not prone to calling out a major funder like Oracle, calls out Oracle's cloud in the following way.[163]

> *"Tier 2 bare bones minimally viable product that's not ready for production workloads" and "Customers need to have a high tolerance for risk"*

But on the other hand, on other occasions, Gartner has sung a different tune regarding Oracle Cloud.

> *"These announcements are more cloud announcements than database announcements," Gartner analyst Adam Ronthal told Techrunch. "They are Oracle coming out to the world with products that are built and architected for cloud and everything that implies — scalability, elasticity and a low operational footprint. Make no mistake, Oracle still has to prove themselves in the cloud. They are behind AWS and Azure and even GCP in breadth and scope of offerings. ATP [Oracle's Autonomous Transaction Processing] helps close that gap, at least in the data management space."[164]*

This quote from Gartner begins by describing well known features of cloud and then soft peddles Oracle Cloud's vast inferiority to cloud with the following sub-quote.

> *"Make no mistake; Oracle still has to prove themselves in the cloud. They are behind AWS and Azure and even GCP in breadth and scope of offerings."*

Who is making a mistake?

Oracle Cloud is horrid and does not exist in the same universe as AWS, Google Cloud and Azure. And is why is having such an ineffectual history in something rephrased as needing to "prove oneself?" Why is Gartner assuming Oracle will?

Furthermore, if this is the end of the quote, then why does the quote begin with...

> *"They are Oracle coming out to the world with products that are built and architected for cloud and everything that implies."*

One would hope that Oracle built the products that they announce. Because if Oracle begins coming out to the world with products built by Salesforce or SAP, then there will obviously be trouble. So yes.....let us agree with Gartner that Oracle is announcing products that

---

163 This is covered in the book Gartner and the Magic Quadrant: A Guide for Buyers, Vendors and Investors
  - http://www.brightworkr.com/gartner/2017/06/14/best-understand-gartners-magic-quadrant/
164 https://techcrunch.com/2018/08/07/oracle-launches-autonomous-transaction-processing-cloud-service/

Oracle built. Furthermore, not only products that it built, but that Oracle both "built and architected."

This quotation is what you get when someone is paid but has to dance around a bit to obscure an obvious truth, and a truth which the payee would prefer the reader to think of differently than the reality would show. We will leave it the reader to guess how much Oracle pays Gartner on a yearly basis. For that type of dancing, let us hope it is a lot.

A review on Quora was a bit more colorful.

> *"Oracle Cloud is an absolute nightmare. All of their IaaS and PaaS solutions are complete sh*t. Nothing works. Support does not exist. It is a leach that should be purged from the industry ASAP. I am a CCNP / RHEL / AWS Architect / Python 3 Developer / DataCenter & Cloud Architect / Senior Engineer with 15+ years of experience. If you do not have my qualifications don't even think about launching your platform in Oracle Cloud. It's a fledgling cloud running alpha code and at best in it's infancy.*
>
> *You have been warned. Also shame on Gartner for reporting that Oracle Cloud was the most innovative, well executed cloud. Gartner has lost all credibility for me at this point. Oracle Cloud will sh*t on you, your reputation, your company, cost you millions, and all the while their "cloud success" engineers will belittle your team. Stay the F*CK away. RackSpace, AWS, Azure, and Google are all viable alternatives."*

We don't mean to violate the virgin ears of our readers, but this type of quotation is not unusual for online comments about Oracle. If you don't like swear words, stay away from Oracle forums as the comments seem to have far more use of expletives than any other vendor that we research. In terms of the number of expletives applied to them, Oracle is the clear industry leader.

All of this makes an Oracle cloud sale nearly impossible for any mature organization. CIOs have to explain why they went with a tier 2 immature provider when they could have chosen a proven and safe leader like AWS, Google, or Microsoft. The only viable solution for Oracle is to start targeting small and medium businesses who use the Oracle database. However, this means they have to compete with Amazon and Google on price and let go of their 80% margin business model.

That will be a problem for Oracle. Discussions around reducing the margin are not responded to well from the top of Oracle.

Disagreement on Oracle's Strategy with Cloud

In September 2018, Thomas Kurian took a leave of absence as head of Oracle Cloud and appeared to be leaving the company.[165]

The reason?

> *"Kurian wants Oracle to make more of its software available to run on public clouds from chief rivals Amazon.com Inc. and Microsoft Corp. as a way to diversify from its own struggling infrastructure, a view opposed by Ellison, one of the people said."*

Larry Ellison has a history of pushing executives out of Oracle (if they disagree with him, or he gets jealous of them), and Thomas Kurian appears to the latest casualty. Kurian should have learned from Safra Catz who has survived by never contradicting Larry. However, Kurian was acknowledging (internally at least, never publicly of course) what people who are objective and have studied the Oracle Cloud know. Oracle Cloud is not a competitive offering. Oracle Cloud is a significant liability for customers that use it and is entirely about locking companies into Oracle products. Oracle's cloud strategy is to "own the entire stack, top to bottom." It wants to run its databases, run its apps, and run its own analytics/BI. Just as with SAP, the business model is not open to other major software providers. Both vendors want to offer IaaS/PaaS to the market, but neither vendor has any capability in the area. In contrast to Oracle and SAP, AWS and Google Cloud are open to all software providers. Even Microsoft, which sells competing software products say in the ERP space, has Azure open to all software providers.

A testament to AWS's growth is that more Oracle databases are running on AWS than on Oracle cloud. This is due, in part, to the substantial lead AWS has over all other cloud providers. However, more importantly, it's because AWS is an open platform that supports all vendors, including open source. Customers can run any product imaginable on AWS, including Microsoft databases and apps, Oracle database and apps, and SAP databases and apps. AWS is not designed or optimized for AWS. AWS is designed and "tuned for everyone." These same things apply to Google Cloud, except the number of options is smaller, but the emphasis on openness is the same. Kurian knew how little chance Oracle Cloud had to create a viable IaaS, Larry Ellison disagreed, and could not take it. One can work as a top executive at Oracle as long as you agree with Larry but disagree and your days are numbered. Acceptance at Oracle is going to be a tricky thing.

---

165 https://www.bloomberg.com/news/articles/2018-09-12/oracle-s-kurian-is-said-to-take-leave-amid-discord-with-ellison?

We interpret this as a significant error on the part of Oracle and a loss for Oracle customers. This is because while Oracle has endeavored mightily, they have managed to coerce very few companies into using their cloud. It is the view of one of the authors, Mark Dalton, that at some point Oracle will come up with a functional cloud offering. However, by the time that arrives, how much further advanced will AWS and Google Cloud be? Right now is a perfect time to be a technical employee at AWS or Google Cloud because Oracle is desperate to improve their cloud, has a lot of money that it is willing to throw at AWS and Google Cloud Engineers however, with all that money, Oracle has shown no ability to develop cloud competency.

Improvement will have to come from hiring employees from AWS or Google or other places, rather than anything novel coming from inside Oracle. However, they have already hired quite a few AWS and Google Cloud engineers. If the current Oracle Cloud is all that they can muster for all those high priced hires, the future of cloud at Oracle does not look good.

Faking Cloud Revenues

Oracle's stock declined when they made an accounting change in how they reported cloud revenues that chose to obscure their cloud revenues. They had to, as the actual story is so different from the projected story. The story Mark Hurd called a "nothing burger" is a "huge juicy In and Out Burger."

Wall Street is finally beginning to figure out that SAP and Oracle are cloud poseurs.

For Oracle, cloud means the following:

1. No upfront license revenue

2. Recurring revenue is not guaranteed since IaaS/PaaS are consumption based

3. Massive CAPEX spending on data centers, cloud DevOps resources, and customer success resources. Hiring engineers from AWS, Microsoft, and Google Cloud is very difficult and very expensive.

4. A massive spending to transition partners to cloud technology

5. An enormous loss in service revenue both for Oracle and their partners since cloud SaaS is not customizable and IaaS/PaaS is automated.

Oracle's cloud strategy is about customer churn containment. Doubling the cost of licensing on competitor clouds is one example. And hiding cloud revenues is another.

Oracle's Illogical Messaging vs AWS

Even though AWS and Google Cloud are incredibly similar, due to AWS's growth, they get the majority of emphasis by SAP and Oracle. Therefore, Google Cloud tends to fly under the radar. However, Oracle messaging versus AWS makes little sense, and it is essential to consider why.

Let us review what AWS is.

AWS is an hyperscale web provider that offers a few of its own (Aurora, Redshift, etc..) databases and can host just about any other database. Oracle is the largest database vendor in the world and has tiny a IaaS that offers Oracle only.

IT Analyst and Wall Street have done a poor job of fact-checking the claims of lock-in vendors like Oracle and SAP dedication and growth in the cloud. The major IT media sources that all take money from Oracle and SAP, barely ever use the term "lock-in." Using terms that your funders don't like is not a good way to run a successful media company. This is particularly true in the era where nearly all of the funding outside of industry sources have dropped out of the equation. These media entities increasingly have positioned themselves like TechTarget (which owns ComputerWeekly among others) to access emails that are then shared with vendors using advanced marketing analytics, as we covered in the article How Computer Weekly is a Front for Marketing Automation.[166]

Oracle will often publish material that goes without any fact-checking. For this book, we decided to review Oracle Cloud on The Register to see what they tended to publish on Oracle and found The Register to be one of the few IT media entities to challenge assertions by Oracle.

Oracle is attempting to position the Oracle database against AWS's homegrown databases. However, that is not the right comparison. The Oracle database can be placed on AWS along with any number of other databases. AWS is not primarily a database vendor; they are a cloud service provider. When Oracle discusses AWS, they tend to present AWS as a database vendor that provides a single on-premises database that competes against the Oracle database.

The fact that Oracle has to draw an improperly framed comparison to AWS (Larry Ellison casting AWS as only competing against the Oracle database) illustrates that Oracle is not comfortable making the case by using the accurate framing. They know under a precise framing, Oracle Cloud will lose in any comparison.

---

166 http://www.brightworkr.com/sap/2017/11/computer-weekly-front-marketing-automation/

But this issue of inaccurate framing generalizes. Oracle makes such bizarre contentions about the cloud, one has to really question whether they study the topic very closely. A good example of this is this quotation from the article The Rise of the Hybrid Cloud.

> *"The common perception that public clouds are the best low-cost option is false. Contrary to this view, on-demand services from public cloud providers may come at a higher premium than in-house cloud services. When you compare the unit economics of a private cloud solution using high convergence density systems, or engineered systems such as Oracle Exadata, with comparable public clouds, it becomes apparent that the private cloud is usually the lower-cost solution. Public clouds still have a long way to go before the virtuous cycle of early public cloud adopters, who help bring down the unit costs, will attract the next wave of adopters. Consider Amazon, one of the leading public cloud providers. It has reduced the price of its public cloud services 42 times in the last six years alone due to this virtuous cycle and increasing competition."*

First things first. What is a "high convergence density system?" We searched for such a term outside of this article and were unable to find one, which means this is a made up term. (which is also undefined by the author).

Other questions from this ridiculous article quickly arise:

- Is it really true that private cloud/hosting **without shared resources** is less expensive than public cloud with shared resources?

- Is Amazon's declining costs evidence of the lower costs of private cloud?

This article by Oracle has to be fully read to be believed. It should come with its own laugh track. We cover this in detail in the article Oracle Writes the Most Stupid Article on Cloud Ever.[167]

Conclusion

It's hard to see the SAP Cloud as anything but an incompetent marketing push to cloudwash SAP to audiences that lack firsthand information about SAP Cloud. Prime targets include Wall Street and higher level executives within customers. It is extremely rare to hear anyone talk about the SAP Cloud on SAP projects and it is evident through testing SAP Cloud that

---

167 http://www.brightworkr.com/saaseconomy/2018/09/17/oracle-writes-the-most-stupid-article-on-cloud-ever/

it has extremely low usage. SAP will, however, keep the SAP Cloud smoke machine up, as it has a purpose for marketing and maintaining the pretense for Wall Street.

SAP has a problem with the cloud for many reasons, but one primary reason is that the programming language that they have used for decades and forced into customers to the detriment of those customers does not work well in the cloud. This means that in a way, SAP is legacy, and not in the good sense (legacy systems can be reliable and low maintenance, but SAP is not low maintenance, and neither are SAP sales reps). SAP has another problem with the cloud in that cloud relies upon openness to work, and SAP is based upon lock-in. SAP cannot produce sincere comments about the cloud, because the more SAP embraces the cloud, the more SAP loses control over their customer base. Therefore, when SAP attempts to entice customers into using their cloud, it is from the perspective of maintaining control. If SAP can move customers to cloud, then can control them, and extract from them by greatly marking up services from AWS, Google Cloud and Azure. SAP's pricing lays bare their plan to milk customers that touch SAP Cloud. However, if SAP loses customers to AWS, Google Cloud or Azure through direct usage, SAP has a serious problem.

Oracle Cloud operates in a substantially similar way, except that Oracle is further behind in accepting the fact that like SAP they will never be a competitive IaaS provider. Larry Ellison has the Oracle Cloud setup for even more irrelevance than the SAP Cloud because they have not yet ceded the IaaS battlefield to the apparent winners.

Oracle's public statements on cloud display not only deception but also confusion as to how the cloud operates. It appears that Oracle is having difficulty processing what is happening around them. This is true even though they have plenty of smart people and have access to all the information. Many articles written by Oracle on cloud quickly devolve into unmitigated nonsense. That is their deception appears to extend to self-deception concerning cloud.

Chapter 7: Where is SaaS/PaaS/IaaS Going in the Future?

Web services are segmented into SaaS, PaaS and IaaS. In this article we will cover their history, and where they are headed.

The Switch in Growth from SaaS to IaaS

IaaS and PaaS were not the first types of remote delivery to become popular. The first was SaaS, which is where a vendor sold access to a centralized multi-tenant web based application.

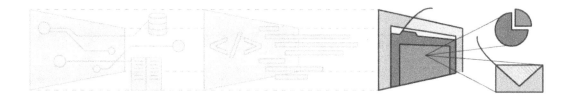

Software as a Service (SaaS):

Software as a Service provides you with a completed product that is run and managed by the service provider. In most cases, people referring to Software as a Service are referring to end-user applications. With a SaaS offering you do not have to think about how the service is maintained or how the underlying infrastructure is managed; you only need to think about how you will use that particular piece software. A common example of a SaaS application is web-based email where you can send and receive email without having to manage feature additions to the email product or maintaining the servers and operating systems that the email program is running on.

AWS's explanation of SaaS. SaaS was thought to change the enterprise software space dramatically, but this has not yet happened. While starting significantly later, it is now IaaS/

PaaS that is growing more rapidly and reconfiguring enterprise software. No SaaS vendor has ever matched the growth that has been experienced by AWS. Although AWS also provides SaaS services also, most of their services are PaaS or IaaS.

While beginning with great fanfare, and receiving large amounts of venture capital funding, SaaS vendors have proven to have grown slowly overall, and profits are hard to come by. The largest SaaS vendor, Salesforce has seen its growth slow, and it now behaves more like an on-premises vendor in many respects than a SaaS vendor with its restrictive terms and conditions. (recall that being cloud has specific requirements and can't be self-ascribed) Moreover, the overall cloud nature of applications is overstated because of companies like SAP and Oracle whose organizational structures are setup for on-premises development, sale and delivery that cloudwash, and try to trick customers and Wall Street as to how much progress they are making moving to the cloud.

SaaS applications certainly have many advantages. And for consumers who access Gmail or a SaaS invoicing application or use Google Docs as examples, it has allowed users to access many applications quickly and easily. However, PaaS/IaaS will ultimately prove to be far more transformational for enterprise customers than will SaaS. Furthermore, PaaS/IaaS is growing far more rapidly than SaaS vendors combined. This is illustrated in the measurement of each category of service, but don't zero in on this graphic too strongly, as we are about to critique its accuracy.

Worldwide Public Cloud Services Revenue, Market Share, and Year-Over-Year Growth, 1H17
(revenues in US$ millions)

Segment	1H17 Revenue	1H17 Market Share	1H16 Revenue	1H16 Market Share	Year-over-Year Growth
IaaS	$11,236	17.8%	$8,138	16.6%	38.1%
PaaS	$8,567	13.6%	$5,702	11.6%	50.2%
SaaS	$43,400	68.7%	$35,310	71.8%	22.9%
Total	**$63,260**	**100%**	**$49,179**	**100%**	**28.6%**

Source: IDC Worldwide Semiannual Public Cloud Services Tracker, 1H17

[168] *Some of the growth in SaaS is not actually growth. For instance, major vendors like Adobe and Microsoft transitioned their on-premises revenues to SaaS revenues. That is it has merely replaced on-premises software revenues. Therefore even the 22.9% growth in SaaS is not entirely "growth." Once that is taken into account, IaaS and PaaS growth looks even more impressive.*

---

168 https://www.geekwire.com/2017/new-data-software-service-industry-revenue-23-year-shift-cloud-continues/

Although again, some of this is also conversion as more IaaS growth means fewer servers being purchased and ultimately less IT employment in companies that use IaaS services. Thus part of this is a redirection of revenues. The PaaS revenue is more distributed among different providers, while AWS has a very big chunk of the overall IaaS revenues. We include this graphic from IDC, but the estimates from different firms on this topic are all over the place. Vendors are cloud washing like crazy, so anyone performing this analysis needs to be able to adjust for that factor, or the numbers won't be accurate.

Gartner proposes the following numbers for 2017 (in millions).

- Cloud Business Process Services (BPaaS) $40,812

- Cloud Application Infrastructure Services (Pass) $7,169

- Cloud Application Services (SaaS) $38,567

- Cloud Management and Security Services $7,150

- Cloud System Infrastructure Services (IaaS) $25,290

- Cloud Advertising $90,257[169]

- Total Market $209,244[170]

If we compare just IaaS, IDC comes to $11,236 million versus $25,290 million. That is a pretty big discrepancy. And there is another problem. Both IDC and Gartner are so commercial and profit maximized, we don't find the reports of either firms on this or other topics to be compelling.

- The book by one of the authors, Shaun Snapp on Gartner found that they follow no established research conventions and markets services to vendors by telling them that by purchasing advisory services they will perform better in various Gartner products.[171] Gartner has a poor record in forecasting, and their forecasts seem to be more focused on garnering attention than on being accurate.[172]

- IDC is part of IDG, which publishes eight of the largest IT media publications (ComputerWorld, CIO and others) and as we covered in the article How IDG Works

---

169 If these numbers are to believed, it means that cloud advertising is by far the largest segment of cloud business.

170 https://seekingalpha.com/article/4073423-amazon-web-services-190-billion-valuation

171 http://www.brightworkr.com/gartner/2016/11/26/gartner-similarities-sales-strategy/

172 http://www.brightworkr.com/gartner/2017/06/15/disregarding-gartners-deeper-technology-insights-predictions/

to Provide Inaccurate Information, their financial bias is deep and their accuracy is extremely low.[173]

The problem is that there are not many entities that track these numbers. However, as we covered in the article The 23 Largest Software Vendors in the World, the largest vendors are not primarily SaaS vendors. There is a discrepancy between the coverage of SaaS and the actual percentage of revenues that are driven by true SaaS.

The Application Versus Data Centric Models

Both AWS and Google Cloud do perform development and are leaders in the software industry. However, they are not vendors, in the traditional sense, as they use software to sell access. This distinction between being a software vendor instead of selling access to computational "things" turns out to have important implications for the approach that it allows customers to take in managing their IT expenditures. Also, one of the most significant changes relates to the ability to become data-centric rather than application centric, which for those interested can read about this in the article How AWS and Google Cloud Enabled Data Centric Development.

Containerization and Microservices

No discussion of the future of SaaS/PaaS/IaaS is complete with an analysis of containerization and microservices.[174] Therefore we will begin by explaining what microservices are and how they work.

---

173 http://www.brightworkr.com/enterprisesoftwarepolicy/2017/08/05/idg-works-provide-inaccurate-information/

174 For those who remembers SOA, it is interesting to compare and contrast SOA with microservices. *"In microservices, services can operate and be deployed independently of other services, unlike SOA. So, it is easier to deploy new versions of services frequently or scale a service independently. In SOA, ESB could become a single point of failure which impacts the entire application. Since every service is communicating through ESB, if one of the services slow down, could cause the ESB to be clogged up with requests for that service. On the other hand, microservices are much better in fault tolerance. For example, if there is a memory leak in one microservice then only that microservice will be affected. The other microservices will continue to handle requests. In both architectures, developers must deal with the complexity of architecture and a distributed system. Developers must implement the inter-service communication mechanism between microservices (if the message queue is used in Microservice architectures) or within ESB and services."* - https://dzone.com/articles/microservices-vs-soa-2

Microservices

Microservices are a way of breaking up the functionality that is generally contained within a monolithic application and monolithic database into smaller pieces increasing the variety in coding languages, databases, and associated tools.

This is explained nicely in the following quotation.

> *"First, to be precise, when talking about microservices, we are actually referring to a microservice architecture. This architecture type is a particular way of developing software, web or mobile applications as suites of independent services – a.k.a microservices. These services are created to serve only one specific business function, such as: user management, user roles, e-commerce cart, search engine, social media logins, etc. Furthermore, they are independent of each other, meaning they can be written in different programming languages and use different data storages. The centralized management is almost non-existent and the microservices use lightweight HTTP, REST or Thrift APIs for communicating between themselves."*[175]

With microservices, modularity is increased as is developer specialization as each microservice has its development which is concentrated on the technologies and the even the business processes for that microservice. New applications or new development will be increasingly likely to be based upon microservices. However, old applications are also being refactored into microservices to receive their benefits. Microservices are the opposite design to the monolithic design approach.

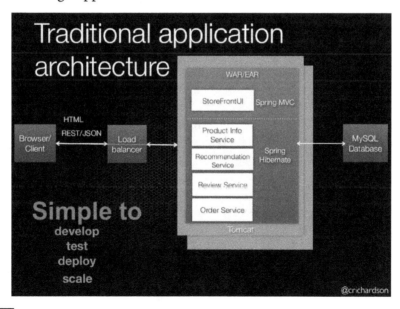

---

175 https://dzone.com/articles/what-are-microservices-actually

This is a slide from Chris Richardson, a well-known thought leader in the field of cloud, which describes the monolithic design.[176] *The monolithic design requires a long-term commitment to a specific technology stack. This can be considered as a type of lock-in to the original design components.*

The long life and "metastasizing" nature of computer programs, and particularly of successful programs, means that a monolithic design limits the flexibility of the program. This is because it begins with a series of development components that invariably would benefit from being altered/upgrades as time passes and new technologies become available. The monolithic design promotes the need for refactoring code rather than being able to add new microservices based upon new technologies, or adding microservices built on different technologies to address an increase in scope.

Microservices & Gateway

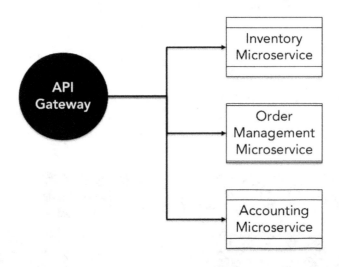

*The objective is to make each component or microservice modular. This means that changes within the module can be tested **without affecting** the other modules. The API is the connection point to other applications or microservices.*[177]

---

176 https://www.slideshare.net/chris.e.richardson/building-apps-with-microservices-svcc-2014

177 As is normal microservices have their own extra overhead. *"The API Gateway also has some drawbacks. It is yet another highly available component that must be developed, deployed, and managed. There is also a risk that the API Gateway becomes a development bottleneck. Developers must update the API Gateway in order to expose each microservice's endpoints. It is important that the process for updating the API Gateway be as lightweight as possible. Otherwise, developers will be forced to wait in line in order to update the gateway. Despite these drawbacks, however, for most real-world applications it makes sense to use an API Gateway."* - https://www.nginx.com/blog/building-microservices-using-an-api-gateway/

Example: *Weather Application*

S3 — *Front-end code for weather app hosted in S3*

User clicks link to get local weather information

API GATEWAY — *App makes REST API call to endpoint*

Lambda is triggered — *Lambda runs code to retrieve local weather information and returns data back to user*

DYNAMODB

Notice the API Gateway in AWS's explanation of Lambda and DynamoDB.[178]

With microservices development, the modules have such a high degree of isolation from one another that they can and often are written in different languages with head microservice having its own **database** (allowing for different database designs). By creating such natural isolation in the design, it means that computer languages can be selected based upon the fit between the language and the purpose. This is particularly efficient because in most cases the different modules (application slices?) are maintained by different teams. This differs from a monolithic design like SAP where the entire application is written in a single language, and uses a single database. The monolithic design means forcing a single language and a single database type do things that they not naturally good at doing, in order to keep a single language throughout the application.

Microservices are enabled by containerization and use containers which can contain a wide variety of items, and even databases.[179] Lynn Langit, calls containers the new VMs, as her following quotation explains.

> *"To me, containers are the new VMs. All this frenzy about containers, and more specifically container management systems — look, somebody has to manage the things. I want to pay the cloud providers to do it so I don't have to."[180]*

---

178 https://aws.amazon.com/dynamodb/

179 MariaDB differentiates itself on how well it can be run from within containers. *"However, the architecture of MariaDB TX enables it to run equally as well on containers and public cloud instances as it does on bare-metal servers – a challenge for databases requiring shared storage for high availability and/or scalability (e.g., IBM Db2 with pureScale and Oracle Database with RAC). In addition, it includes the world's most advanced database proxy featuring a powerful database firewall and denial of service protection."* - https://mariadb.com/sites/default/files/content/assets/wp/mariadb_enterprise_comparison_wp.pdf?aliId=48162144

180 https://read.acloud.guru/serverless-superheroes-lynn-langit-on-big-data-nosql-and-google-versus-aws-f4427dc8679c

Containers

A container is a discrete encapsulated and emulated operating system that allows portability of codes and dependencies between physical or virtual/emulated servers.

Containers benefit from the automated management and performance benefits of container management systems like Docker. Docker is widely thought to have significantly simplified the usage of containers and also increased the general usage of containers. Docker's capabilities provide a higher incentive to use containers, because of the all the container management that comes with Docker.[181]

Docker is only slightly less popular with programmers than this cartoon would suggest.[182]

---

181 *"So the ability to do containerization is over 15 years old, but why has it become famous only recently? It is because Docker has simplified it to the point where it only takes a few commands to create namespaces and connect them in a usable manner."* - Hybrid Cloud for Architects

182 http://turnoff.us/geek/docker-panacea/

A great explanation of container is as follows:

> *"Container-based development dictates the architecture of the application. In container-based development, the application is broken into small pieces (containers) that are replicated within the network. Each container is networked together so that if one is overloaded by a request, a copy of the container can step-in to handle the incoming requests while the overloaded container reboots and gets back online"*[183]

> *"Containers have impacts on the cost of managing resources credence as a way to build apps directly from the developer's laptop with much of the process automated and packaged. They have impacts on the cost of managing resources"*[184]

All of these containers must be "orchestrated" (organized to work together) which is where Docker or the Docker Engine comes in.

In Docker's own words, the Docker Engine is the following:

> *"Docker creates simple tooling and a universal packaging approach that bundles up all application dependencies inside a container. Docker Engine enables containerized applications to run anywhere consistently on any infrastructure, solving "dependency hell" for developers and operations teams, and eliminating the "it works on my laptop!" problem."*[185]

> *"Docker operates on top of the infrastructure and syncs with the way to ship, build, run and deploy applications. It's an open platform for distributed apps. It works wherever Linux does, which is essentially anywhere; it also works on Windows. Docker is not reliant on a separate operation system; it just takes advantage of already built technology."* [186]

---

183 https://medium.com/@GoRadialspark/heroku-alternatives-aws-azure-and-google-cloud-platform-870ae316527e
184 The New Stack: The Docker and Containers Ecosystem eBook Series. - https://thenewstack.io/ebooks-thank-you?pid=2336881&bid=2336883
185 https://www.docker.com/products/docker-engine
186 The New Stack: The Docker and Containers Ecosystem eBook Series

The rise of microservices and containers is evidenced by the fact that Docker is one of the fastest growing products currently in programming circles, but the overall use of containers be it with Docker or Kubernetes, or AWS Container Service is seeing enormous growth.[187]

Containers are described by Docker as follows.

"In a micro-services architecture, many small services (each represented as a single Docker container) comprise an application. Applications are now able to be deconstructed into much smaller components which fundamentally changes the way they are initially developed, and then managed in production."[188] [189]

The entire purpose of the container is to launch microservices. These containers provide a high degree of autonomy. Moreover, this allows each container to use a different coding language. The reason this is beneficial is simple. Various tasks are better addressed with different coding languages.

For instance, our application, the Brightwork Explorer which we show as a case study in the end of the book, only does math.[190] Therefore we started the initial development and testing in R which is better for early testing when the focus is on just the math, and then transitioned the code to Python, when one wants to operationalize the math in an application (although Python has a lower overall math capability than R). These are two excellent languages for math, each with their advantages and disadvantages.

In addition to being written in any language, or the best language for the task, microservices have the freedom to store data as is best for each microservice. This is why IaaS is such a boon for microservices (and vice versa). For instance, within Google Cloud's App Engine (its PaaS), multiple microservices can be deployed within one App Engine, or as the following quotation explains, there is another option.

"If you don't want to rely on these patterns to achieve isolation and you want a more formal enforcement of separation, you can use multiple App Engine projects.

---

187 *"Overall Docker adoption increases to 49 percent from 35 percent in 2017 (a growth rate of 40 percent). Kubernetes sees the fastest growth, almost doubling to reach 27 percent adoption. The AWS container service (ECS/EKS) leads among the cloud provider's container-as-a-service offerings at 44 percent adoption."* - https://www.rightscale.com/blog/cloud-industry-insights/cloud-computing-trends-2018-state-cloud-survey

188 https://goto.docker.com/rs/929-FJL-178/images/Docker-for-Virtualization-Admin-eBook.pdf

189 Docker began its life connecting to or as an extension of Linux LXC. However, to enable platform independence, it developed its own execution driver and this eventually became something known as containerd. Containerd is actually now a container which can be used inside of Kubernetes. - https://www.amazon.com/Docker-Deep-Dive-Nigel-Poulton-ebook/dp/B01LXWQUFF

190 http://www.brightworkr.com/brightworkexplorer/

There are pros and cons to using projects instead of services, and you must balance the tradeoffs depending on your situation. Unless you have a specific need for one of the advantages offered by using multiple projects, it's best to start with using multiple services within a single project because performance will be better and the administrative overhead will be minimized. Of course, you can also choose some hybrid of the two approaches. It means that the developers for each microservice can look at the full menu of storage and databases offered by the IaaS and pick and choose the best that meets the needs of the individual microservice. The performance implications are enormous, because under the monolithic development approach, the entire development team could only store data in the single database type, say the Oracle DB. Under the IaaS model, particularly with open source databases, there is little "fixed cost." That is customers are charged by usage. This means any number of databases can be leveraged by any number of microservices."[191]

When Is an Application Finished in Development?

The microservice architecture sees no endpoint for development. Microservices are a design that accounts for this **continual development**, and effectively manages the long term growth and modification of the application.

When analyzed by those with the most in depth understanding of software, it increasingly seems that software is like a "thing" at any one point in time. That is because of its constantly changing nature, and its constant maintenance and adjustment, as well as its natural growth, it can also be viewed as a process. Alternatively, a thing **in the process of becoming something else.**

Many have compared software to a biological organism. It has a lifecycle, parts of it are continually being updated, pieces being thrown away. This is how the developer sees the software, although the user of the software tends to view software as more of a "thing," as they are not as privy to what goes on in the background.

---

191 https://cloud.google.com/appengine/docs/standard/python/microservices-on-app-engine#app_engine_services_as_microservices

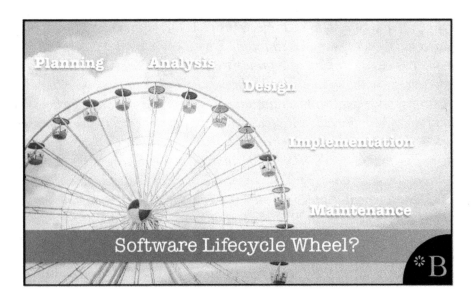

What is the most accurate and functional mental model for software development and maintenance? One view is that the software development lifecycle has a definitive endpoint. This is what project managers would like people to believe. However, isn't software more of a wheel, where after maintenance, further changes are implemented, and the software evolves years after the initial go live?

Once one begins to consider software in an organic context, how does that alter the way that you build software? Monolithic vendors tend to present the go live as the end point. While this may sell well to corporate buyers, this is not a functional mental model that helps with optimizing software development.

Microservices are often more efficient for many types of development (not necessarily all types) than the monolithic strategy where a single database and single code base is used. This coordination of microservices is controlled by a service mesh, which is a "dedicated infrastructure layer built right into an app."[192]

This is explained in the following quotation from the Heroku blog.

> *"The first force that led to the surge in microservices was a reaction against traditional, monolithic architecture. While a monolithic app is One Big Program with many responsibilities, microservice-based apps are composed of several small programs, each with a single responsibility. This allows teams of engineers to work relatively independently on different services. The inherent decoupling also encourages smaller, simpler programs that are easier to understand, so new*

---

192 https://www.redhat.com/en/topics/microservices

developers can start contributing more quickly. Finally, since no single program represents the whole of the application, services can change direction without massive costs. If new technology becomes available that makes more sense for a particular service, it's feasible to rewrite just that service. Similarly, since microservices communicate across a language-agnostic protocol, an application can be composed of several different platforms - Java, PHP, Ruby, Node, Go, Erlang, etc - without issue."[193]

Adjusting from the Monolithic Model

The vast majority of applications that have ever been developed have been developed under the monolithic design. One might think, quite naturally, that because microservices are new that the majority of microservice applications are **new development**, but in fact, the majority of containerized applications are **legacy** applications that have been ported to containers.

Daniel Stori {turnoff.us}

Monolithic designs can be created quickly, but can have long term maintenance implications that were not considered in the development stage.[194]

The reason this is possible is that conversion is possible from a monolithic application to containers, **without** performing coding.[195]

Monolithic designs have their place, and we are not covering this topic to simply treat them like a piñata. However, decades of history with the monolithic design has demonstrated some clear disadvantages.

---

193 https://d1.awsstatic.com/whitepapers/DevOps/running-containerized-microservices-on-aws.pdf
194 http://turnoff.us/geek/the-depressed-developer-17/
195 https://www.docker.com/solutions/mta

- *Code Redundancy:* A monolithic application generates a lot of code redundancy. And to integrate with any functionality of a monolithic application, one must integrate to the overall database of the "monolith." However, if a monolithic application is broken into many microservices, those microservices can be connect to any other microservice, there is little dispute that this is a more flexible design.

- *Decreasing Development Efficiency with Growth*: Monolithic applications are quick to develop...**in the beginning**. However, as the application grows, the development slows, and the interdependencies increase, and the limitations of the approach quickly catch up with the software monolith.[196] And the larger the application becomes, the slower the future development and the more bugs begin to appear. Monoliths require more time analyzing code as it is more difficult for the programmers to understand. This is because it is far more difficult to control the interdependencies as the application or its code base grows. Unfortunately, in their haste to develop quickly, vendors often select the monolithic approach in order to hit the early deadlines to show fast progress.

- *Lack of Tool Variety/Choice:* Monoliths primarily use a **minimal number of tools**. This is a disadvantage. Monolithic designs use one database type, one coding language, etc.. This cuts out the leverage that comes from using multiple components. If we consider how languages are created, each computer language does some things better than others.[197] In databases, no database performs all types of database processing equally well. Also, of course, different loads work better on some hardware configurations versus others (that one is easy for people to understand, the earlier two examples require more hands-on exposure, but are just as relevant). The degree to which tools are limited is the degree to which the overall final application is limited. A perfect example of this is an ERP system, which is the mother of

---

196 *"Monoliths are significantly easier and faster to build... in the beginning. Your entire application can be managed in a single IDE. All of your data lives in a single database. You can cross-query against an assortment of disparate parts to assemble reports. You can ensure data integrity by wrapping codependent inserts/updates into a single transaction that can be rolled back in the event of a failure. Your controllers can easily pull in data from different related models without the need to create an API. This type of development absolutely leads to the ability to get a lot of features out the door, very quickly."* - https://blog.codeship.com/ exploring-microservices-architecture-on-heroku/

197 *"Heroku removes most of the upfront investments involved in developing with a microservice architecture. It makes working with a virtually unlimited number of pieces fairly trivial, which is exactly what you need in order to keep track of microservices in a way that keeps you sane. Without dedicated IT staff, microservices using more than a single language can create a lot of DevOps issues, and Heroku alleviates the vast majority of those so you can focus on your application."* - https://blog.codeship.com/exploring-microservices-architecture-on-heroku/

all monoliths. Moreover, this is an excellent time to take a slight detour to fully appreciate the scope of the ERP influence on software design.

The Mother of All Monoliths, the ERP System and Its Influence on Present Day IT

The ERP industry is massive and because of this infrequently criticized because of its enormous economic power. When ERP systems first were marketed, consulting companies became partners with packaged software companies, effectively parroting everything they said. Even to the point where almost no one in IT is aware that academic research going back to the 1980s on packaged ERP systems consistently show the same results, which is a negative ROI. One author of this book, Shaun Snapp covers this in the book The Real Story on ERP: Separation Fiction from Reality.[198]

All of this is why the ERP system can be viewed as a Trojan Horse as is covered in the article How ERP System Was a Trojan Horse.[199]

ERP implementations were instant money makers. ERP consulting firms were careful to never expose any of the problems with the ROI ERP systems. Everyone "knew" that ERP systems benefited companies. Also, if you had any doubt, you could read a report from Gartner that would say how good ERP systems were. You know, Gartner, a "trustworthy" firm with significant undeclared revenues from ERP vendors.

198 http://www.brightworkr.com/scmfocuspress/erp-books/the-real-story-behind-erp/
199 http://www.brightworkr.com/erp/2016/04/09/erp-systems-trojan-horse/

ERP sales reps have done their job well, with software "stuffing" after the initial ERP sale being quite ordinary. Moreover, the maintenance of ERP systems has proven to be higher than anyone imagined. The estimates on this topic vary, but let us review some we were able to find.

- According to Rimini Street, the 89% of the average IT budget is dedicated to keeping the lights on, leaving only 11% for innovative projects.[200]

- *"Some agencies are spending 90 percent or more of their IT budgets on operations and maintenance, a report released last week found. The IDC Government Insights report found 77.7 percent of proposed agency IT budgets for fiscal year 2017 are going to operations and maintenance, with the remaining sliver dedicated to systems development and enhancement."*[201]

- *"The federal government spent more than 75 percent of the total amount budgeted for information technology (IT) for fiscal year 2015 on operations and maintenance (O&M) investments."*[202]

IT departments are so stuffed with unused or little used software that a major complaint of SAP and Oracle sales reps is that they can't get more growth from their current customers, which is why "net new" customers, which is customers who have never been SAP or Oracle customers, are considered so highly valued.

In the case of SAP, the question is how to unlock value from the large investment made into both the ERP system and the associated systems purchased by SAP customers. (Hint: it is not by buying more SAP).

- In some cases, it is decommissioning some SAP applications. Leveraging cloud services is a primary way to improve the investments made into SAP and into ERP systems generally.

- There are so many ways to unlock value from SAP environments, but they aren't from leveraging more SAP, or from leveraging most of what SAP has to offer as most of the new things that SAP offers don't work out.

The first step is to stop listening to SAP or to the SAP consulting partners that won't tell their clients anything independent but repeating whatever SAP says. All of the advice from these entities leads right back into buying more of what SAP has to offer. And when it comes to cloud, SAP is just a big pile of liability.

---

200 https://www.riministreet.com/Documents/Collateral/Rimini-Street-eBook-10-Telltale-Signs-Change-Database-Strategy.pdf
201 https://www.fedscoop.com/new-report-highlights-skyrocketed-agency-o-m-spending/
202 https://oversight.house.gov/wp-content/uploads/2016/05/2016-05-25-Powner-Testimony-GAO.pdf

Containers and Microservices Are the "New Shiny" (Actually No Longer New as "Serverless" is the True "New Shiny") But Why Containers Are Not Unflawed

Containers and microservices have many advantages over the monolithic design, but even if they offered nothing but benefits and no disadvantages, there would still be costs in adjusting to these newer technologies.

This is emphasized in the following quotation.

> *"Just as container management systems present new sets of questions, so too do new organizational structures. If a company decides to adopt Holacracy as part of its mission to improve agility, it will have to navigate and structural change happens through experimentation, failure, and adaptation."*[203]

Companies have reported shortages of skills in this new way of performing and managing development. There is simply a lot to keep up with, for all the changes in the programming space.

DANIEL STORI {TURNOFF.US}

---

203 The Docker and Container Ecosystem - https://thenewstack.io/ebooks-thank-you

Of course, as with anything new, not everything is roses. And we would be remis if we did not include this cartoon on microservices versus the monolithic approach.[204] [205]

The issue illustrated in the previous cartoon is of finding the microservices is a real issue, and is one of the reasons for the rise of services like Docker that help manage and deploy microservices. Docker manages the "containers" which support the microservice. A container may run within a virtual machine or on "bare metal."[206] And they can be ported between virtual machines (say on different IaaS providers) or between a virtual machine and bare metal. But in most cases, they are run from within virtual machines. In fact, the container can address any resource within its host virtual machine. And containers are, while newer than virtual machines, considered to provide similar benefits to virtual machines, but to have even more advantages as containers *"virtualize the operating system rather than the hardware."[207]* Because of this they use far fewer resources and containers are more portable than virtual machines.[208]

---

204 http://turnoff.us/geek/are-you-ready-for-microservices/

205 This issue highlighted in the cartoon is related to the findability of microservices, the obvious solution to is a directory. This is addressed by Netflix, one of the leaders in the use of microservices in the following quotation. *"One of the problems introduced by microservices is the large volume of services that must invoke other services in the system. Each of these services must know where to find the services it consumes, and attempting to manage the resulting configuration manually is intractable. To solve this problem Netflix created the Eureka server. A Eureka server is a service registry. It's like a phone book for your microservices. Each microservice registers itself with Eureka, and then consumers of that service will know how to find it. This is similar in spirit to a DNS service but with additional features such as host-side load-balancing and region-isolation. Eureka also keeps track of health, availability and other metadata about the service. That makes it an ideal place to start when building your own microservices architecture."* - https://blog.heroku.com/managing_your_microservices_on_heroku_with_netflix_s_eureka

206 https://blog.docker.com/2018/08/containers-replacing-virtual-machines/

207 https://www.docker.com/resources/what-container

208 *"In a VM-centered world, the unit of abstraction is a monolithic VM that stores not only application code, but often the stateful data. A VM takes everything that used to sit on a physical server and just packs it into a single binary so it can be moved around. But it is still the same thing."* - https://goto.docker.com/rs/929-FJL-178/images/Docker-for-Virtualization-Admin-eBook.pdf

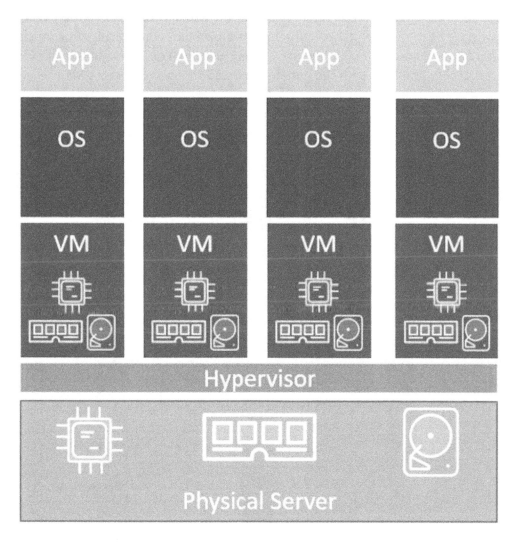

This diagram is from the book Docker Deep Dive. Moreover, this diagram does one of the best jobs in explaining virtual machines. Notice that each virtual machine has what is emulated hardware for each VM. This provides much flexibility as each VM can be a different OS, but it also uses many resources. The use of VMs made sense when containers had not arrived yet on the scene. However, due to its resource consumption, it makes more sense to limit the number of VMs on a server, and let containers do more of the work. We are now seeing fewer VMs and more containers. VMs are still critical components, but there will be fewer of them used.[209] [210]

209 https://www.amazon.com/Docker-Deep-Dive-Nigel-Poulton-ebook/dp/B01LXWQUFF
210 *"Virtualization technology from companies like VMware sits below the operating system and virtualizes the server, not the application. Wherever the virtual machine goes, the operating system has to go with it."* - The New Stack: The Docker and Containers Ecosystem eBook Series

This reduction of VMs is an essential change in infrastructure as it is widely considered that VMs have been over implemented which is a problem considering how much in the way of hardware resources VMs consume versus bare metal or the traditional server stack. Moreover, this is combined with the human overhead in managing the VMs.

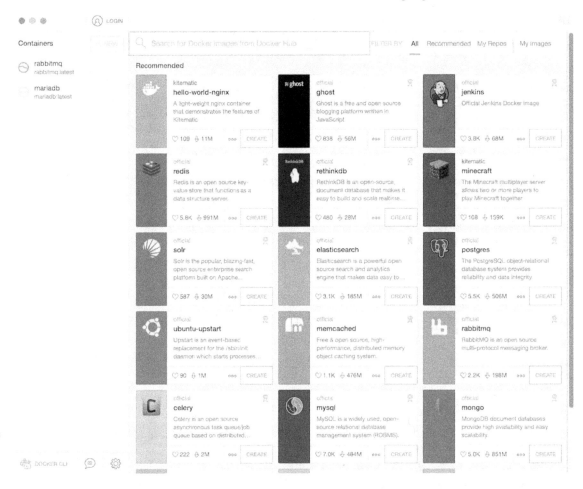

These are all Docker containers that are available for me to open on my local computer. The containers can be ported from my operating system to any server, to either the bare metal or to a VM on premises on in the cloud. If one were to have a VM on a local computer instead and then port that VM to a different location, it would be a much more involved affair. Notice that some of these containers are databases. In the past, the database was a resource that ran

on a VM, which was addressed from within a container. Now databases (some of them) are themselves within containers.[211]

Containers can and are often ported between virtual machines, or between virtual machines and bare metal. Moreover, when Docker is used, they can be migrated between virtually any operating system. They also separate the data from the container as is covered in the following quotation from Docker.

> *"So, how does a sysadmin backup a Docker container? They don't. The application data doesn't live in the container, it lives in a Docker volume that is shared between 1-N containers as defined by the application architecture. Sysadmins backup the data volume, and forget about the container. Optimally Docker containers are completely stateless and immutable."[212]*

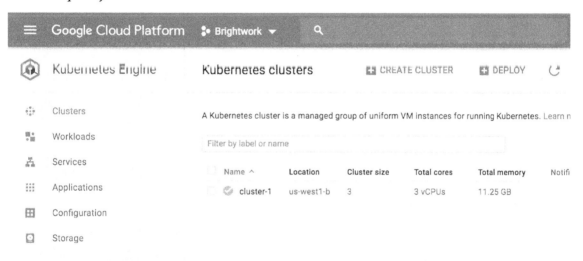

---

211 An interesting comment on the benefits of running databases from within containers. *"Want to move the MySQL instance to a different server? No problem, just mount the same volume and go for it. Is the image for your minor version of MySQL updated? Update it with a single command. Did your server restart, albeit on purpose? Docker will start your container automatically for you. Wanna use the server you're using now for something else? Stop and remove the mysql container, your system is now clean and can run anything else. Or run your containers alongside of your MySQL instance if you want to, without worrying about any other process conflicting with others."* - https://myopsblog.wordpress.com/2017/02/06/why-databases-is-not-for-containers/

212 https://goto.docker.com/rs/929-FJL-178/images/Docker-for-Virtualization-Admin-eBook.pdf

Containers can be managed by Kubernetes. Kubernetes is an open source orchestration project begun by Google for managing containers.[213]

The Kubernetes Engine is a primary service offered in Google Cloud (as well as AWS, called EC2 Container Service. Kubernetes has been a primary factor in Google Cloud's growth.[214]

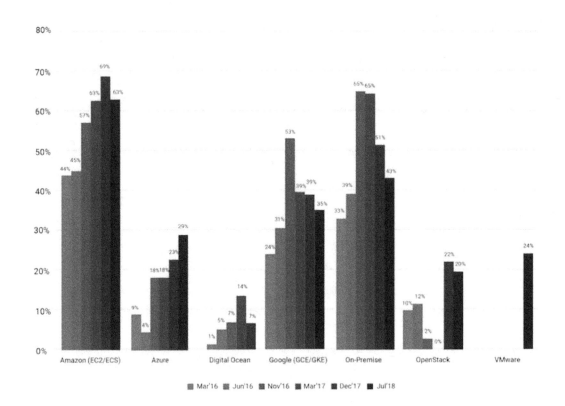

Your company/organization deploys containers to which of the following environments?

---

213 https://resources.codeship.com/hubfs/Codeship_Continuous_Deployment_for_Docker_Apps_to_Kubernetes.pdf

214 *"Well, here we are. Kubernetes turns four years old this month—technically, on June 7, 2018—the very same platform that brings users and data center administrators scalable container technologies. Its popularity has skyrocketed since its initial introduction by Google. Celebrating the project's birthday is not the only thing making the headlines today. Amazon recently announced the general availability of its Elastic Container Services for Kubernetes (EKS), accessible via Amazon Web Services (AWS)."* - https://www.linuxjournal.com/content/kubernetes-four-years-later-and-amazon-redefining-container-orchestration

This graphic is from the Cloud Native Computing Foundation. Even though Google Cloud is substantially smaller than AWS, notice how prevalent the use of containers is on Google Cloud. In total the usage of containers on Google Cloud is close to that of on-premises, the second most common place containers are implemented.[215] [216]

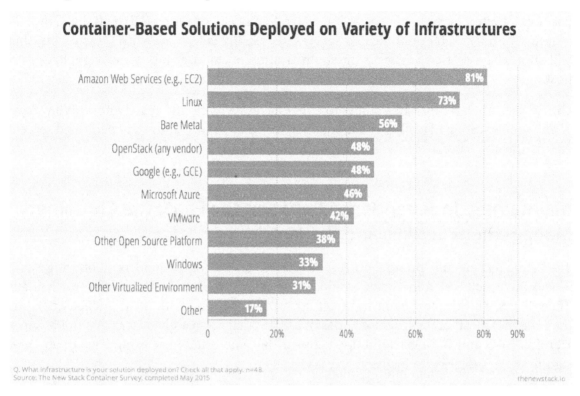

This graphic shows the frequency with which containers are run on various infrastructures.[217]

Another way of improving the management of microservices is through the use of a PaaS. This is covered in the following quotation from the PaaS provider Heroku.

> *"That said, microservices are not a free lunch. Each service has its own overhead, and though that cost is reduced by an order of magnitude by running in a PaaS environment, you still need to configure monitoring and alerting and similar*

215 https://www.cncf.io/blog/2018/08/29/cncf-survey-use-of-cloud-native-technologies-in-production-has-grown-over-200-percent/

216 *"I would hazard a guess that GCP was never that high on people's list for a cloud provider until Google released Kubernetes. It's reasonable that the best-managed option would originate from the company behind the birth of the project."* - https://resources.codeship.com/hubfs/Codeship_A-Roundup-of-Managed-Kubernetes-Platforms.pdf

217 Survey: How the IT Landscape Will Shift to Accommodate Containers, The New Stack Book, Lawrence Hecht

services for each microservice. Microservices also make testing and releases easier for individual components, but incur a cost at the system integration level. Plan for how will your system behave if one of the services goes offline."[218]

AWS and Google Cloud are offering this not as virtualization have been attempted in the past on a limited number of servers but against an ocean of servers. Essentially, Oracle is arguing for bare metal or dedicated servers (as usually is the case with Oracle), but this will always have a price, and lacks the sophistication of cloud, as it puts one right back into hosting.

Oracle does not have the same ability to either have AWS's cloud capacity nor do they have AWS's sophistication in containerization. Therefore they have to argue that dedicated servers are the way to go because this is what Oracle has to offer.

Maintaining Independence Between the PaaS, the Container Management Service and the IaaS

The IT media generally presents SAP, Oracle, AWS and Google Cloud as all offering PaaS. This is incorrect. SAP and Oracle would like to offer PaaS, but don't yet offer much at all. Their "PaaS" allows a few items to be set up (very slowly and with great inefficiency), but they lack nearly all of the functionalities of a PaaS, that are readily observable in PaaS like Heroku. AWS and Google Cloud don't appear that interested in offering PaaS of any real significance, preferring to focus on just IaaS.

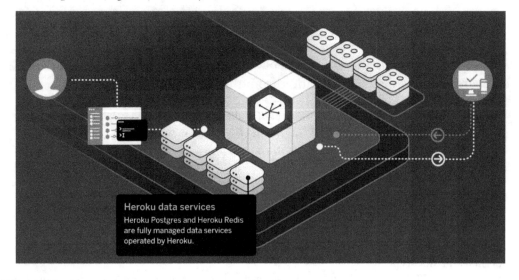

Heroku data services
Heroku Postgres and Heroku Redis are fully managed data services operated by Heroku.

---

218 https://blog.heroku.com/why_microservices_matter

Heroku is a pure PaaS. It configures the IaaS, but offers far less choice than the IaaS. This is a great video on Heroku.[219]

Developers give Heroku high marks for keeping the things they don't want to worry about such as scaling, version and release management, DNS and SLL, and managing development boxes in the background and allowing them to focus on the code.[220] Furthermore, the collaboration aspects are a strong motivator to use Heroku.

This is expressed in the following quotation from Heroku.

> *"The Heroku Platform is designed so you can focus on what matters the most: the app. Getting apps out in the wild, in front of real users, and then iterating fast, is what can make or break companies. Heroku lets companies of all sizes embrace the value of apps, not the hassle of hardware, nor the distraction of servers — virtual or otherwise. The Heroku Platform is great for the early part of the app lifecycle, but it really shines when you go into production. Heroku seamlessly supports every step of the app lifecycle — build, run, manage and scale. Heroku Postgres provides trusted database options at terabyte scale. Dyno choices to suit your needs, including performance dynos for your highest traffic apps — all scalable in an instant. Heroku keeps the kernel up-to-date with the latest security patches. All backed by the trust and reliability of Salesforce."[221]*

We developed our application, Brightwork Explorer without Heroku, but the more we looked into it, the more we wished we have leveraged Heroku. PaaS solutions like Heroku allow companies to scale their development far more efficiently, as is covered in the following quotation.

> *"Fundamentally, a PaaS provides you with a container, an abstraction in which you house your software. All of the supporting technologies discussed above, from load balancing to independent scaling and process monitoring, are provided by the platform, outside of your container. Without such providers, deploying even a single monolithic app can take whole teams of IT operations specialists. However, with a PaaS, the range of people qualified to deploy applications grows to include generalists like application developers or even project managers, reducing deployment effort to near-zero. For instance some of our customers have no one devoted full-time to IT operations, and can deploy to countries all over the*

---

219 Heroku is a pure PaaS. It configures the IaaS, but offers far less choice than the IaaS. This is a great video on Heroku at the Heroku website. https://www.heroku.com/

220 DNS is controls how the traffic is sent to the appropriate server.

221 https://www.heroku.com/platform

world made by any developer on the team. With the advent of PaaS, microservice deployment has become a reasonable endeavor."[222]

The overall PaaS market is a confusing mixture of development environments which includes Heroku, Outsystems, Apprenda, and Engine Yard, with each having various pros and cons. The use of the right PaaS requires a deep understanding of the development requirements and one of the issues with selecting a PaaS is that they usually have specific advantages for some programming languages versus others. For instance, Heroku started as a project for the Ruby language, but then added other languages later. In 2012 Gartner predicted that the PaaS market would become 2% of the overall revenues for the cloud market. The PaaS market seems quite "siloed," and while IaaS has grown enormously and grabbed the headlines, the PaaS market appears to have stagnated.

Our interpretation is that AWS would rather farm that work out to partners as they grow Lambda. AWS sees the platform market as overhyped with low long-term value add. Eventually, everything will be a service invoked on one of the Function as a Service (FaaS) frameworks. Moreover, There are now Azure Functions and Google Functions, and others, but practically speaking Lambda dominates this space. Google Cloud appears similarly unfocused about the PaaS market. The closest thing Google Cloud offers to a PaaS is their App Engine. However, this is also like Elastic Beanstalk more of deployment tool than a PaaS. That is one interpretation, another is that IaaS providers are not particularly adept at creating PaaS environments.

If we looked at an outsiders view of the PaaS offering it might look something like the following table.

---

222 https://blog.heroku.com/why_microservices_matter

PaaS	Container Service	VM Service	IaaS
Google App Engine	Google Kubernetes Engine	Google Compute Engine	Google Cloud
Amazon Elastic Beanstock	Amazon EC2 Container Service	Amazon (Elastic Computer Cloud) EC2	AWS
Heroku	Dynos Manager	Google Compute Engine	Google Cloud
Heroku	Docker	Amazon (Elastic Computer Cloud) EC2	AWS
Heroku	Docker	Google Compute Engine	Google Cloud
Heroku	Dynos Manager	Amazon (Elastic Computer Cloud) EC2	AWS
SAP Cloud	Kubernetes	SAP Cloud Platform VM	SAP, AWS, Google Cloud, Azure
Application Container Cloud	Container	Compute	Oracle Cloud

With cloud componentry, the devil is really in the details. The first problem with this table is that of the services offered by SAP, Oracle, AWS or Google Cloud, only Google Cloud's App Engine and Elastic Beanstalk can be considered to be a PaaS. Also, even there we are shrinking the scope of PaaS from what we think is ideal or what we would recommend. Realistically, while it makes sense to use App Engine, it makes the most sense to use it more to simply setup components to be addressed by an outside PaaS than as a PaaS itself. Alternatively, to run functions against "serverless" services. The App Engine restricts the development in multiple ways to the Google Cloud.[223]

Nevertheless they are all commonly placed with the classification of PaaS providers.

---

223 *"In fact easy, no-frills sandboxing is a major App Engine's forte, together with the ability to quickly and easily scale horizontally for load-balancing. Still, many have complained that App Engine's proprietary, read-only nature results in tedious and unnecessary code refactoring; apps have to be written specifically with App Engine in mind, API's have to be written specifically for App Engine, even standard Java code has to be extensively altered to fit into the App Engine environment. Another sore point is that Google insists on App Engine customers only using its Big Table non-relational database, although they have also recently added some support for Cloud SQL."* - https://www.upguard.com/articles/heroku-appengine

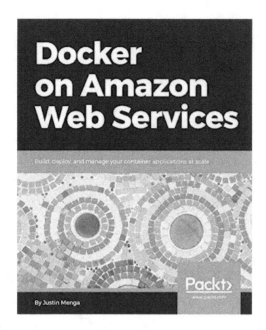

There are plenty of books that explain how these different components can be used in conjunction with one another. Again, because of the ability to test, items can be selected to use based upon using them to try to get work done. Docker is quite popular, but there are other container management services as well such as Cloud Foundry. Cloud Foundry also works well with either Docker or AWS EC2 Container Service or Google Cloud Kubernetes. Cloud Foundry emphasizes the exact issue of independence in the following quote.

> *"Cloud Foundry removes the complexities of developing applications by decoupling the application from its infrastructure, so that organizations can make a business decision on where to host workloads – on premise, in public clouds, or in managed infrastructures."[224]*

A second important feature illustrated by this table is that is shows if one selects a true PaaS like Heroku allows IaaS independence. If one chooses to use AWS Elastic Beanstalk or Google Cloud App Engine, one not only loses out on PaaS functionality, but independence is also lost.

---

224 https://www.cloudfoundry.org/multi-cloud/

Connecting Independent Cloud Components

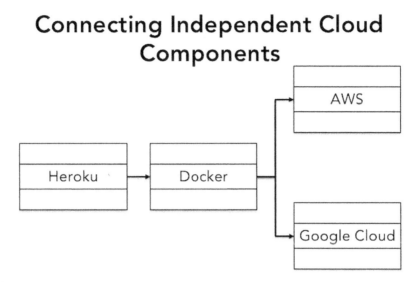

Using both an independent PaaS and container management system is an excellent way to maintain IaaS independence. As the costs of AWS and Google Cloud are incurred by usage, it is not a scenario where one must choose to use only one or the other. Doing so reduces the flexibility and will potentially increase the costs of the overall solution. Furthermore, we only cover AWS and Google Cloud in this book, but there also may be other IaaS providers that have a beneficial service that is desirable to access, if only in a limited way. Docker has an enormous amount of support in the IaaS providers. This is generally referred to as the multicloud approach. This means not only running on multiple IaaSs but also on private, public, hybrid environment. Cloud Foundry proposes it can allow companies to move applications between environments in "90 seconds."[225]

Multicloud is the most common approach to using cloud services, as is covered in the following quotation from the Rightscale 2017 State of the Cloud Report.

> *"Companies that use public cloud are already running applications in an average of 1.8 public clouds and experimenting with another 1.8 public clouds. While fewer companies are using private clouds, those that do use more, running applications in an average of 2.3 private clouds and experimenting with an additional 2.1 private clouds."[226]*

---

225 https://www.cloudfoundry.org/multi-cloud/

226 https://www.rightscale.com/blog/cloud-industry-insights/cloud-computing-trends-2017-state-cloud-survey

What is interesting is how much this increased in the same study the following year.

> *"Respondents are already running applications in 3.1 clouds and experimenting with 1.7 more for a total of 4.8 clouds."*[227]

However, maintaining PaaS and IaaS independence does have a downside. That downside is that any technical issues between the PaaS and the IaaS can often leave the customer in a no man's land, where neither the PaaS provider nor the IaaS provider will take the support ticket.

Furthermore, using Docker combined with Heroku (or other independent PaaS) allows for both the PaaS and the container service to be independent of the IaaS. Moreover, for the advantages of Heroku versus Google Cloud App Engine is highlighted in the following quote.

> *"In terms of databases, you have both relational and non-relational choices in PostgreSQL, MongoDB, Cloudant, and Redis. This highlights Heroku's massive advantage over AppEngine – Heroku's database-platform choices reflect a collection that is in widespread use already in the wider world. It's relatively easy to port your DB from Oracle to PostgreSQL because they are both relational, for example, but good luck trying to move your relational DB to the non-relational BigTable. It can be done, but it's an expensive (in terms of time) and painful exercise. Heroku's infrastructure is hosted on Amazon's EC2 could servers.*
>
> *Overall though, the sentiment in the developer community (that's the crowd that mainly uses PaaS's) is that AppEngine is a missed opportunity by Google because of its closed-in, proprietary nature and lack of platform choices. Heroku offers few restrictions on what can and can't be done in your hosted app, and you also have powerful access to the user space your application runs in."*[228]

Now Heroku offers a proprietary container management solution called Dynos Manager, but for us it makes more sense to use Docker, again keeping the PaaS and the container management solution independent.

This is key, because when a new development is begun, it may not be immediately apparent which IaaS it should access. With PaaS/Container Management System/IaaS independence

---

227 https://www.rightscale.com/blog/cloud-industry-insights/cloud-computing-trends-2018-state-cloud-survey

228 https://www.upguard.com/articles/heroku-appengine

one can switch between IaaS providers when the opportunity presents itself.[229] [230] Secondly, a deep functionality PaaS like Heroku provides enormous collaborative development benefits.

This is a good time to point out that the term PaaS means different things to different people. This elasticity in the term only serves to increase the confusion around PaaS. We are using the term in its broader sense to describe solutions that we considered to support development fully. When others write on the subject of PaaS, they often include offerings that we would find too bare bones.

It should also be considered that using independent components in this way will typically reduce the direct costs paid for the various components (Heroku is a premium priced component for instance), but may reduce the overall costs or the total costs. The total costs include the efficiency of developers and others involved in the process.

FIGURE 1. **Google Cloud Platform Pricing Advantage vs. Amazon Web Services**

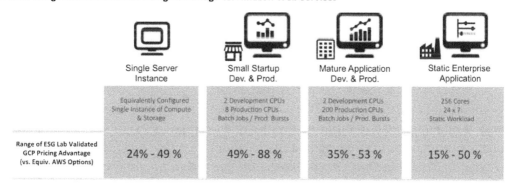

Source: Enterprise Strategy Group, 2015.

Even AWS, when compared to Google Cloud, does not have the same costs, with AWS being higher, but compensating with a broader offering. Of course, that by no means ends the discussion, as there all manner of other implication to using AWS versus Google Cloud – and one may want to use some AWS services with Google Cloud services. We, of course, have

---

229 This table shows the normal combination of cloud components. However in the cloud things change rapidly. AWS has a service called Fargate, which allows customers to run containers without any server or virtual machine. The logic presented by some is that virtual machines are increasingly adding costs without a corresponding value. This argument is made in the following article. - https://thenewstack.io/aws-fargate-the-beginning-of-the-end-for-infrastructure-management/

230 Fargate is a variation on Lambda in that the container can be run with what amounts to a self-configured AWS server. If Fargate were to be utilized, it means that Heroku could be connected to Docker and then directly to Fargate. - https://aws.amazon.com/fargate/

accounts with both. Moreover, an independent PaaS and container management systems allow you to connect to both.[231]

We, of course, can't produce a cost breakdown in this book of all the components used together under every possible use case. We merely acknowledge that these decisions to impact both the immediate costs and the total costs.

If we think of SAP and Oracle, their entire orientation is to lock in customers to their "full cloud stack" even though SAP and Oracle lack a true cloud stack. Moreover, when, for instance, SAP connects to an IaaS, (as we illustrated earlier in the book) their pricing vis-à-vis AWS shows that they markup the IaaS cost enormously, essentially taxing customers at the highest possible margins to access a service that anyone can access from AWS (or Google Cloud or Azure) for one-tenth of the prices. These specifics should make it apparent why it is difficult to take anything that SAP or Oracle say about the cloud seriously.

The Future is PaaS, or Wait Maybe FaaS?

AWS describes Lambda, their "serverless" compute service as follows:

> *"Lambda can be described as a type of serverless Function-as-a-Service (FaaS). FaaS is one approach to building event-driven computing systems. It relies on functions as the unit of deployment and execution. Serverless FaaS is a type of FaaS where no virtual machines or containers are present in the programming model and where the vendor provides provision-free scalability and built-in reliability."*[232]

"Serverless" allows effortless scaling. This is possible because AWS and Google Cloud have in effect no capacity limitation and they have developed the capabilities to adjust resource consumption based upon the load. "Serverless" is having the impact of taking over some of the services selection from the developer. When a non-"serverless" services is used the customer can set autoscaling and selects sees the supporting items (which database, which memory, etc). However, with "serverless," the customer leaves that to AWS or Google Cloud.

"Serverless" can also be thought of as the following:

> *"Cloud computing, which started with Infrastructure-as-a-Service (IaaS), Platform-as-a-Service (PaaS), and Software-as-a-Service (SaaS), is fast moving into a Function-as-a-Service (FaaS) model where users don't have to think about servers. Serverless applications don't require the provisioning, scaling, or*

---

231 https://cloud.google.com/files/esg-whitepaper.pdf
232 https://d1.awsstatic.com/whitepapers/serverless-architectures-with-aws-lambda.pdf

management of servers, as everything required to run and scale the applications with high availability is provided by the platform itself. This allows users to focus on building their core products, instead of worrying about the runtime infrastructure demands; and to pay only for the actual compute time and resources consumed, instead of the total uptime

Another remarkable feature of serverless functions is their near-infinite scalability — the ability to scale from virtually nothing to literally tens of thousands of concurrent instances — which makes them perfect candidates for handling highly variant and highly unpredictable loads, such as traffic for a real-time sports score app.."[233]

All non-"serverless" services is sometimes referred to as "serverfull."

According to AWS in order for a service to qualify as "serverless" is must offer the following capabilities:

1. No Server Management

2. Flexible Scaling

3. High Availability by Default

4. No Idle Capacity[234]

AWS states that the following services can support "serverless."

- AWS Lambda

- Amazon Athena

- Amazon API Gateway

- Amazon Simple Storage Service

- Amazon DynamoDB

- Amazon Simple Notification Service

- Amazon Simple Queue Service

- AWS Step Functions

- Amazon CloudWatch Event[235]

---

233 https://dzone.com/articles/introduction-to-serverless
234 https://d1.awsstatic.com/whitepapers/serverless-architectures-with-aws-lambda.pdf
235 https://d1.awsstatic.com/whitepapers/serverless-architectures-with-aws-lambda.pdf

Daniel Stori {turnoff.us}

Some people think that "serverless" creates mass unemployment among servers. But it's not true! There is still plenty of work available for servers.[236]

Function as a service is part of "serverless" computing essentially skips over containers and functions against a "serverless" service or a self-configured services like AWS Lambda (the "serverless" function is called a "lambda").[237] [238] Lynn Langit, describes serverless as the following:

> *"A service that abstracts away the management of containers."*[239]

---

236 http://turnoff.us/geek/serverless-economic-impact/

237 This quote does a nice job of explaining some of the tradeoffs with Lambda. *"Overall, running a serverless function on Lambda costs a lot more than setting up an EC2 instance that is tailored to your application and running your application there. But what Lambda offers that EC2 on its own does not is the ability to execute an application (or part of an application) very quickly, and to run it only for a limited amount of time. For certain types of workloads, these Lambda benefits are well worth the price."* - https://containerjournal.com/2018/05/23/aws-fargate-what-it-is-and-why-it-matters/

238 *"Lambda is a stateless computer service, meaning it works on the data and delivers the output to another service"* - The Continuum: From Containers to Serverless Architecture and Unikernels, The New Stack Book, Alex Williams

239 https://read.acloud.guru/serverless-superheroes-lynn-langit-on-big-data-nosql-and-google-versus-aws-f4427dc8679c

Google Cloud's "serverless" service is called Google Functions. Google Cloud calls Google Functions as the "simplest way to run code in the cloud." Moreover, while the effort involved in configuring servers comes way down, so does the amount of code written, which is normally considered a small fraction of the amount of code required for the traditional approach. Therefore, while the category focuses on the configuration reduction as the named benefits, that is only a part of the benefits offered by "serverless."

Once setup, functions can be easily copied.

AWS Fargate

A second "serverless" variation on the EC2 service is AWS Fargate. Fargate is used for longer run processes that you don't intend to be running permanently (so test environments) as opposed to which Lambda tends to work better for shorter-term processes.[240] Obviously, legacy or monolithic applications are more difficult to migrate to "serverless"/auto configured server services.[241] Fargate does not isolate functions while Lambda does. This makes Lambda scale better.

Fargate is less known that we think it should be for a few reasons, but one being that it is not its own service, but a modality or a configuration of the EC2 service. So it requires an EC2 instance to use, but it takes care of all the EC2 setup automatically.

Called "containers on demand" by AWS, also known as "Lambda, but for your containers," Fargate interacts with containers, and at Mark Dalton's AutoDeploy they ported all of their JDE migration product to it. AutoDeploy finds auto-scaling to provide amazingly impressive results. The overall service is a high-end value add.

How Fargate is brought up is explained in the following quotation.

> "AWS ECS supports two launch types, EC2 and Fargate. With the EC2 launch type, EC2 instances are started to run Docker containers. The Fargate launch type, which was introduced recently (November 2017), hosts tasks that encapsulate Docker containers. The tasks are directly made accessible to the user via an Elastic Network Interface. The EC2 instance on which Fargate is provisioned are not accessible to the user and are not directly accessible."[242]

Therefore with the Fargate launch type the infrastructure is entirely managed by Fargate. The ideal is to get to only the functional unit of code. The intent is to get as much as possible into a container.

---

240 The uses of Fargate are explained in more detail in this quotation. *"So, if you have a containerized application that you want to spin up quickly, Fargate may be a good solution. This is especially true if you don't expect to be running the application permanently. Otherwise, ECS or EC2 are probably better solutions for your container-deployment needs."* - https://containerjournal.com/2018/05/23/aws-fargate-what-it-is-and-why-it-matters/

241 *"There are many cases where AWS Lambda just is not an option: legacy application migration, unsupported languages, long-running-processes. In these situations Docker is the best path to immutable and fully automated infrastructure. Historically, however, the added complexity of Docker host and cluster management had been a huge downside."* - https://www.trek10.com/blog/is-fargate-serverless/

242 https://www.amazon.com/Amazon-Fargate-Quick-Start-Guide-ebook/dp/B07FY8VFGL/

Is FaaS Really Much Different Than PaaS?

What will most likely happen with "serverless" or self-configured servers is that current PaaS providers like Heroku and Cloud Foundry simply become the tool for "serverless" and therefore address functions (through Google Functions, AWS Lambda).

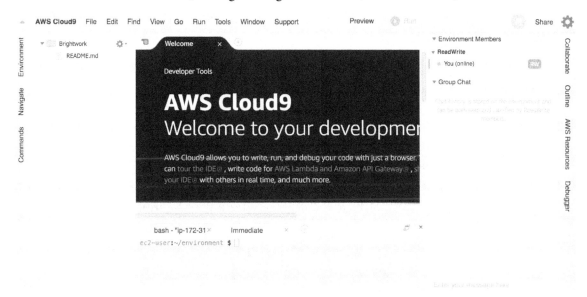

If we look at Cloud 9, which was an IDE acquired by AWS, it is now promoted as a "serverless" or function framework. Cloud 9 has some collaborative features, but it appears to be more of an online IDE than a PaaS.

Options Galore with AWS and Google Cloud

AWS does offer some internally developed products (the Aurora database being one), and Google Cloud offers both the Spanner database and the Go coding language, but the vast majority of AWS's and Google Cloud's revenue comes from providing services for items they did not have a hand in developing. Kubernetes is an open source project initiated by Google, which has helped increase the popularity of Google Cloud; however Kubernetes is not controlled by Google.

Some of these items that AWS and Google Cloud offer services for are open source and some are commercial license products. This "universal" revenue stream places AWS and Google Cloud in a far less biased position than a software vendor that is trying to sell its licenses first (which leads directly to the most profitable thing SAP and Oracle sells which is support), and it is the cloud as a distant second. Both Oracle and SAP have very small cloud businesses compared to AWS or Google Cloud.

This choice was explained by AWS in the following quotation.

> *"The days of the one-size-fits-all monolithic database are behind us," he said. "Our customers are changing how they develop applications and they need particular databases to do that."*

This is particularly prevalent in the space for databases that are analytical in nature rather than designed to support an application (because of the lower degree of lock-in due to application certification). Moreover, what have we observed in this market? Increasingly, the data from applications is being moved into data lakes or data staging areas at a lower degree of normalization (increasing the size of the data, but reducing its maintenance) and being pushed out of more structured higher maintenance databases like Oracle (version 18 presently) and into databases like Hadoop or MongoDB. However, SAP and Oracle are trying to "get into" this open source environment by declaring that their commercial software is necessary. Let us review a graphic in this area.

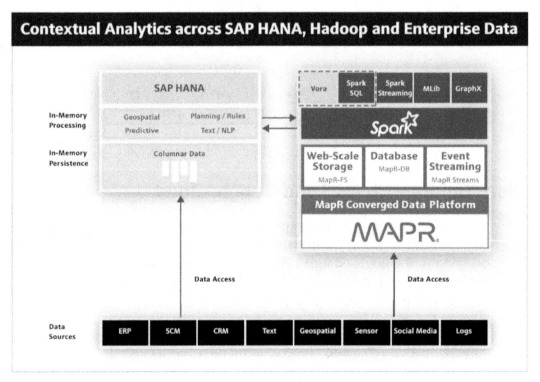

Notice the data coming from SCM (SAP) goes to HANA, then to MAPR. However, the sensor and social media data (which is not from SAP, goes directly to MAPR). What is the benefit of

HANA in this design? SAP makes several proposals, but non-SAP projects are pleased with 100% open source Hadoop. If the ERP, ECM, CRM (SAP) data is in Oracle, it can go directly to MAPR. However, if any application sits on HANA, it must then go through a second HANA database due to indirect access rules enforced by SAP. There is no reason for SAP to have HANA in this design, except to infiltrate the open source MAPR solution.

Oracle offers a variety of database types, but its primary strength is in the structured (highly normalized) relational database design. However, growth in the database market is more in the unstructured database design (which in practice often means its holds less normalized data than a database that supports an application that requires highly normalized data). There are many people with excellent database knowledge like Werner Vogels that propose the highly normalized relational database design has been over applied. Less normalized databases are dominated by open source offerings rather than commercial offerings. Moreover, of course, Oracle has no interest in using its Oracle Cloud to allow companies to host non-Oracle databases or applications. Secondly, the Oracle Cloud is such an uncompetitive offering to AWS or Google's Cloud Services **that it would make little sense to use Oracle Cloud even if Oracle were interested in opening up to other vendors and to open source**. The Oracle Cloud, much like the SAP Cloud is for hosting Oracle databases and applications. That is the extent of Oracle's vision for the Oracle Cloud. AWS, by contrast, offers the ability to test all of the different databases (including SAP and Oracle databases), and this dramatically increases the ability of a company to test different databases and to compare and contrast the offerings.

One such area to test is covered in the following quotation.

> *"And, if you've mixed online transaction processing (OLTP) and analytics-style data access, moving from a one-tool-for-everything Oracle setup to using a separate warehouse for reporting and analytics can improve both your application responsiveness and your analytics capabilities. There are options to create a dedicated Postgres-XL–based warehouse or use Amazon Redshift as a powerful managed warehouse."[243] - **David Rader***

Increasing the Type of Databases Put Into Use

This increase in the types of databases put into use. For years SAP and Oracle and even IBM have been telling customers they offer the database processing types that they needed and that various processing types could be met their RDBMS databases. When SAP promoted

---

243 https://aws.amazon.com/blogs/database/challenges-when-migrating-from-oracle-to-postgresql-and-how-to-overcome-them/

their HANA in-memory RDBMS database as superior to all other databases, Oracle and IBM copied SAP by adding column-oriented "in memory" capabilities to the Oracle and IBM RDBMS database.[244] Bloor Research questioned whether this was really worth the extra overhead as we covered in the article How Accurate Was Bloor on Oracle In-Memory?[245] The sizing each of their databases is by itself a lengthy process, and the commitments for specific hardware have greatly restricted testing the proposals by SAP and Oracle. When the performance does not match what SAP or Oracle say, some excuse is often given. After the customer has purchased the software and the hardware and paid for the implementation, the vendor has the power in the relationship.

In terms of options, AWS offers EC2, which is a AWS's computer cloud. With EC2, AWS offers over 60 different instance types that are categorized by the following types.

1. General Purpose

2. Computer Optimized

3. Memory Optimized

4. Accelerated Computing

5. Storage Optimized

AWS's RDS has 35 different instance types, these change depending upon the number of CPUs, the amount of memory, whether the instance is EBS optimized and the speed of the network.

AWS S3, which is a storage offering has four different storage classes (Standard, Standard-IA, One Zone-IA, and Glacier). It also has options concerning access control. In each AWS offering, SAP and Oracle customers will observe options that they are not accustomed to in SAP or Oracle. Also, all of these options are public; they do not need to be communicated through an account rep.

All of this allows AWS to support new approaches to data management, as is covered in the following quotation by Werner Vogels, the AWS CTO.

> "If there's a unifying theme to AWS's disparate set of databases, he said, it's that they're all aimed at supporting cloud-native methods of creating applications that

---

244 The story is a more involved than this, as IBM had in memory capability combined with DB2 before SAP created HANA, but they had not emphasized its development until in their database until pressure from the market (created by SAP's claims around HANA) promoted IBM to emphasize in-memory in DB2.

245 http://www.brightworkr.com/saphana/2017/08/01/accurate-bloor-research-oracle-memory/

aren't driven by the way the data needs to be stored in a single kind of database. Instead, the cloud application, often composed of smaller bits of code widely distributed in multiple data centers and the cloud, drives the way the data needs to be accessed and used. That, Vogels contends, requires different kinds of databases for different kinds of applications."[246]

Also, there is just no way for SAP or Oracle to provide such a variety of databases on their cloud offerings. One reason is both SAP and Oracle are very opposed to open source options. SAP is an expert at taking open source offerings and then making them closed source. SAP has a product that is a copy of the open source Spark component, called Vora, that connects HANA to Hadoop (as we covered in the article How Accurate is SAP on Vora?[247]). Also almost no one uses it. Nor should anyone. Hadoop does not need HANA, and a company that is intelligent enough to figure out Hadoop will also figure out that there are far better column oriented in-memory databases to connect to Hadoop rather than HANA. SAP is always coming up with some intrusion into open source with a commercialized offering. Oracle's history with open sources has been one of hostility and neglect. Several very prominent examples include the following:

- Oracle purchased Java, OpenSolaris, OpenOffice.org and MySQL and others, and is widely considered to have worsened each of these open source offerings.

- Oracle's acquisition of MySQL is a significant factor which drove the growth of other open source database projects like MariaDB and PostgreSQL.

AWS is opening up the horizons of their customers in a way the customers have not had in the past as explained by Werner Vogels.

"More generally, Vogels contended, AWS' own enterprise customers were looking for alternatives. "With many of our enterprise customers migrating from on-premises into the cloud, there's a desire to move away from commercial databases, mostly because of the licensing restrictions and the lack of control over the cost."[248]

And AWS is the best in the market at offering these options.

"Now, he noted, a lot of companies are using multiple Amazon databases for various parts of their business. "What we're seeing in AWS customers is they're using a multiplicity of databases," he said. "They're looking for the best tool for each application, or maybe multiple tools."

---

246 https://siliconangle.com/2018/06/21/amazon-cto-cloud-offers-database-need/

247 http://www.brightworkr.com/saphana/2017/07/12/accurate-sap-vora/

248 https://siliconangle.com/2018/06/21/amazon-cto-cloud-offers-database-need/

> *"For instance, Airbnb Inc. uses DynamoDB for storing users' search history, ElastiCache for storing site sessions for faster site rendering, and MySQL on another AWS relational database, RDS, as its main transactional database. Besides Elasticsearch, Expedia also uses Aurora, ElastiCache and Amazon's Redshift data warehouse."*

This is a fundamental change in how databases are evaluated and then used. This means that the structure and row-oriented database that was overapplied is giving way to a multitude of specialized database types. AWS emphasizes the educational challenge in leveraging these different database types in the following quotation.

> *"The biggest challenge is education; there is another way, but it means learning something new," Jim Webber, chief scientist at the graph database maker Neo4j Inc., also told SiliconANGLE. "If all I've got is a hammer, then every problem is a nail. Relational is a beautiful hammer."*

Conclusion

Changes are afoot in software development that are intertwined with the cloud. The cloud is reinforcing these changes. This is because the cloud is making so many options available to developers. These changes are reinforced by specific cloud providers, not all of them. SAP Cloud and Oracle Cloud make it very difficult to bring up services and have all manner of quality problems. SAP and Oracle are overpromising in the cloud to the degree that it is difficult to believe what they say about their cloud offerings. AWS and Google Cloud offer so many services that SAP Cloud and Oracle Cloud that there is no way to draw a comparison between these two sets of the cloud. Two clouds have more significant numbers of users logging in and trying new things, and using their clouds in production, and two other clouds are more brochureware designed to help those companies that are opposed to the cloud and opposed to open source projects cloudwash for Wall Street. One of the authors of the book, Ahmed Azmi recently tested SAP Cloud for a prospect, and it was a resounding "pass." In AWS, Azure, and GCP we can spin up/dispose of a container within a few seconds. On SAP Cloud, containers take as long as 8 minutes to start. That's not an ideal environment for building lightweight microservices.

These changes are allowing a movement from monolithic designs with little choice, to containers where the number of choices seems endless, and where much more time must be spent in evaluating individual components rather than simplistically choosing to use the Oracle database because one is an Oracle shop, or to use ABAP because SAP says that it is "standard SAP." This means multiple programming languages being used, and multiple databases being used to develop applications that are "composites" of multi-container applications. It also means being able to leverage custom and in many cases self-configured hardware in a way that was not possible before and that removes the necessity to perform sizing.

Never before in IT has there been such a necessity to perform testing, or such a fast and straightforward way to perform that testing. The previous on-premises approach where vendor sales reps were able to make assertions that could not be first be tested before purchase is diminishing. These are all positive developments, but they mean a new day for IT departments, and that the structure of previous IT departments is not the appropriate structure required to leverage the new cloud lead alternatives.

Now that we have covered how the four different clouds compare, let jump into what the cloud means for the data warehouse and data lake.

Chapter 8: Sliming and Re-platforming the Data Warehouse into the Data Lake with Cloud Services

Cloud is causing major changes in the data warehouse, and data lake spaces. Cloud is going to result in a significant reconfiguration of the data warehouse market and is already leading to increases in choice and a move away from monolithic data warehouses. And on AWS one of the components that supports this change is Amazon Athena and Amazon Glue.

Amazon Athena and Glue

Amazon Athena is one of the most quizzical or unexpected serverless services. Athena works on files to be uploaded to an S3 bucket. The load is supported by AWS Glue, which is an ETL service which simplifies preparing and uploading data. Glue discovers data and the associated metadata, and once cataloged, the data is "immediately searchable, query-able and available for ETL."[249] We will discuss Glue in relation to Athena, but it also works with RDS, DynamoDB, Redshift, as well as S3 (which is how it integrates with Athena).

AWS describes glue as follows:

> *"AWS Glue is a fully managed ETL (extract, transform, and load) service that can categorize your data, clean it, enrich it, and move it reliably between various data stores. AWS Glue crawlers automatically infer database and table schema from your source data, storing the associated metadata in the AWS Glue Data Catalog. When you create a table in Athena, you can choose to create it using an AWS Glue crawler."[250]*

---

249 https://aws.amazon.com/glue/
250 https://docs.aws.amazon.com/athena/latest/ug/what-is.html

The ability of AWS Glue to do this means it creates an AWS Glue "data catalog." This reduces the time between data ingestion and use because AWS Glue can begin working with the new data with little processing, as we will illustrate with Athena.

Amazingly, Glue is not only compatible with multiple data sources, but it also works across different data sources.

The AWS Glue Crawler will create a metadata repository called the AWS Glue Data Catalog that allows a virtual database to be created.[251]

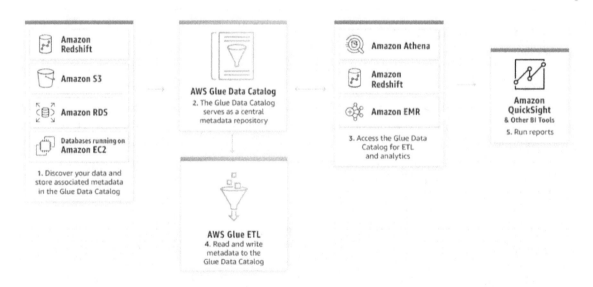

Notice the relationship between the AWS Glue Data Catalog and other components.[252]

This topic is explained in the following quotation.

---

251 https://aws.amazon.com/glue/
252 https://aws.amazon.com/glue/

"The AWS Glue Data Catalog provides a unified metadata repository across a variety of data sources and data formats, integrating not only with Athena, but with Amazon S3, Amazon RDS, Amazon Redshift, Amazon Redshift Spectrum, Amazon EMR, and any application compatible with the Apache Hive metastore."[253]

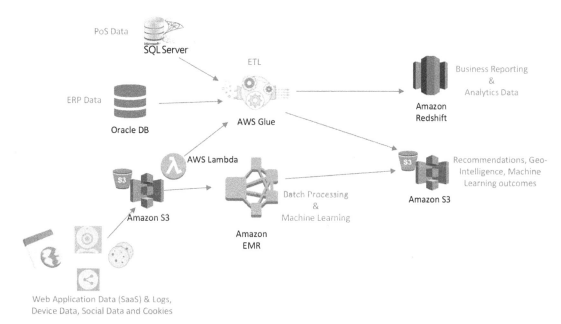

Observe how AWS Glue can tie together many different data sources. But note also that AWS Glue can also interact with Lambda.

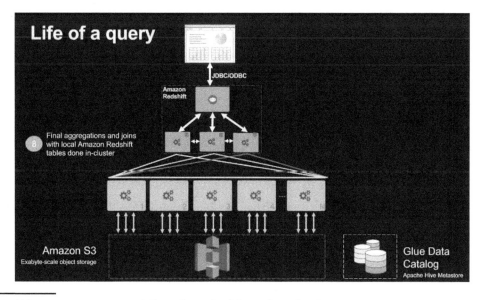

---

253 https://docs.aws.amazon.com/athena/latest/ug/glue-athena.html

Notice the AWS Glue Data Catalog. It connects the various data sources through discovery. In this case the queries are being run from Amazon Redshift, AWS's data warehousing solution to S3 to data outside of Redshift.[254]

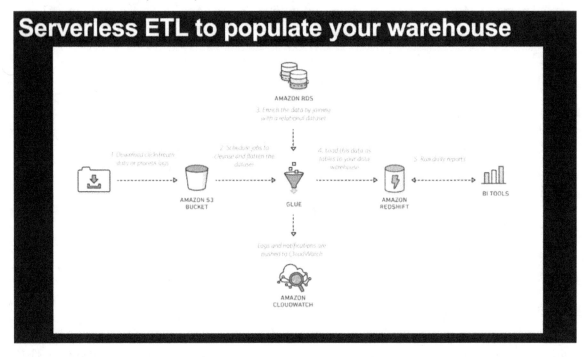

This is another view of how Glue fits into the data warehouse design.[255]

AWS Glue also allows data to be moved between data stores.[256] However, there is something quite appealing about when Athena is used with only S3, which is that it means one does not need to spend time structuring and organizing data before performing queries on data. Athena is a service that allows SQL queries, and normally ad-hock or in-frequent queries to be run against a logical schema is flexibility and quickly applied to a text file or text files. The logical schema is superimposed on the files loaded into S3. AWS describes Athena this way.

> *"In Athena, tables and databases are containers for the metadata definitions that define a schema for underlying source data. For each dataset, a table needs to exist in Athena. The metadata in the table tells Athena where the data is located in Amazon S3, and specifies the structure of the data, for example, column names,*

254 https://www.youtube.com/watch?v=fORJ6y572gs
255 https://www.youtube.com/watch?v=fORJ6y572gs
256 https://docs.aws.amazon.com/glue/latest/dg/what-is-glue.html

data types, and the name of the table. Databases are a logical grouping of tables, and also hold only metadata and schema information for a dataset"[257]

AWS Glue, Athena and S3 begin to call into question the different distinctions or dividing lines between constructs like data warehouses and data lakes. Let us review the definition of these two terms.

Characteristics	Data Warehouse	Data Lake
Data	Relational data from transactional systems, operational databases, and line of business applications	Non-relational and relational data from IoT devices, web sites, mobile apps, social media, and corporate applications
Schema	Designed prior to the data warehouse implementation (schema-on-write)	Written at the time of analysis (schema-on-read)
Price/Performance	Fastest query results using higher cost storage	Query results getting faster using low-cost storage
Data Quality	Highly curated data that serves as the central version of the truth	Any data that may or may not be curated (i.e. raw data)
Users	Business analysts, data scientists, and data developers	Data scientists, data developers, and business analysts (using curated data)
Analytics	Batch reporting, BI, and visualizations	Machine learning, predictive analytics, data discovery, and profiling

This table is from AWS only.[258]

Notice the data warehouse is a structured data lake. Data warehouses have been with us for decades. However, the term data lake is relatively new. When comparing the two descriptions, the data warehouse described an end state to a process that never occurs. This is because new data is continuously being brought into the environment. Therefore it seems logical that one must have both a data warehouse and a data lake. It is not an "either/or" situation. Proposing that a data warehouse exists without a data lake would be like proposing that all of the files on your computer are organized. Some of them are organized (the ones you use) but many of them are not organized, and others never will be. Not all of the data

---

257 https://docs.aws.amazon.com/athena/latest/ug/what-is.html
258 https://aws.amazon.com/data-warehouse/

that comes in needs to be placed into a rigid schema or placed into an RDBMS. It is not worth the effort. Every IT department we have seen has far more data than they can ever reasonable manage, so perfectly manicured data sets is not on the table as an option. (or as we like to say, optimal has left the building).

Furthermore, many of the initiatives that are begun around data warehousing are not completed, or not completed as advertised. This is covered in the following quotation from Snowflake.

> "*Many organizations do not have an enterprise data warehouse or data lake. In some cases, they've been disappointed by their attempt to create one. Their data sits in multiple, on-premise systems: some used for OLTP, some used for OLAP and some data sits in file systems just waiting to be analyzed. Changing platforms is viewed as an ideal time to re-architect, or architect for the first time a fully functional data platform capable of scaling with the business.*"[259]

Secondly, with a service like AWS Glue, queries can be run not only on one data source but instead on multiple data sources (so-called federated queries). Some of those data sources could be Athena, and other sources could be RDBMSs. Alternatively, they might be a key value database like DynamoDB, or a column-oriented database like Redis, but with Elasticache in front of it.

It all depends.

That is some of the queries will be local, and some will be cross data source queries. Moreover, when this capability is enabled, it means a federated database or virtual database is created. Wikipedia calls this a virtual database is there is no integration between the database. Instead, queries are run across the federation.[260]

---

259 Migrate to the Cloud: The How and Why of Modernizing Your Data Warehouse
260 https://en.wikipedia.org/wiki/Federated_database_system

```
SELECT accounts.account,
       accounts2.sector,
       accounts2.year_established,
       accounts2.subsidiary_of,
       accounts.revenue
  FROM siyeh.`crm-account-stats`.external_account AS accounts2, accounts
 WHERE accounts2.account = accounts.account
```

siyeh/crm-project   Copy code   ● Run query

account	sector	year_established	subsidiary_of	revenue
Acme Corporation	technolgy	1996		1,100.04
Betasoloin	medical	1999		261.41
Codehow	software	1998	Acme Corporation	2,714.90

This is an example of a federated query. This runs a select statement for a table called accounts in one system versus a dataset outside of the system called crm-account-stats.[261]

It is amazing to learn that the concept of federated databases goes back to the 1980s, but they are now only recently appearing in reality, and they are doing so because of the cloud.

When reviewing the lifecycle of data, it just does not make sense to assume that all data eventually moves to the RDBMS. Some will, some won't, and there is a triage process where the company should determine *"is it worth the effort to place this data into a rigid schema?"* If it isn't, then don't. However, one way or another, a data warehouse is going to have a data lake attached.

Furthermore, there may be opportunities to bring new data or data set into the data lake, for example, to perform a correlation with already existing data that is only used intermittently. That is a perfect data set to keep in S3.

Let us review the last row of the table which explains the difference between data warehouses and data lakes concerning analytics.

---

261 https://docs.data.world/documentation/sql/concepts/dw_specific/federated_queries.html

Analytics	Batch reporting, BI, and visualizations	Machine learning, predictive analytics, data discovery, and profiling

A natural question might be, why not perform both types of analysis on data in the data lake. That is batch reporting, BI and visualizations on data warehouse type data sources, and machine learning, predictive analytics, data discovery, and profiling on data lake type data sources? Moreover, after all, as the data sources are held together in AWS with AWS Glue that allows cross-source queries, why conceive of a dividing line between the data warehouse and the data lake?

The SAP Business Warehouse (BW)

When we think of the new approach possible in data warehousing, it is instructive to compare it to the old way in SAP and Oracle. The most popular data warehouse in SAP is BW. SAP also purchased Business Objects, but BOBJ has been in a decline since SAP's acquired them, with new development as well as support in a long term continual decline.

SAP BW is an extremely difficult data warehouse to work with, and it has appalling productivity. We reviewed SAP BW in this article MUFI Rating and Risk SAP BW/BI.[262] SAP BW followed a somewhat typical pattern of overweight and encapsulated data warehouses in that the reports sit in a lengthy queue, and when the report is received, it often does not meet the initial requirement or has taken so long to be developed that it is no longer relevant to the business. SAP does provide an ad hock front end for BW called the BEx Web Analyzer, but it is a weak offering.

SAP has had the most success with their HANA database both commercially and in real terms by porting BW to HANA. This speeds BW, but it also undermines many of the reasons for BW as much of BW is a Data Workbench that allows structures to be created that speed queries when BW sits on a row-oriented data store. However, SAP follows the data warehouse concept where data is staged and is not analyzed before being pushed through the process where it is placed into a rigid schema. However, SAP does have an answer to how to connect to the data lake. For this, they propose connecting HANA to Hadoop.

---

262 http://www.brightworkr.com/softwaredecisions/mufi-rating-risk-sap-bibw/

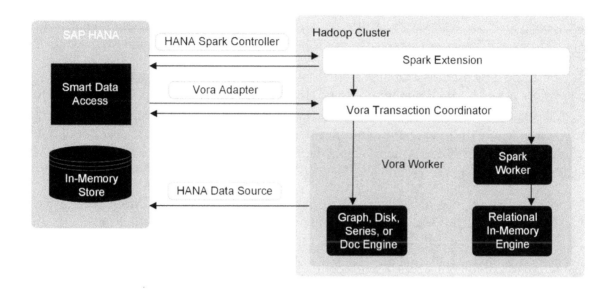

SAP likes publishing these types of diagrams. However, there is a significant problem with this. BW is SAP's primary data warehouse, and it has been demonstrated to be inefficient. HANA speeds BW, but at great expense. Now SAP wants companies to connect Hadoop to their problematic combination of BW with HANA. Overall, SAP is trying to get companies to take an RDBMS centric approach to data warehousing, but the difference being that the RDBMS is now connected to Hadoop.

SAP has had many years to demonstrate capabilities and the cost-effectiveness with BW and has failed to do so. For this reason, SAP is intent on convincing customers that their offering is still relevant given all the changes that are afoot, and one of the ways of doing this is in co-opting new items. For whatever reason, SAP has spent most of their marketing effort in co-opting Hadoop. SAP interpreted Hadoop as the most significant threat to their data warehouse revenues. SAP has spent time influencing customers that Hadoop will not replace the data warehouse. SAP does not say this because it is true, but because SAP sells a data warehouse.

Notice the quote from Timo Elliott from SAP on this exact topic.

> *"Does this mean that you'll be able to do more with Hadoop in the future? Yes. Is it going to be easier to make applications? Yes. Is forty years of business process and data warehousing technology and expertise going be obsolete any time soon? No!"*[263]

---

263 https://timoelliott.com/blog/2014/04/no-hadoop-isnt-going-to-replace-your-data-warehouse.html

Loosely translated, Timo Elliott would like to ensure that SAP customers keep playing licenses on SAP BW. SAP wants as little adjustment as possible to the current scenario with BW. This scenario does not serve customers, but it keeps money flowing to SAP.

However, the new options available to customers for data warehousing and the data lake is far more extensive than merely Hadoop. Moreover, to query Hadoop, it turned out that NoSQL turned into SQL, and running SQL on Hadoop structures meant putting energy into some degree of organization and increase the relations. As we just described, AWS Glue combined with S3 and Athena – along with other components, means that the RDBMS centric approach to data warehousing/"data laking" makes less sense.

As with SAP, Oracle is also trying to promote the idea of an RDBMS centered data warehouse. Recall that Oracle is only dominant in one database type, the RDBMS. Is this the best technical solution? No, but it is what Oracle has to offer. Therefore, for Oracle, every problem looks like a nail, that an RDBMS will be "just perfect for." Their marketing and sales are directed toward getting companies to see data warehousing as a perfect problem for the Oracle RDBMS. However, using data for analytical purposes means de-normalizing that data that is then aggregated. RDBMSs are optimized for highly normalized data (for transaction processing) that is not aggregated.

Thus why are RDBMSs the center of SAP and Oracle's data warehousing strategy?

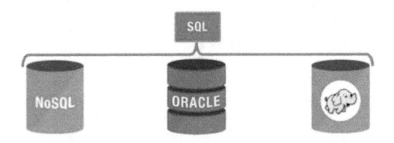

Query any data across Hadoop, NoSQL, and Oracle Database - Oracle Big Data SQL is a unique innovation from Oracle. It is a new architecture for SQL on Hadoop, seamlessly integrates data in Hadoop and NoSQL with data in Oracle Database. Oracle Big Data SQL radically simplifies integrating and operating in the big data domain.

This is how Oracle likes customers to see it in the data warehousing/data lake. Oracle's RDBMS is right in the center of it. However, the RDBMS was never designed for analytics, or that is for read performance. An RDBMS is not optimized for anything other than transactions that require commit/rollback. An RDBMS does as much writes and locks as reads, while a data warehouse does read operations only. So why is Oracle saying that it is?[264]

The problem with what Oracle is proposing is covered in this quotation from Dan Woods (#2).

> *"The model of having just one data warehouse is a throwback to a simpler time. In any organization of significant size, there will be a need for multiple repositories. The CDW should participate in federated queries both as a query aggregation point and as a source for queries aggregated by other systems."[265]*

Another concerning thing about Oracle is that they state analytics can be performed using the column oriented store that is within their RDBMS. This is explained in Oracle's documentation.

> *"Database In-Memory uses an In-Memory column store (IM column store), which is a new component of the Oracle Database System Global Area (SGA), called the In-Memory Area. Data in the IM column store does not reside in the traditional row format used by the Oracle Database; instead it uses a new columnar format. The IM column store does not replace the buffer cache, but acts as a supplement, so that data can now be stored in memory in both a row and a columnar format.*
>
> *Oracle Database In-Memory accelerates both Data Warehouses and mixed workload OLTP databases and is easily deployed under any existing application that is compatible with Oracle Database. No application changes are required. Database In-Memory uses Oracle's mature scale-up, scale-out, and storage-tiering technologies to cost effectively run any size workload. Oracle's industry leading availability and security features all work transparently with Oracle Database In-Memory, making it the most robust offering on the market."[266]*

That sounds good, but Oracle, does not compare their offering to other offerings that are less complex and perform better because they are purpose built for analytics, rather than an adjustment to an application database (RDBMS) design. Oracle does not address the maintenance overhead of adding extra workload capability to an already very complex Oracle database. For example, purpose-built and inexpensive in-memory databases like

---

264 https://www.oracle.com/technetwork/database/bi-datawarehousing/overview/index.html

265 https://www.forbes.com/sites/danwoods/2016/08/31/what-should-the-data-warehouse-become-in-the-cloud/#5ebbceaa1d2a

266 https://www.oracle.com/technetwork/database/in-memory/overview/twp-oracle-database-in-memory-2245633.pdf

Redis or an in-memory data store Elasticache can be integrated connected to any RDBMS. These services can be easily tested as independent items without having to go through the overhead of maintaining those items in Oracle. In fact, as Elasticache can be flexibly assigned, it can be used in front of virtually anything that requires extra performance. Also, as those services are specialized, they will be better than Oracle's in-memory addition to RDBMS. Furthermore, as Oracle continues to add more items to their monolith, the more overhead their RBBMS develops. This evaluation with respect to Oracle applies equally to SAP's HANA and IBM's DB2. In the past it would have been far more difficult for customers to test services like Redis or Elasticache, but now they can be brought up in minutes and thoroughly tested. This is reducing the power of the commercial database vendors, hence the need for the misleading propaganda to get customers to do things that are against their interests, but good for the monopoly vendors.

Oracle is asking customers to invest more into their monolithic database and not to follow a microservices approach to database selection, which is based upon database specialization. No doubt, Oracle would be fine with microservices, as long as the Oracle database is used and everything is kept Oracle-centric.

> *"The ability to easily perform real-time data analysis together with real-time transaction processing on all existing database workloads makes Oracle Database In-Memory ideally suited for the Cloud and on-premises because it requires no additional changes to the application."*

The issue here is that that is not true. Oracle is not as suited for the cloud as Aurora or DynamoDB or Spanner. These databases have been specifically designed for the cloud. Furthermore, the Oracle RDBMS was not even designed for data warehousing!

A mixed type database such as an RDBMS with a column store, like (like Oracle RDBMS and SAP HANA) will never perform as well and will come with extra complexity over a pure column-oriented database like Redis for analytics. If even more speed is required, than ElasticCache can be placed in front of Redis, and it can be added quite inexpensively. The weakness of Oracle's inability to leverage the multibase approach shows itself in the designs that they present to customers. This is also a problem when analyzing Oracle's pronouncements about their RDBMS's performance or its complexity. The question should always be "to what end." The RDBMS has a limited window where it beats other database types, and it is particularly suitable as an application database. However, Oracle pushes their RDBMS into places where it is not competitive.

Moreover, Oracle has done this for decades. When there were fewer alternatives and because they were more difficult to access (pre-IaaS) Oracle was very successful with this strategy.

But now with a cornucopia of databases so quickly brought up on IaaS providers, Oracle's presentation of the universality of their RDBMS is increasingly being challenged.

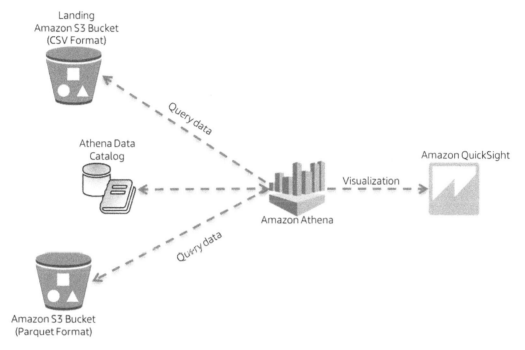

With Athena, Amazon Quickview can be used as the analytics frontend. QuickSight is an analytics service on AWS.

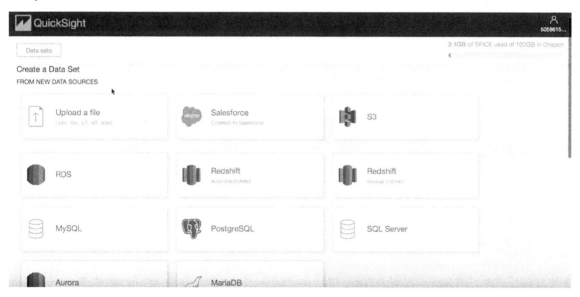

QuickSight runs on AWS and can easily connect to any AWS data sources.

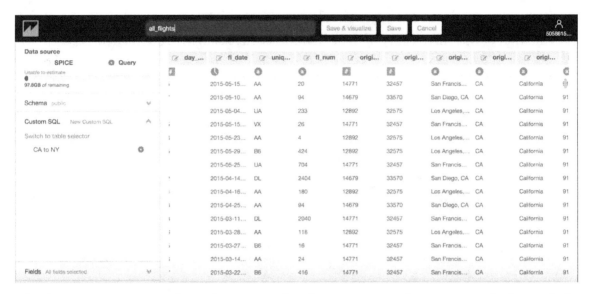

The data comes in extremely easily. It uses either direct query mode or SPICE, which stands for Super-fast, Parallel, In-memory, Calculation Engine is how the data is stored into the SPICE memory store.[267] [268]

---

267 https://www.youtube.com/watch?v=x9RUtTzqpr0

268 SPICE is *"..a combination of columnar storage, in-memory technologies enabled through the latest hardware innovations, machine code generation, and data compression to allow users to run interactive queries on large datasets and get rapid responses." - https://aws.amazon.com/quicksight/*

QuickSight is quite impressive. It allows analytics to be performed right on the data sources at AWS. Coming from SAP projects, it seems like a different world regarding productivity beginning at the data and following the string all the way to the analytics layer.

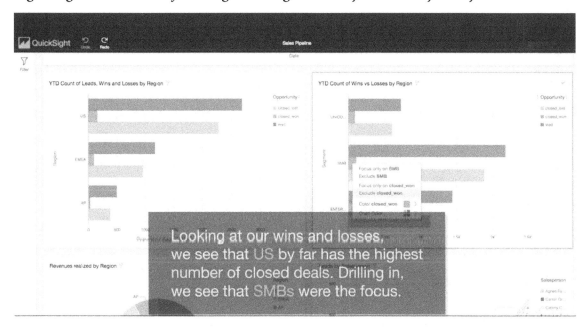

Right now on SAP and Oracle projects, there are massive queues of reports that are waiting to be processed. Moreover, there is one self-evident reason for this. SAP and Oracle's data warehousing solutions are significantly behind the cloud. For example, SAP Cloud Analytics (supposedly supplanting the visualization application and "Tableau killer" Lumira) is still barely operational, and that does not count the data supply chain.

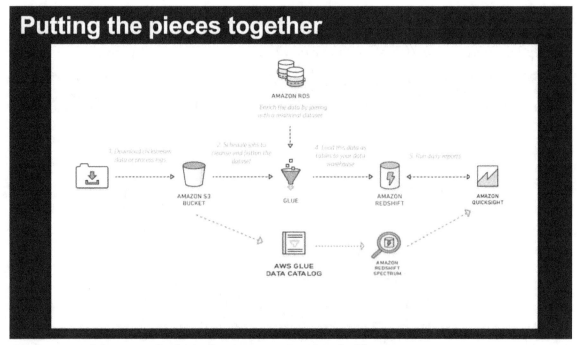

One potential data supply chain for Amazon QuickSight.[269]

Oracle and SAP data warehousing projects have the feel of extreme hierarchy. The users are asked to "wait outside," while the "priests" or the data mungers and data structure builders do their work on the inside. Moreover, dropping a visualization tool onto the environment does not help the overall scenario very much. At many customers that we have seen with both SAP and Tableau, the most popular analytics tool is Excel.

The eternal question for users on SAP projects after they pass away.

---

269 https://www.youtube.com/watch?v=fORJ6y572gs

The Importance of Access to Compute

Companies focused on data warehousing that is not focused on the cloud will face increasing difficulty in maintaining the illusion that their approaches are desirable. This is explained in the following quotation from Dan Woods (#2).

> *"The cloud is the land of cheap storage and on-demand compute. The CDW should radically separate storing data from the engine that does the computation. This will allow as much data as possible to be stored and as many different type of engines as needed to process it to be created. This separation significantly changes the economics of the data warehouse because you don't have to build a large system to handle your peak storage needs inside an on-premise system.*
>
> *The of the complexity of a data warehouse is decreased by the cloud's ability to start up as many different computing engines as needed to handle your workloads. Some of these engines will wake up and stay running, handling on-demand requests or waiting for batch jobs. Others will wake up and process just one workload and then disappear. The point is that each of these engines is created on a separate infrastructure that doesn't compete with the others. This simplifies the implementation."*[270]

How All of This Applies to Google Cloud

This chapter has discussed AWS; however, this applies similarly to Google Cloud. We showed this table earlier, but Google Cloud has similar services that are data warehouse/ data lake ready.

---

270 https://www.forbes.com/sites/danwoods/2016/08/31/what-should-the-data-warehouse-become-in-the-cloud/#5ebbceaa1d2a

Category	AWS	Google Cloud
Storage Bucket	S3	Google Multi Regional Storage Bucket
Data Warehouse	Redshift	BigQuery
ETL	Glue	Data Flow
PaaS/FaaS/Compute	Lambda	Functions
Analytics	QuickSight	Data Studio

As with AWS, Google Cloud allows a conglomerated approach which flexibly combines a data lake with a data warehouse and can allow for federated queries across a virtual database.

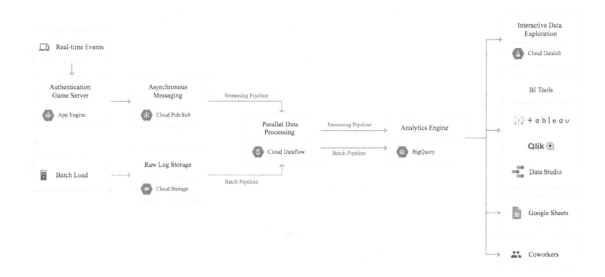

Google Cloud does not have an analytics application that we consider as good as QuickSight, but here there are many options.

One of the most interesting data warehousing use cases is not something we would ordinarily consider a data warehousing application as it is such a short time lag use case. This is published on Google Cloud's website and is a real-time inventory management system. In most cases, inventory management is handled by the ERP system. However, there is nothing to say that an ERP system has to be used for this purpose. ERP systems usually are costly implementations and impose considerable inflexibility upon a company. As we cover in the case studies, ERP systems typically have poor supply chain planning capabilities. An ERP system could be used, or not be used with this use case, which is shown in the graphic below.

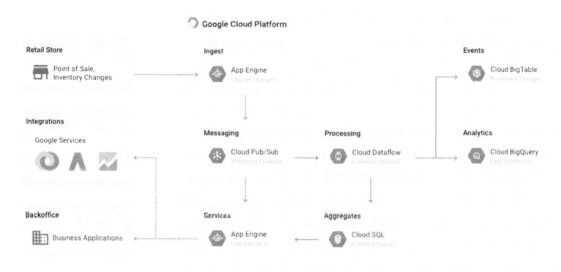

Here the point of sale information comes from retail stores. The current inventory position is held in the back-office applications (which may contain an ERP system). The various Google Cloud components are used to combine retail store point of sale data with the back-office applications.[271]

Conclusion

Data warehousing projects are known to be engines of scope creep in companies and delivery far less output than expected at the beginning of the project. This is yet another monolithic approach where an enormous number of data sources are brought together in a single place. SAP and Oracle's entire concept of a data warehouse is dated and locks customers into a high overhead and inflexible design that has already ample evidence not be able to come close to meeting the expectations set for data warehousing. The future of data warehousing is leading away from the approaches and heavy lock-in promoted by SAP and Oracle.

Data warehousing vendors and consulting companies have become accustomed to long-running projects, where again, the final result is not verifiable until a lengthy period of

---

271 https://cloud.google.com/solutions/building-real-time-inventory-systems-retail

time has passed and a lot of money has been spent. Once purchased, they prove incredibly sticky, and the vendor sets the agenda in what has been a monolithic design where they stipulate the tools and everything ends up being around what the vendor decides will be used. However, cloud data warehousing/data laking can be brought up much more quickly, and the more savvy customers will leverage this rather than continuing to take what the data warehousing industry has been serving up.

AWS and Google Cloud offer the opposite of what the traditional data warehousing industry with its high lock-in and long-running projects.

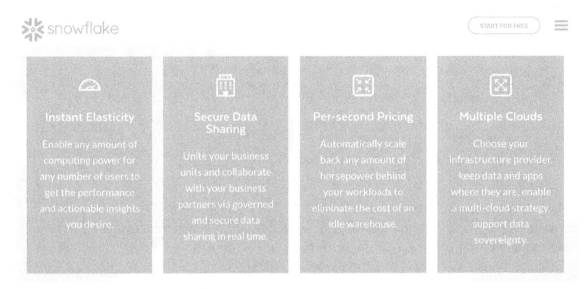

Snowflake obtained a peculiarly high score on Gartner's ODMS Magic Quadrant. For a vendor that is rated at 119th in overall popularity, it seemed odd. That is until we found how much capital Snowflake had raised (and therefore its budget for promotion). Yet if you look at the items, it lists on its webpage (Instant Elasticity, Secure Data Sharing, Per Second Pricing, and Multiple Clouds), those are all capabilities already inherent to both AWS and Google Cloud. The market will determine if there is enough value add with Snowflake over the inherent data warehousing capabilities in AWS, Google Cloud and Azure.

Snowflake was able to raise $450 million in capital in 2018 alone.[272] And the investors in Snowflake are making a bet that the data warehouse market is ready for an all cloud provider.

---

272 https://en.wikipedia.org/wiki/Snowflake_Computing

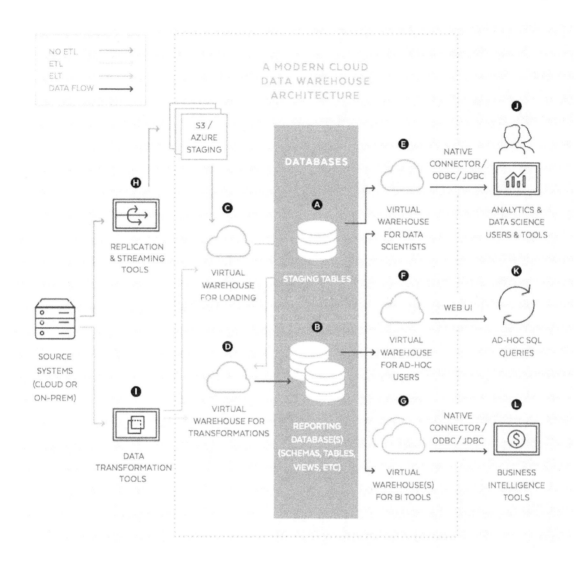

This is Snowflake's vision of the multicloud data warehouse.[273]

273 https://resources.snowflake.net/data-warehousing-modernization/migrate-to-the-cloud

Chapter 9: Speed: How AWS and Google Cloud Speed the Implementation of SAP and Oracle: Why You Can't Listen to SAP and Oracle Consulting Firms About AWS and Google Cloud

Both SAP and Oracle rely upon an ecosystem of consulting partners to implement their software. These partners can sell both licenses and consulting services, but most only have consulting services to sell, and their consulting services are based upon billing hours. The agreement between these vendors and the consulting entities is to gain recommendations from consulting companies in return for receiving implementation work.

The following are important things to consider regarding these consulting partners.

- As the consulting company does not use the software after it is implemented, their primary concern is the billing hours, not the software that works the best for their clients.

- Each of the SAP and Oracle consulting companies maintain aggressive targets regarding the number of billing hours and the margin that must be sold each year for a member of these consulting companies to attain and retain their senior level status and their compensation. This is why consulting companies aren't able to help their clients with software selection in a way that puts the client's interests ahead of the interests of the consulting companies. The selection has already been performed **before** the consulting companies evaluate the requirements. This is because the consulting company has already dedicated its consultants to specific modules within a specific vendor. SAP or Oracle consulting companies will typically use the RFP process to backward engineer the RFP (regarding the questions in the RFP) to match the software for which they already consult. Any senior member who did not do this and allowed the client to choose an application the consulting company could not implement (and thus bill hours for) would lose their position in that company as well as the respect of their peers. This is covered in the article How to Understand the

Logic of the Software RFP.[274] For consulting companies the RFP functions to place an aura of legitimacy over the software selection process.

Therefore the SAP and Oracle consulting companies primarily function to **funnel IT expenditures** to SAP and Oracle applications and databases. This of course results in SAP and Oracle implementations.

Of all the vendors, SAP has the most significant partner consulting network with the top 18 consultancies employing over 250,000 consultants globally. There are many other smaller consultancies and independent consultants that increase that number significantly above 350,000 consultants. In the book SAP Nation 2.0, the global SAP ecosystem was estimated at roughly the size of the GDP of Ireland or Norway. In the book, Vinnie Mirchandani observed that he could receive no assistance from any of the well-known IT analyst firms in estimating the global yearly spend on SAP and SAP services as the IT analyst firms said that the total number was "sensitive." Such an estimation is only sensitive because the major IT analyst firms are paid by SAP to push SAP products. Also, therefore SAP is a client, and hence the sensitivity, or should we say the reluctance to offend such a well-paying customer.

SAP's consulting ecosystem has grown to be the largest in the world because SAP projects are the most remunerative in the world. That is the consulting companies followed profit maximizing principles when selection which vendors to push. In consulting companies that have both an SAP practice and an Oracle practice, in most cases, the SAP practice is larger. The remuneration obtained from SAP projects is a function of the number of consultants that can be staffed on an SAP project multiplied by the length of each SAP project, and SAP has the most extended projects in the industry.

SAP has introduced one accelerated methodology after another for decades, beginning with ASAP in the 1990s that were proposed to increase implementation speed. We covered one such methodology in the article How to Best Understand the Faux SAP RDS.[275] Our conclusion is that much like the implementation methodologies of the SAP and Oracle consulting companies they are primarily written by the **sales and marketing arms** of these entities, and they don't speed implementations. Neither SAP nor Oracle implementations have changed much in their implementation durations.

How long do these implementations for SAP and Oracle take? Well, SAP's flagship ERP application, called ECC, is typically thought not to be implemented in less than a year, with multi-year implementations being the norm. At the outer edge of the typical timeline,

---

274 http://www.brightworkr.com/softwareprojectrisk/2018/06/02/how-to-understand-the-logic-for-the-software-rfp/

275 http://www.brightworkr.com/sapprojectmanagement/2017/06/best-understand-faux-sap-rds/

a recent SAP failure at the grocery chain Lidl went on for seven years until it was finally canceled. While a significant loss for Lidl, it was extremely remunerative for KPS as the consulting partner. KPS which would have consumed an ample percentage of the estimated 500 million Euros that were spent on that project over that extended timeline. This is because the consulting company always makes a significant multiple of the funds received by SAP for the license (although recall that support is paid to SAP on a yearly basis, even after the implementation ends). Even after the failure, the project has still declared a success on the KPS website as we cover in the article KPS Continues to Keep Promote HANA for Retail for Lidl After Failure.[276]

Curiously, KPS complained that the timelines for performing customization were too short, which seems like an odd complaint for a project that went on for seven years. Still, a large number of SAP consultants leaped to KPS's defense, declaring that in their "considered opinion" it would have to have been the client's fault. This is standard practice. When projects fail, the SAP consultants that comment nearly always blame either the customer or the systems integrator. And this is done ordinarily without actually reading the case study. By the time developers start work, the contract is already signed and its already too late. Whenever an SAP project fails, the post-mortem is typically performed by SAP consultants (or by Oracle consultants for Oracle), which is a problem as they have a strong financial bias to blame the client, which they ordinarily do. In each case, the apologists are careful never to highlight their financial bias when they provide their explanations for SAP project failures. These sources also have a habit of denying that poor quality information flows to the customer/client in the beginning.

Both SAP and KPS told Lidl many inaccurate things. We know this because this is a feature of how SAP projects are sold and because credible sources have told us who were involved **in the project**. Because the duration was so long (no doubt the project became delayed from an originally shorter duration), this meant that it took Lidl a long time **until they finally learned that many of the areas of information presented to them were incorrect**. The eventual outcome was that Lidl ended up preferring to stay with their previous systems rather than move on to SAP. SAP consultants see this as a "failure of leadership" at the customer.

It is well known, and we have documented this in the article How SAP Used and Abused the Term Legacy,[277] that SAP nearly always overrepresents how easily SAP's applications can take over for the prospect's existing applications. Oracle did the same thing to the Air Force in a well-publicized case of sales overreach, proposing that Oracle's ERP functionality

---

276 http://www.brightworkr.com/sap/2018/08/kps-continues-to-keep-promote-hana-for-retail-for-lidl-after-failure/

277 http://www.brightworkr.com/sap/2017/04/sap-used-term-legacy/

could replace highly specialized military systems that had been custom developed over decades (Which we covered in the article How to Understand Overmapping Functionality to ERP).[278] [279] In both cases, the length of the project, along with its eventual (mandatory?) delays pushed out the date when the customer figured out that the information given in the sales process was radically inaccurate.

How Can AWS and Google Cloud Improve This Situation?

Because AWS and Google Cloud offer ready to deploy infrastructure, it means that sales contentions can be tested far more quickly than they can in an on-premises environment. Under the on-premises model, merely the sizing exercise, which is unnecessary when one has access to a reliable IaaS environment, pushes out the date from trying out the software. Both SAP and Oracle continuously pledge their newfound allegiance to the cloud. However, they don't run their companies as cloud vendors. They have for their entire existence operated on the on-premises sales model, where contentions are not checked until a significant amount of time has passed, and the longer the lag between the purchase the decision and learning the reality, **the more likely the customer is to "stay the course"** the less likely they are to admit they made a mistake.

Something else which is essential to consider is that both SAP and Oracle consulting companies operate with almost no independent verification of the information they provide to customers. We/Brightwork Research & Analysis receives details of communications from all over the world, and the accuracy of the consulting company provided information turns out to be quite low, something we cover for SAP in the article A Study into The Accuracy of SAP. We have not performed such an exhaustive study for Oracle, but our individual analysis of Oracle such as with the autonomous database (as covered in How Real is Oracle's Autonomous Database?) indicates that Oracle would also not fare very well in this analysis.[280]

As with SAP and Oracle, AWS and Google Cloud also have consulting partners. However, the orientation is entirely different from the relationship between SAP and Oracle and their consulting partners. First, AWS and Google Cloud have created such a magnet with their capabilities, that AWS and Google Cloud do **not** rely upon partners anywhere near the way that SAP and Oracle do for lead generation. If these partners want to participate with AWS, then they can, but AWS does not "need" them. Furthermore, the multiple that consulting companies have come to expect from SAP and Oracle is not going to fly with

---

278 http://www.brightworkr.com/erp/2017/04/01/how-to-understand-overmapping-functionality-to-erp/

279 https://www.nytimes.com/2012/12/09/technology/air-force-stumbles-over-software-modernization-project.html

280 http://www.brightworkr.com/saphana/2018/04/18/how-real-is-the-oracles-autonomous-database/

AWS. Therefore, the consulting companies will most likely find AWS and Google Cloud related consulting to be a poor substitute for SAP and Oracle consulting, because there is no financial substitute for SAP and Oracle consulting.

One way or another AWS and Google Cloud will grow because their offering is that good. This also extends to sales. AWS and Google Cloud's business is mainly inbound, or the SaaS/cloud model of acquisition. AWS has hired some salespeople from Oracle and other vendors, but AWS (nor Google Cloud) will never have the number of salespeople compared to their revenues or customers as SAP or Oracle. SAP and Oracle are so heavy with salespeople that there are constant turf battles between the sales reps for territory within both vendors.

AWS and Google Cloud Tools for Speeding Implementation

All three of those involved in this book are experienced implementations. As such we are highly suspicious of accelerators promoted by vendors and consulting companies and view them more often than not as sales tools. However, when reviewing AWS and Google Cloud documentation called Quickstart, we were pleasantly surprised.[281] Unlike with SAP or Oracle, these are not just methodologies (i.e., PowerPoint decks) they are actual components that can be leveraged within AWS. Let's take a look at some of them.

AWS's QuickStart covers the following categories.

- Databases & Storage
- Big Data & Analytics
- Data Lake
- Data Warehouse
- DevOps
- Security
- Compliance
- Messaging and Integration
- Microsoft Technologies
- SAP Technologies
- Networking and Remote Access
- Additional

---

281 https://aws.amazon.com/quickstart/

Each one of these categories has coverage for multiple items. If we take just one, which is the first on the list, Databases & Storage we see the following items.

- CloudStax Cache for Redis
- CloudStax NoSQL DB for Cassandra
- Couchbase
- DataStax Enterprise
- MongoDB
- ONTAP Cloud for NetApp
- Oracle Database
- SAP HANA
- SIOS DataKeeper
- Spectrum Scale
- SQL Server
- StorReduce

AWS is serious about each of these Quickstarts. Each one of them have a comprehensive guide. If we take just the first Quickstart on the list, the CloudStax Cache for Redis, it is 23 pages long.

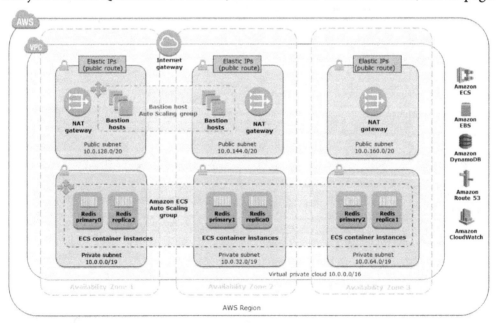

Here is a graphic from the CloudStax Cache for Redis Quickstart document explaining the architecture of Redis.

Each Quickstart guide lists the prerequisites to using the Quickstart. For the CloudStax Cache for Redis, the following are listed as prerequisites:

- Amazon EBS
- Amazon EC2
- Amazon ECS
- Amazon Route 53
- Amazon VPC
- Redis
- CloudStax FireCamp

The guide then explains the technical requirements, the deployment options, the deployment steps, how to launch the quick start, how to test the deployment, information around data persistence, data backup, Redis configuration, security, troubleshooting, links to GitHub to download more templates and scripts and how to share customizations with others. Finally, there is an extensive listing of additional resources.

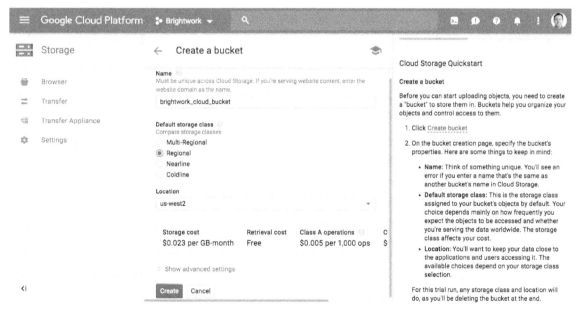

Google Cloud also has Quickstarts. They can be found as separate documents like AWS's Quickstarts, but also pop out to the right while performing tasks in the console.

Evaluating this documentation leaves one with the distinct impression that the Quickstarts were not merely conceived as marketing tools, senior members didn't write them at AWS or Google Cloud or by their sales groups (as is the case with Oracle and SAP methodology and accelerator documentation). Instead, they were written by technical resources at AWS. Once again, this makes sense. AWS and Google Cloud are not trying to sell software or to create a giant consulting ecosystem. They are trying to get customers up and working as quickly as possible. The sooner customers can begin using AWS and Google Cloud services, and the faster they can start using more services, and more advanced services, the more that AWS and Google Cloud can charge them. That is, while SAP and Oracle's revenues models are loosely based upon the usage of their products (and for SAP and Oracle's consulting partners their consulting services), AWS, and Google Cloud's revenues are tightly connected to the utilization of their services.

Another part of AWS's rapid approach is the free and paid training that AWS offers.[282] AWS offers quite a bit of good quality free training. AWS breaks its training tracks into the following:

- Cloud Practitioner Path

- Architect Path

- Developer Path

- Operations Path

While AWS offers offline courses, AWS, as is usually the case, differentiates itself by providing training online. While SAP and Oracle treat training as profit centers, AWS treats training as a way to get customers and consultants scaled up on AWS as quickly as possible.

We signed up for and tested AWS's training ourselves while researching this book to validate its quality.

---

282 https://aws.amazon.com/training/

This will of course change, but when we filtered for Digital courses in English, we found 230 courses that we could take from AWS. They ranged from 7 hours to 5 minutes.

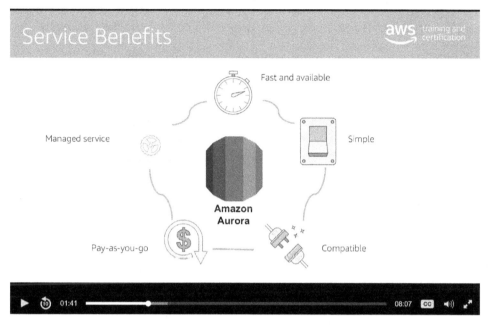

AWS training is quite good. Here is a slide from a video explaining the benefits of Amazon Aurora. We learned quite a bit about Aurora from the AWS training on the topic.

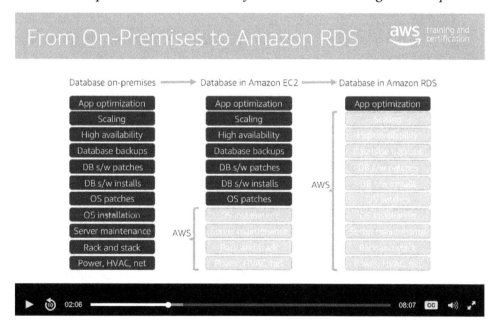

For example, the Aurora training did an excellent job of explaining what parts of the stack are managed by AWS, with the EC2 service managing one level, and the RDS managing essentially the entire database. This is not a slide or training that SAP or Oracle want anyone to see. This is because neither of these vendors can offer what AWS can for the fully managed database.

Google Cloud also offers quite a bit of inexpensive training options.

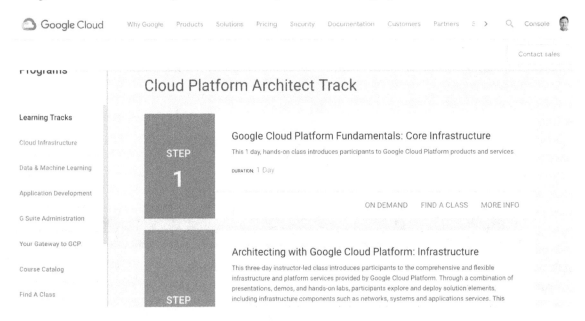

Google Cloud also has a wide number of training options available online. Google Cloud uses a company called Coursera.

All of this leads into the topic of how reliable SAP and Oracle consulting companies are on the subject of AWS and Google Cloud. First, these consulting companies will have a problem with AWS and Google Cloud as AWS, and Google Cloud provide the ability to both shorten implementations, and to bring down the time between when the sales process occurs, and therefore when the information about software finally is available to the customer. As so many SAP and Oracle projects have such a wide variance between what is promised and what is true, this is not a welcome development for SAP, Oracle or their consulting partners. It does nothing but increases the likelihood their customers will confront them on inconsistencies.

Secondly, the shortened time frame reduces the potential revenues for these consulting companies. For example, consultancies like Accenture and CapGemini have begun AWS practices.

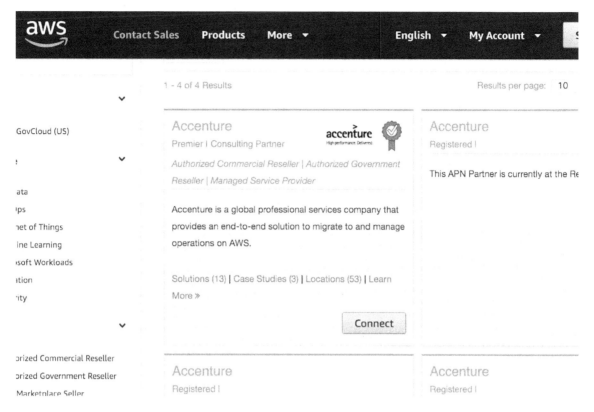

*Accenture is an AWS partner. But this is not what these consulting firms actually want. Accenture and others with SAP practices will make far less money client with **AWS than they will with SAP consulting**. SAP consulting, according to the book SAP Nation 2.0 supports a $300+ billion ecosystem, as we covered in the article SAP Nation 2.0 on The Overall SAP Ecosystem Spend.[283] (29% of which is consulting).*

The historical behavior of these firms makes us wonder whether these are good companies to listen or use to when it comes to AWS.

- These companies are accustomed to a high multiple between the vendor or service expenditure and consulting.

- IIow will they adjust to cloud, which is supposedly about efficiency?

- Will these firms find it as straightforward to access cloud skills as on premises skills? Many cloud skills are based upon open source, something big SAP and Oracle consulting firms don't have much history in working with.

---

283 http://www.brightworkr.com/sap/2018/09/sap-nation-2-0-on-the-overall-sap-ecosystem-annual-spend/

- These firms for decades have been very focused around specific vendor practices. How will they adjust to an environment that requires true systems integration? That is their ability to select the best tool for the job?

For this book, we reached out to Accenture and several other large consulting partners that also have SAP consulting practices. When we asked questions, we were met with the same overpromising that it is so typical from these companies on SAP projects. Everything was explained as "very easy," and there was a desire to move us quickly to the next stage of the sales process where we would meet with a solution architect. We are quite confident that these consulting firms will "lift and shift" their business practices from SAP and Oracle consulting to AWS and Google Cloud consulting.

Thus it is not only SAP and Oracle that are "addicted" to the on-premises sales and delivery model, but also their consulting partners. They are all hugely successful following their current processes and have not adjusted their organization structure and staffing to be successful in the cloud. SAP and Oracle along with their consulting partners have fought and will continue to fight movement to the cloud as it fundamentally undermines their business model. The implications of the cloud are not only the consulting firms it is not being considered by governments and policy setters, as we covered in the article How Cloud Changes the Labor Needs in IT.[284]

Conclusion

Up until this chapter, we focused primarily on the functionality offered by AWS and Google Cloud. That is why it was so essential to have a chapter that just focused on development speed because this is one of the lesser discussed topics around cloud services. Services are so easy to bring up on AWS and Google Cloud that development can experiment faster than they ever could before. The introduction of "serverless" provides enhanced development speed because not only is sizing unnecessary but server component selection is also unnecessary. The on-premises vendors were offering none of these things. Quite the contrary, the SAP and Oracle were quite happy with the status quo.

However, it is not merely a matter of leveraging AWS and Google Cloud services. SAP and Oracle consulting firms are embedded at SAP and Oracle accounts, and one of their primary roles is to put the brakes on leveraging the innovation in AWS and Google Cloud. They need to push their clients to SAP and Oracle cloud to maintain their relationship with SAP and Oracle. This is why self-reliance and finding entities that are not part of the current status quo on SAP and Oracle projects are so important to be able to leverage AWS and Google Cloud for SAP and Oracle environments.

---

284 http://www.brightworkr.com/saaseconomy/2016/04/08/saas-changes-labor-needs/

Chapter 10: Responding to Oracle Arguments

Oracle has a long history of publishing information that critiques every alternative to Oracle as well as asserting that customers owe them money that they aren't. We read these publications with amusement, but they are less funny if they are successful in tricking customers into making a bad decision. We will cover several of these arguments against AWS. AWS is usually the mentioned party, but the arguments would also apply to Google Cloud.

Oracle Argument 1: Do Serious Databases Not Run on Virtual Machines?

Oracle proposes that AWS is not ready for enterprise workloads. This is a common argument on the part of Oracle that only its offerings are indeed "enterprise ready."

The following quote covers this argument.

> *"The problem for AWS, is that their architecture was not originally designed to run Database workloads. Back in 2002 when AWS was first architected (I was at Sun when several of my friends/colleagues went to AWS so I know the history), the intent was to just sell what unused compute and storage capacity wasn't being used by Amazon themselves. And over the last 15+ years, AWS just heavily invested in building out this, what I call generic/basic architecture worldwide-leveraging the Asian OEM/ODM builders to get cheapest costs.*
>
> *But the problem & challenge for AWS is that it's (still today) 100% fully virtualized (until their bare metal instances finally go live) and as we all know, serious Databases don't run on virtualized environments and why AWS realizes they need bare metal to eliminate needing virtualization."*

This is essentially the bare metal argument again. Bare metal does have better performance than virtualization, but bare metal puts one back into performing hosting rather than being in the cloud. Also, all the benefits of the cloud are lost when this is done. AWS does not offer bare metal, but it is not where AWS gets most of its revenue. It is well understood that bare metal has specific use cases, but Oracle is attempting to make the entire situation about performance. If what Oracle said were true, AWS and Google Cloud and Azure would not even exist (as they do) because they could not add benefits over bare metal hosting. Secondly, the problem with the cloud is bandwidth, not database speed. All commercial and databases have a sub-second response time on many operations.

This is covered in the following quotation from AWS.

> *"Amazon RDS provides a fully managed relational database. With Amazon RDS, you can scale your database's compute and storage resources, often with no downtime. Amazon DynamoDB is a fully managed NoSQL database that provides single-digit millisecond latency at any scale. Amazon Redshift is a managed*

petabyte-scale data warehouse that allows you to change the number or type of nodes as your performance or capacity needs change."[285]

The problem is not the database response time. For decades development has focused on making databases faster, applying better hardware to the database, essentially focusing on different aspects of the database. However the bottleneck is less frequently the database and instead the bottleneck is cloud latency when a data center is located 10,000 kilometers away. That's why AWS invests heavily in building DCs everywhere. The speed of light in fiber is still constant. AWS investments and capabilities get into great detail to optimize network performance as the following quotation explains.

> *"In AWS, networking is virtualized and is available in a number of different types and configurations. This makes it easier to match your networking methods more closely with your needs. AWS offers product features (for example, Enhanced Networking, Amazon EBS-optimized instances, Amazon S3 transfer acceleration, dynamic Amazon CloudFront) to optimize network traffic. AWS also offers networking features (for example, Amazon Route 53 latency routing, Amazon VPC endpoints, and AWS Direct Connect) to reduce network distance or jitter."[286]*

Furthermore, AWS, Google Cloud and Azure all support HTTP 2.0. The newer protocol (released 2015) supports multiplexed requests across a single connection. Instead of buffering requests and responses, it handles them in streaming fashion. This reduces latency and increases the perceived performance of your application.

HTTP 2.0's multiplexing and concurrency, dependency streaming, header compression, and server push decrease web resource load time by at least 200% compared to HTTP 1.1.

---

285 http://d0.awsstatic.com/whitepapers/architecture/AWS_Well-Architected_Framework.pdf
286 http://d0.awsstatic.com/whitepapers/architecture/AWS_Well-Architected_Framework.pdf

Oracle Argument 2: Customers Should Use Bare Metal?

Now let us get to a second Oracle argument against AWS is a more direct argument for bare metal versus cloud.

> *"Let's assume you own Oracle Database licenses and now with Oracles new "BYOL" (bring your own license) program, you can decide where to deploy those licenses. You can chose on-premise of course, but now can choose Oracle Cloud, AWS or even Azure. Everyone here I am sure has the perception that it will be far cheaper, easier and faster to run on AWS, right?"*

> *"Well, take a look at this research report blog from AVM Consulting who actually consults migrations to AWS, Azure and recently Oracle Cloud. They just tested/ Benchmarked running Oracle DB in Oracles BYOL DBaaS against AWS RDS. They ran an open source Database testing tool, SLOB, written by the (in)famous Kevin Closson, formerly of Oracle and now at AWS.*

> *As you can see from the comparison tests on pricing and performance, there is just no comparison! Here are a few quotes from the article located here."(see footnote)*

> *"The results suggest that Oracle's infrastructure (OCI) is between 7 and 10 times faster in I/O than the AWS counterpart, using only a quarter of the time to load the same amount of data. Furthermore, OCI outperformed AWS significantly in wait times for critical I/O events, which indicates a superior I/O latency on OCI. Finally, the TCO of running the system on AWS is twice as high as the bill would be if the system was run on OCI. Oracle's performance dominance can be partially explained by the unique and differentiated capabilities of Oracle's next generation Bare metal infrastructure, which is very different to the architecture of AWS"*[287]

This is a study by AVM Consulting which is pro-Oracle. Therefore, Oracle is presenting a study that is ostensibly from a neutral source, when it is not a neutral source. The AVM Consulting study could be found on Oracle's website!

Oracle was run on a bare metal configuration with NVMe SSD. On AWS NVMe SSD was not used. Therefore the hardware is not equivalent. Oracle knew this study was misleading, and yet choose to reference it and further imply that the source was independent.

---

287 https://www.avmconsulting.net/single-post/2017/12/09/AWS-RDS-and-OCI-DBaaS-Performance-Benchmark

The initial test case should state the following:

> *"Here's why you should use NVMe SSD."*

Here are the problems with the AVM Consulting study:

- The study does not hold the hardware constant.

- There are also issues that undermine the comparison with the versions of Linux used.

- This analysis breaks the question down between virtualization or containers and bare metal. However, there have been changes afoot that call into question this simple dichotomy.

Oracle seeks to emphasize bare metal, and they are nowhere near as adept at containerization for the cloud as is AWS or Google Cloud. Everything that AWS and Google Cloud offer is left out of the equation in Oracle's analysis.

As of May 2018, AWS began offering bare metal instances. AWS describes when it makes sense to use their bare metal.

> *"These instances are ideal for workloads that require access to the hardware feature set (such as Intel® VT-x), or for applications that need to run in non-virtualized environments for licensing or support requirements. Bare metal instances allow EC2 customers to run applications that benefit from deep performance analysis tools, specialized workloads that require direct access to bare metal infrastructure, legacy workloads not supported in virtual environments, and licensing-restricted Tier 1 business critical applications. Bare metal instances also make it possible for customers to run virtualization secured containers such as Clear Linux Containers. Bare metal instances enable VMware to run their full suite of software, including vSphere Hypervisor, directly on EC2 managed infrastructure."*[288]

Notice that AWS does **not list** performance as a reason for using AWS's bare metal instances.[289]

In Oracle's argument, they entirely leave out bare metal's disadvantages, which are covered in this quotation from Denis Myagkov.

---

[288] https://aws.amazon.com/about-aws/whats-new/2018/05/announcing-general-availability-of-amazon-ec2-bare-metal-instances/

[289] Interestingly, Google Cloud still does not offer a bare metal server service.

> *"In AWS I'm able to take any database as a service and logging system as a service and run my solution in production in a few months with a small team. With bare metal I will need a team of system administrators, database administrators, DevOps, managers to handle them… I will spend several months to settle the team only. With AWS I'm able to increase overall complexity of solution slowly and comfortably, while with SAP and Oracle it's necessary to start immediately from bloody enterprise hardcore."*

Overall, the argument advanced by Oracle is both false in its contentions but leaves out all the other ways that AWS adds value to infrastructure. The framework proposed by Oracle imagines database services like RDS as merely hosting, or virtualized hosting, which is incorrect.

Oracle Argument 3: Is AWS Inappropriate for Enterprise Workloads?

One common criticism of AWS by Oracle is that AWS is not appropriate for enterprise workloads. This is the official story on whether the largest database vendors have been moving to the cloud. Let us review the following quotation.

> *"Customers with the largest Databases in the world have or in process of moving to Oracle Cloud. For example AT&T is moving 1000's of Databases that are all in the TB of size. Several petabyte in total. They are largest Telecom in the world and I believe are in top 3 of having largest databases in world. CERN, the European Organization for Nuclear Research, is one of the world's largest and most respected centers for scientific research, in running quite a bit of services & Databases in Oracle Cloud. They I believe are in top 5 largest Databases in world. Sprint also a huge Oracle and Oracle Cloud customer. They're also in top 5 largest Databases.. Generali, Unilever, and thousands of very large companies are migrating and/or running in Oracle Cloud. Here's the ones that have been documented.*
>
> *And by the way, you do know that Amazon runs Oracle Database (they pay Oracle ~$60M a year) just like many of the born in the cloud companies like SalesForce, SuccessFactors, Concur, Ariba, etc. And majority of largest Databases in the world are Oracle Databases including #1, World Data Center for Climate (WDCC)."*

While this has some truthful examples, this is an extension of a common argument presented by Oracle. No matter what the application, only Oracle can run "enterprise workloads." We have observed its usage so many times that we refer to it as the "Gatorade Argument." The Gatorade Argument is where some niche capability (in this case electrolyte drinks) which are only necessary for extreme endurance activities, is sold to the people that do not engage in such activities. In the past, Oracle made this argument against other database vendors, now they have adopted this argument against AWS, even AWS runs Oracle!

Oracle frequently talk about "Customers with the largest Databases in the world." We congratulate Oracle for having these types of use cases, but these upper end case studies, as repeatedly pointed out by one of this books authors Ahmed Azmi comprise roughly 2% of the market. The World Data Center for Climate's online database is designed to grow by 1 petabyte per year. What is the relevance of that database size to the vast majority of customers?[290] Should the typical customer use what the World Data Center for Climate uses? Furthermore, Oracle seems to readily overlook many very large installations that don't run Oracle. You know who does not run Oracle? Google. Google not only does not run the Oracle database, but they also moved away from Oracle's MySQL in 2013.[291] Google is also, like the World Data Center for Climate, one of the ten largest databases in the world. Oh, and MariaDB is open source, so see the price comparison at the beginning of this book to see how much money Google is saving (not that they even need to save money).

The mainstream doesn't run the largest databases in the world and they don't need scorching fast HPC database performance. Speeds and feeds are never a priority for mainstream customers.

---

290 https://www.comparebusinessproducts.com/fyi/10-largest-databases-in-the-world

291 An interesting quotation from this decision found in this article is how and why Google moved away from MySQL *"Even though it's easy to suggest that this mass migration from MySQL to MariaDB is some sort of comeuppance for Oracle, the truth probably lies in the history of Oracle's handling of the MySQL community to date—Oracle has made its bed of spikes with the MySQL community, and now it has to lie in it."* https://readwrite.com/2013/09/14/google-waves-goodbye-to-mysql-in-favor-of-mariadb/

Oracle Argument 4: Does AWS Have Noisy Neighbors?

Noisy neighbors are when different customers share computing resources interfere with one another causing performance to degrade. This is another of Oracle's critiques against AWS. The following quotation explains this "concern."

> "The other problem for Databases on AWS, is what's called noisy neighbors. Yes, AWS does offer dedicated compute, but that doesn't necessarily guarantee that the virtual machine running across several dedicated compute environments, aren't being consumed by outside resources. So you can't get consistent performance, throughput, latency, IOPS, etc. And that's why AWS doesn't even provide an SLA on performance because they can't guarantee it. So as long as the service is available, even at 1% of total performance, the customer isn't covered by any SLA."

AWS is not only offering virtualization, they are offering more advanced types of virtualization called containerization. AWS has their own definition of containerization.

> "Containerization is an operating-system-level virtualization method for deploying and running distributed applications without launching an entire virtual machine (VM) for each application. Container images allow for modularity in services. They are constructed by building functionality onto a base image. Developers, operations teams, and IT leaders should agree on base images that have the security and tooling profile that they want. These images can then be shared throughout the organization as the initial building block."[292]

The cloud is always not about performance; it is also about flexibility. To obtain that flexibility, a tradeoff can be accepted of (for example) 5-10% from maximum performance. However, in exchange, one can enable new servers or release existing servers whenever they are required. Of course, better performance can be achieved on-premise or with colocation, but then the result is a rigid solution. Also, the results of having these rigid systems are well known at this point. When new servers are required, the customer has to go to the vendor and wait several weeks.

Of course, a mixed strategy can fit the requirements. That is some rigid components, like an accounting system or a master database instance can be on-premise while web components, like analytics or file archives, are deployed in the cloud.

One does not need to go 100% in either direction.

---

292 https://d1.awsstatic.com/whitepapers/DevOps/running-containerized-microservices-on-aws.pdf

Oracle Argument 5: Does AWS Have a Problem with Scalability?

The next argument moves to the scalability argument.

> *"And finally, what happens when your AWS Database workload seriously gets big, as in TB's or PB's? Can you move your AWS Database on-premise? No, they are public-cloud only. What if you have governance requirements for the Database and can't run it on AWS as they don't have a location that's in-country? Well, don't have an option their either. So again, you become locked-in to AWS and as we know, the Database is probably the worst of lock-ins and where it resides is probably second. So choosing the right Database and location is probably the biggest IT decision being made."*

After spending a lot of time analyzing Oracle's arguments, This is a standard strategy by Oracle, which is to take one particular case study and to try to generalize from it and make it appear more significant than it is.

Yes, AWS is offering public cloud. Public cloud with security (as we covered in the VPC topic earlier in the book), but public cloud. Private cloud or hosting loses most of the advantages of the cloud. There is a great debate as to how much more of an advantage a private cloud is from merely being on premise. Therefore, this does not hold interest for AWS. AWS is interested in businesses, or sections of a business that can be scaled, and that is a public cloud. While Oracle is talking up its private cloud, AWS is building public cloud capabilities that it now appears that neither SAP nor Oracle, with all of their resources, are not able to replicate.

The reason is not a lack of financial resources, but because neither SAP nor Oracle has experience managing scaled multitenancy (of course, as SAP and Oracle have ex-AWS and ex-Google Cloud employees, specific employees do have that experience, but it was attained while at other companies). The experience of SAP and Oracle is replicating the same items at hundreds of thousands of accounts. That is implementing applications and databases in a job shop manner on-premises but in hundreds of thousands of customers. Imagine factories where factory workers (i.e., the consultants) were trying to make the production process as expensive as possible, and this would be a rough approximation of SAP and Oracle environments.

This is a primary reason why SAP and Oracle are so expensive, while both being immense companies they follow more of a job shop model rather than a mass production model. Everything from how software is sold to how it is installed is the same repeating model, which is inefficient.

As for Oracle's assertions of cloud lock in, is this really an argument Oracle should be making?

Oracle Argument 6: Does AWS Not Provide Sufficient Uptime?

Oracle has questioned these SLAs as is presented in the following quotation.

> *"AWS's SLAs, like those of most competitors (except Oracle Cloud), only guarantee uptime, not performance. The upfront fees paid to reserve EC2 instances are not taken into account in the calculation of the service credits.*

> *"Oracle Cloud SLAs cover these 3 key customer requirements:*

> *Availability SLA*

> *----------------*

> *Compute and Block Volume storage have external connectivity, and are available to run customer workloads >99.95% of the total customer provisioned time-Object Storage and FastConnect external connectivity, and are available to run customer workloads >99.9% of the total customer provisioned time*

> *Manageability SLA*

> *----------------*

> *APIs provided to create and manage IaaS services are available >99.9% of the time*

> *-not offered by any IaaS competitor today*

> *Performance SLA*

> *---------------*

> *Block storage, local NVMe storage, and cloud networks are delivering normally expected performance levels-SLA coverage for performance degradation providing service credits if disk or network performance drops below 99.9% of expected levels, not offered by any IaaS competitor today*

> *Enterprise SLAs Information*

> *https://cloud.oracle.com/en_US/iaas/sla*

> *Enterprise SLA Press Release*

https://www.oracle.com/corporate/pressrelease/oracle-iaas-sla-021218.html

Detailed Terms of Service

http://www.oracle.com/us/corporate/contracts/paas-iaas-pub-cld-srvs-pillar-1117-4021422.pdf

Expected levels is the level of performance that Oracle has documented. They all should be listed in here: http://www.oracle.com/us/corporate/contracts/paas-iaas-pub-cld-srvs-pillar-1117-4021422.pdf

Oracle is providing a true performance guarantee SLA which you cannot get with any other cloud vendor."

There is some important context to provide to these comments.

- Performance is adjusted elastically on AWS and Google Cloud. While there are frequent complaints about Oracle meetings its guarantees, this is not an issue with AWS and Google Cloud.

- The performance is known to move in lockstep with the chosen configuration of the AWS or Google Cloud service. Secondly, when and if Oracle does not meet its performance guarantee, the customer is forced into the support pathway, and Oracle does not offer customers well regarded or responsive support.

Oracle Argument 7: Is AWS Only Migrating Non Critical Databases?

Oracle has argued that the databases migrated to AWS aren't mission critical.

> *"So, sure, you can do test/dev and run small non critical Databases as many have been doing for years on VMWare. This is what AWS continues to report in their "XXK Successful Database migrations to AWS". But if you look at how many are true "Oracle Database" workloads, you will see that they are less than .1% of the total."*

AWS had $6.11 billion in revenue in the 2nd quarter of 2018 and is growing its revenues year over year at close to 50%. Does Oracle expect companies to believe that RDS is only for small and non-critical databases?

One customer we are aware of runs Oracle Database for EnterpriseOne on AWS. They have almost a terabyte of production data. They moved off of Secure-24, a hosting provider, and are experiencing more uptime, better database response time, the better overall response time from WebLogic servers on AWS. This is not an isolated story; there are many stories like this.

Oracle has a long-term history of discounting every other offering in the market and no matter Oracle's position; Oracle is the best possible option, the only problem, according to Oracle, is people just don't "understand" how great the Oracle option is.

There usually are two positions that you can hold in the eyes of someone from Oracle. One is a position that agrees with Oracle. The other is the position of idiots that questions any of Oracle's superiority.

Oracle Argument 8: If the Number of vCPUs or Virtual CPUs on Amazon EC2 or RDS is Reduced, The Licenses to be Purchased Should be the Total of CPUs that Could Have Been Used

This is completely false.

The number of licenses to be purchased is the number of CPUs that are running as observed by House of Brick.[293] Oracle is well known for merely asserting additional licenses are needed, and they lose nothing by making the assertion. It is the customer's job to figure out if Oracle is telling the truth.

---

293 http://houseofbrick.com/oops-they-did-it-again-debunking-oracles-claims-of-needing-to-license-prospective-events-in-the-cloud/

Oracle Argument 9: Is Replacing Oracle Databases Hard?

Oracle CEO, Mark Hurd told analysts that he felt very safe from database replacement in Oracle customers. And he gave a specific reason related to the history of databases.

> *"The third largest database in the world is IBM DB2, and it's been going out of business for 20 years," Hurd said in a characterization that IBM (IBM, -0.64%) would dispute. "If it was so easy to replace databases, DB2 market share would be zero."*

> *"That is because most databases—which companies rely on as the basis for core accounting and financial operations—run custom programming, which is hard to move."[294]*

Mark Hurd should not feel so comfortable. This is because there are very important differences between IBM DB2 and the options available in AWS and Google Cloud.

1. The past 20 years did not have the cloud options that we have today or the number of open source databases that we have today. For decades Oracle and IBM could say the open source alternatives were not ready for the "big time." But not anymore. It is increasingly difficult for this assertion to be made and to be accepted.

2. RDS and Cloud SQL offers cloud migration and testing and the ability to bring up and close down instances without committing to hardware.

Therefore, while it is true, there is "stickiness" in databases, with the most substantial sticky factor being application certification. However, the growth of AWS is undeniable. Companies are migrating; Oracle is going to lose a lot of business because of these cloud alternatives combined with open source alternatives. And we predict customers will be the winners.

---

294 http://fortune.com/2017/04/12/mark-hurd-oracle-data-centers/

Oracle Argument 10: Can Oracle Compete with AWS and Google Cloud With Far Fewer Data Centers?

Oracle has needed to cover up for the inconsistency of their statements around their dedication to the cloud versus their relatively small investment in data centers. For context, while the aggregate spending of AWS, Google Cloud and Azure were $31 billion in 2016, Oracle's was only **$1.7 billion**.

Mark Hurd, CEO of Oracle addressed this issue in the following quotation.

> *"We try not to get into this capital expenditure discussion. It's an interesting thesis that whoever has the most capex wins," Hurd said in response to a question from Fortune at a Boston event on Tuesday. "If I have two-times faster computers, I don't need us many data centers. If I can speed up the database, maybe I need one fourth as may data centers. I can go on and on about how tech drives this.*
>
> *Oracle has said it runs its data centers on Oracle Exadata servers, which are turbocharged machines that differ fundamentally from the bare-bones servers that other public cloud providers deploy by the hundreds of thousands in what is called a scale-out model. The idea is that when a server or two among the thousands fail—as they will—the jobs get routed to still-working machines. It's about designing applications that are easily redeployed."[295]*

Mark Hurd is not interested in getting in any discussion where the facts are obviously against his position. And why are discussions around CAPEX, or Oracle's measured investment off limits?

Is there some taboo about discussing questions of investment?

One has to wonder about the honesty of a person who when confronted with a very reasonable question which goes directly to the storyline being proposed by Oracle (that they are competing on their data center investments), states they are "not interested in getting in a discussion" around that topic.

The underinvestment on the part of Oracle contrasts with AWS which places three locations or data center into any region it enters. This is to allow for redundancy in the region. Using

---

295 http://fortune.com/2017/04/12/mark-hurd-oracle-data-centers/

Exadata servers at one location does not resolve that issue.[296] As per Oracle's explanation of its cloud posted as of October 19, 2018, Oracle only has 4 regions worldwide. These are Phoenix, Ashburn, London and Frankfurt.[297] That small number of regions naturally increases the distance to consumers of the services and is far behind AWS and Google Cloud. That means more network latency, and it is not something that will be addressed by Mark Hurd's statements about Exadata, even if it were true.

The truth is that Oracle isn't investing much into the cloud. Oracle has leased data centers that rely on the Internet instead of dedicated fiber to communicate.

- Oracle has followed monopolistic practices through continual acquisition. However, there is a problem with Oracle extending this strategy to the cloud.

- The acquisition approach doesn't work in the cloud. Thus, Oracle's approach has been to play defense and delay cloud adoption in its install base as much as possible. This is for instance by raising database license costs for running on AWS/Azure, pushing hard for on-premise deployments of its own hardware, limiting choice by refusing to license the database for Google and IBM.

Hiding their cloud revenue in June of 2018 and changing how they reported cloud revenue was a striking indicator for a company that had to cover for previous cloud projections that have not come true. It also triggered many analysts to question what Oracle was hiding. Last year, Google, Microsoft, and Amazon each spent more than 10 billion dollars on data centers each. How did Oracle spend its money? **On $12 billion buying back its own shares.** A better translation for Mark Hurd's comments is that he does not need as much investment into data centers, when he can use that same money to buy back stock. Curiously, when discussing CAPEX, Mark Hurd left out how much stock Oracle repurchased that year. This highlights just one example of how Oracle is managed for the short-term financial benefits of its top executives. Much like SAP, Oracle prefers not to make investments that they need to make to match the claims made by their marketing department.

Furthermore, this statement was made by Mark Hurd in April of 2017. But notice Mark Hurd's statement on February 2018?

> *"The Redwood City, Calif., company said in February it planned to quadruple the number of giant data-center complexes over the next two years, taking on the market's biggest spenders: Amazon.com Inc., Microsoft Corp. and Alphabet Inc.'s Google."*[298]

---

296 https://perspectives.mvdirona.com/2017/04/how-many-data-centers-needed-world-wide/
297 https://www.youtube.com/watch?v=CgBtKvSWKKY
298 https://www.wsj.com/articles/oracle-results-beat-revenue-and-earnings-targets-1529444704

Why would Oracle need to do this? Remember, according to Mark Hurd, Oracle's faster servers and databases should allow it to compete with AWS, Google Cloud and AWS with a far smaller investment. Wasn't that the story in April of 2017? Alternatively, perhaps does using Exadata servers with the Oracle database not help overcome Oracle's lack of cloud investment?

But even if Oracle's investments were where they needed to be, there is no evidence that they would be able to do what AWS and Google Cloud are able to do with their investments. That is every dollar that Oracle spends on cloud infrastructure would not be as effective as a dollar spend on AWS or Google Cloud infrastructure. Therefore, the argument is the exact opposite of the one proposed by Mark Hurd regarding comparative CAPEX. To match AWS or Google Cloud, Oracle would need to significantly exceed AWS or Google Cloud's CAPEX.

This is explained in the following quotation.

> *"The exact number of servers in Google's arsenal is "irrelevant," Garfinkel says. "Anybody can buy a lot of servers. The real point is that they have developed software and management techniques for managing large numbers of commodity systems, as opposed to the fundamentally different route Microsoft and Yahoo went.*
>
> *Of particular interest to CIOs is one widely cited estimate that Google enjoys a 3-to-1 price-performance advantage over its competitors—that is, that its competitors spend $3 for every $1 Google spends to deliver a comparable amount of computing power. This comes from a paper Google engineers published in 2003, comparing the cost of an eight-processor server with that of a rack of 176 two-processor servers that delivers 22 times more processor power and three times as much memory for a third of the cost.*
>
> *But although Google executives often claim to enjoy a price-performance advantage over their competitors, the company doesn't necessarily claim that it's a 3-to-1 difference. The numbers in the 2003 paper were based on a hypothetical comparison, not actual benchmarks versus competitors, according to Google. Microsoft and Yahoo have also had a few years to react with their own cost-cutting moves."[299]*

AWS and Google Cloud can get scale economies with their investment that is difficult for other IT companies, even giants like SAP, Oracle, and Microsoft to match. That is scale economies running server farms specifically. Again, SAP and Oracle began their lives as vendors, selling software, not running software. This gives them a huge advantage over vendors like SAP and Oracle that are in business to sell software and outsource implementation to someone else.

---

299 http://www.baselinemag.com/c/a/Infrastructure/How-Google-Works-1/6

Conclusion

The technical arguments advanced by Oracle are much like the arguments they advance for why they are owed more money on software licenses. Oracle's culture is to try any argument to see if it works. Oracle want to find any reason for customers to move to Oracle Cloud and they can't. First, they claimed their infrastructure was new, and AWS's was old. Then they claimed that their database was fast, so they don't need as many locations. A year later, they announced a bunch of new locations, illustrating that their earlier arguments were nothing but a ruse to trick Wall Street. Then they turned to bare metal for performance advantages and talked about the noisy neighbor problems in public cloud. AWS responded with dedicated instances then dedicated hosts both virtual and bare metal.

Oracle's act of making up arguments that consume time in analyzing is getting a bit old.

Chapter 11: Responding to SAP Arguments

SAP consulting partners usually will only know how to repeat the arguments that come from SAP. An SAP consulting partners intends to denigrate both the other systems used by a customer and to promote SAP Cloud. This is true even though very few SAP consultants use SAP Cloud. In the mind of the SAP consulting partners, SAP works best when 100% SAP is used. The use of SAP applications, SAP databases, SAP infrastructure, SAP development tools is strictly supported, without ever needing to justify usage. In the mind of SAP and SAP consultants, any lack of ability of SAP's applications to meet requirements can be attributed to either a lack of business process re-engineering or to custom coding in SAP, using SAP development tools and SAP's proprietary coding language. It is the preferred strategy to recode any "legacy" application used by the customer into SAP.

SAP's Connection to IaaS Providers

SAP has made accommodations for non-SAP IaaS. One can use SAP on AWS, Google Cloud and Azure. We covered the topic in SAP's Multicloud Announcement.[300]

---

300 http://www.brightworkr.com/sap/2017/05/best-understand-saps-multicloud-announcement/

SUSE Linux Enterprise Server for SAP Applications 12 SP3

★★★★★ (0) | Version v20180814 | Sold by Amazon Web Services

Starting from **$0.43/hr** or from **$1,118.00/yr** (up to 70% savings) for software + AWS usage fees

SUSE Linux Enterprise Server for SAP Applications is the one solution that meets your needs for SAP applications and HANA databases in the Amazon cloud. In addition to the...

Linux/Unix, SUSE 12 SP3 - 64-bit Amazon Machine Image (AMI)

SAP HANA One

★★★★★ (20) | Version Rev 122.60.0 | Sold by SAP Inc (CAE)

Starting from **$0.99** to **$0.99/hr** for software + AWS usage fees

This is a production-ready, upgradable to latest HANA SPS version (by Addon), single-tenant configured SAP HANA database instance. Perform real-time analysis, develop and...

Linux/Unix, SUSE Linux Enterprise Server 11 SP 4 - 64-bit Amazon Machine Image (AMI)

SAP HANA One 244GB

★★★★★ (3) | Version Rev 122.244.0 | Sold by SAP Inc (CAE)

Starting from **$3.99** to **$3.99/hr** for software + AWS usage fees

This is a production-ready, upgradable to latest HANA SPS version (by Addon), single-tenant configured SAP HANA database instance. Perform real-time analysis, develop and...

As of this book's publication, there are 92 SAP related items available on the AWS Marketplace. This is however misleading as many are slightly different versions of the same basic thing. Most of the offerings are either HANA or the Adaptive Server Enterprise. The Adaptive Server Enterprise is one of the most confusingly named products, and it is a database. It was renamed from the Sybase DB, which SAP acquired.[301]

---

301 https://en.wikipedia.org/wiki/Adaptive_Server_Enterprise

The Real Point of Offering HANA and Adaptive Server Enterprise on AWS

Looking at the HANA offerings, they appear to be more out on AWS for marketing purposes or that is more specifically to get traction for these products and exposure rather than serious usage. The problem is that SAP's databases are not competitive versus the other items AWS offers.

If we take the HANA database, it is a problematic database both from the perspective of cost and maintenance overhead. If HANA is used with all manner of liabilities, both technical as well as license/legal, as we covered in the article The HANA Police and Indirect Access Charges.[302] SAP is offering license-free versions for developers to work with, once a company tries to activate it for production, the costs will dramatically rise, and then they will run into other limitations such as HANA's limitations in clustering.

This is how SAP "boobie traps" its AWS offerings. Furthermore, HANA is a way for SAP to take over the data layer at companies, proposing that every database that touches HANA must either be HANA or must pay extra fees to SAP.

It is true that there are limitations in running SAP on AWS and Google Cloud. However, the problem is that SAP resources are not a good source of information on this topic, as they are told by SAP that the objective is to get customers to adopt the SAP Cloud, as it is standard. This is particularly true if the SAP consultant works for a company that is a partner with SAP. As we cover in the article How to Best Understand the Pitfalls of Vendor Partnerships with SAP, consulting companies that are SAP partners lack any autonomy from SAP.[303]

Conclusion

The best way to handle SAP's objections that customers should access the SAP Cloud instead of alternatives is by having the real story about how SAP setup their cloud to work against their customer's interests, and to reinforce SAP's account control.

The information provided to customers about both SAP Cloud and AWS and Google Cloud is unreliable. SAP allows customers to access AWS, Google Cloud and Azure, but not in a way that makes any sense to use SAP Cloud. We can see no justification for using SAP Cloud when customers can open AWS and Google Cloud accounts and access so many more options and without SAP's exorbitant markup. If customers use SAP or SAP consultants

302 http://www.brightworkr.com/saphana/2017/02/07/hana-police-indirect-access-charges/
303 http://www.brightworkr.com/sap/2017/09/best-understand-pitfalls-vendor-partnerships-sap/

to consult on the cloud, it will lead to inferior outcomes. First, SAP has no idea what they are talking about when it comes to cloud, and second, all advice will lead right back into the clutches of SAP. SAP is also struggling with how to jam as much of their investments into on-premises technologies in the cloud context. ABAP is a perfect example of this, but there are many others. The SAP consulting firms are incentivized to redirect any customer questions about cloud back to SAP Cloud, which a non-starter as far as all three of the authors of this book are concerned. Those customers looking for advice on how to leverage AWS or Google Cloud (that is real cloud) for their SAP environment need to find advisors who are not SAP partners.

Chapter 12: The Hybrid Cloud: AWS for On Premises with VMware Cloud for AWS and AWS Services for On Premises

AWS is becoming increasingly popular, but until very recently there was an extra hurdle if you wanted to introduce AWS into your on-premises environment. And most of the infrastructure globally is by far on-premises. There are an enormous number of virtual machine or VMware instances on corporate data centers and on-premises virtualizations is one of the ways that allow companies to leverage the cloud.

The advantages of using VMware include the following:

1. *"Cost Reduction: While most, if not all, of the remaining advantages, also contain the potential for cost savings, this deserves a mention of its own. Direct cost reductions come in the form of server consolidation, and operational efficiencies that are not available otherwise.*

2. *Optimize Licenses: Oracle and SQL Server are two prime examples of RDBMS products that license according to underlying hardware specifications. By optimizing the hardware, we can reduce the license footprint, while still gaining the other advantages listed here.*

3. *High Availability: HA solutions for Oracle and SQL Server databases are complex, costly, difficult to maintain, or altogether non-existent. VMware provides a lower cost, yet highly effective HA solution that is optimal for many workloads.*

4. *Recoverability: If your DR solution is for the database only, you are missing out on DR coverage for the rest of the application stack required to make that database work. VMware encapsulates the application stack and, when coupled with proper configuration and testing of replication, provides as close to perfect recoverability as any solution can get.*

5. *Development Process: Developers need systems and data that are like production in every way possible. When they get quick access to production-like development environments, development time is reduced, and features are more robust on release.*

6. *Test/QA: The optimum environment to test on is production itself. That can be risky, however, since the production system needs to keep your organization running. VMware allows you to provide an exact copy of the production environment to the Test/QA team without impacting your critical systems.*

7. *Deployment Flexibility: Do you want to move your database workload from one licensed server to another? Do you want the advantages of a private, hybrid, or public cloud environment? Do you want to create live datacenters that are thousands of miles apart, and be able to swing back and forth between them? VMware virtualization, coupled with stretch storage solutions from EMC can facilitate these options.*

8. *Security: Not only does VMware create a minimalized attack profile with its small footprint hypervisor, but also advanced security features like Trusted Execution Technology from Intel allow virtual machines to validate security down to the chip level."[304]*

As we discussed in the book there are many changes afoot with these on premises VMs.

1. The number of VMs is being reduced as containers are becoming more prevalent, and containers reduce the need for as many VMs. This reduces "VM bloat," and has the positive consequence of increasing server capacity due to the lower hardware overhead of containers.

2. VMs are increasingly ported between on-premises and cloud, whereas in the past they stayed on premises. This trend intersects with containers, as containers are more portable than VMs.

---

304 http://houseofbrick.com/wp-content/uploads/2016/08/2016_HoB_RDBMS_Licensing-White-Paper.pdf

AWS, Google Cloud and Azure are based on Linux LXC, which is an operating system based containerization.[305] [306] [307] [308] A major contributor of containerization code to the Linux kernel was Google.[309]

Yes, you heard it right.

Microsoft Azure works on Linux! All clouds based on virtualization and every single server works as an application server. That is a SQL database, NoSQL database, video broadcaster and anything else. Cloud providers assign specific **instances to servers** in proportion to the resources they demand.

And here is the problem. Virtualization or containerization is not applicable to SAP. Most of SAP's products require their own server. The only choice is the physical location of such server (cloud or on-premise).

This is why SAP's inclusion of VMs and containers in the SAP Cloud are more of brochureware than anything serious that customers will end up leveraging.

And again, those VMs and containers are actually on AWS, Google Cloud or Azure with SAP not offering a PaaS and not doing much more than marking up AWS, Google Cloud and Azure services by in many cases a factor of ten (as we covered earlier in the book).

Curiously, while VMware created great opportunities for infrastructure efficiency, because of the adoption of far lower quality infrastructure tools that are proposed to IT departments as "standard" SAP environments suffer from deep inefficiencies. On SAP projects the client always tells us to make changes in their development system or their quality system. However, once we begin using the development system or their quality system, we find that the systems are useless because **they are not maintained.**

305 https://en.wikipedia.org/wiki/LXC
306 https://en.wikipedia.org/wiki/Operating-system-level_virtualization
307 Linux LXC *"First introduced in 2008, LXC adopted much of its functionality from the Solaris Containers (or Solaris Zones) and FreeBSD jails that preceded it."* - https://www.linuxjournal.com/content/everything-you-need-know-about-linux-containers-part-ii-working-linux-containers-lxc
308 Prior to this point in the book we spent a lot of time covering containers. The following quote explains the strong relationship between containers and virtual machines. *"Virtualization is not independent of container technology. VMware, for example, has developed a platform that uses virtual machines to insulate containers. Photon OS, as it's now called, will serve as the agent that gives VMware's vSphere management system visibility into the operations inside containers. from containers that don't include it. It is an alternative platform to vSphere. This new Photon Platform, as VMware has dubbed it, is intended for "cloud-native" containers only — for data centers intending to deliver intends to be established."* - The New Stack: The Docker and Containers Ecosystem eBook Series
309 https://www.amazon.com/Docker-Deep-Dive-Nigel-Poulton-ebook/dp/B01LXWQUF

On SAP projects it is widespread for all of the boxes are years out of synch with each other. If VMware were being used and used correctly, these old instances would be blown away and replaced by recent copies of production. However, only some SAP components, like the SAP APO optimizer, can be placed on virtualization. This means that SAP projects it is commonly thought that a full system refresh is not possible, and instead, it seems these SAP environments are using some SAP tool to do a "system copy."

The system copy tool that is used by recommended by SAP. And the outcome of this system copy tool? The result is all of the boxes on SAP accounts are far out of date with production, and asking for a recent copy is like asking for the moon. As we have been told on SAP projects…

> *"It would be nice to make a complete duplicate of an SAP box, but it is not possible."*

This is odd because, on projects where SAP infrastructure tools are not used, this is commonplace. A new image can be made in less than an hour, yet for SAP customers controlled by the SAP paradigm, doing it is something that is planned for weeks. For some strange reason, the SAP System Copy tool works within SAP.

Why would that make any sense?

VMware copies the entire stack. SAP promotes customers to use SAP software over all other non-SAP software because the SAP software is "standard." VMware is not standard. If SAP System Copy is the official tool for SAP, then according to SAP consulting firms, customers should implement it. After decades these SAP consulting companies and SAP "Platinum Consultants" will attest that the best course of action is to go 100% SAP. Anything can be critiqued as not SAP by stating "it is not standard SAP."

VMware benefits from being used by all environments and VMware as the company is the premier virtualization vendor in the world, and thus know and are capable of all manner of virtualization that SAP is not capable of performing. This gets into an infrastructure efficiency question around what is called SAP Basis. With Basis on SAP projects, everything seems to take so long and is so hidden. However, when one pops around AWS or Google Cloud, everything is right there, and one has transparency. The fact is that SAP infrastructure efficiency is very low. It is controlled by Basis resources which are used to the SAP ways of doing things.

There is a growing chorus of companies with on-premises environments would like to leverage AWS to at least some degree. In response to this, AWS introduced VMware Cloud on AWS.

VMware Cloud on AWS is a full VMware vSphere cloud that is deployed and runs on AWS. We have a screenshot below.

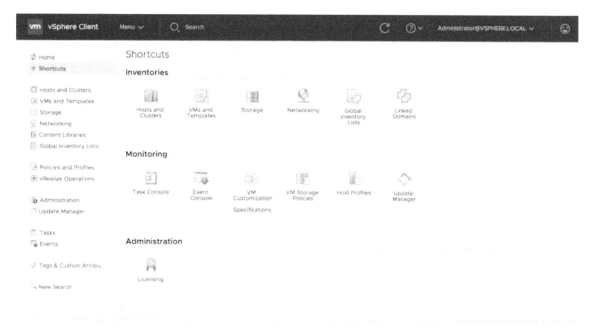

vSphere is VMware's environment for hybrid clouds. vSphere supports many different types of workloads. (3D graphics, big data, HPC, machine learning, in-memory, and cloud-native) vSphere has been around for years and is widely used. VMware Cloud for AWS is an extension of vSphere for AWS.

Using VMware Cloud for AWS allows for on-premises companies to leverage AWS more easily. This means that privately hosted VMware deployment in a data center. VMware Cloud for AWS brings AWS's Relational Database Service (RDS) to these corporate data center customers. This is designed to make the transition to the cloud more accessible to customers. All the standard databases apply. However, it also allows AWS Lambda, Simple Queue Service, S3, Elastic Load Balancing, DynamoDB, Redshift and much more.

This is a major development, as it simplifies the speed and simplicity of managing the migration to AWS.

How AWS Supports the Hybrid Cloud

AWS begin in the cloud, and for the longest time, the argument was between cloud providers like AWS and Google Cloud versus on premises. However, AWS's value proposition has begun to extend to on premises. Also, the natural connection is through the on-premises virtual machine.[310] This is a massive change in the value offered by AWS. When AWS extends its services into on premises, it is now leveraging its software and not offering its hardware. Hybrid cloud is when workloads and data reside in **both on-premises and the cloud.**

AWS has clearly targeted growth into the on-premises environment. The following are a few more examples:

1. AWS Firehose

2. AWS EC2 or Elastic Computer Cloud

3. AWS CodeDeploy

4. AWS Storage Gateway

5. CockroachRB/AWS RDS

Let us briefly get into each one.

AWS Firehose

AWS Firehose is used for hybrid environments to move the actual data to AWS. The VMWare Cloud on AWS provides a high-performance network through the Amazon Virtual Private Cloud (VPC).

AWS EC2 or Elastic Computer Cloud

EC2 or Elastic Compute Cloud's console can be used to manage on-premises instances. This means that a single console can provide a company of the full picture of what they are managing. It costs AWS very little to do this, but it makes even more likely that that customer will enable more AWS services.

AWS Storage Gateway

AWS Storage Gateway can be used for backup and archiving, disaster recovery, cloud data processing, storage tiering, and migration.

---

310 This quotation provide an important distinction on virtualization. *"It's important to note that virtualization environments typically lack key capabilities of cloud systems – such as self-service, multi-tenancy governance, and standardized instances."* - https://assets.rightscale.com/uploads/pdfs/Designing-Private-and-Hybrid-Clouds-White-Paper-by-RightScale.pdf

This is covered in the following quotation from AWS.

> *"The gateway connects to AWS storage services, such as Amazon S3, Amazon Glacier, and Amazon EBS, providing storage for files, volumes, and virtual tapes in AWS. The service includes a highly-optimized data transfer mechanism, with bandwidth management, automated network resilience, and efficient data transfer, along with a local cache for low-latency on-premises access to your most active data."[311]*

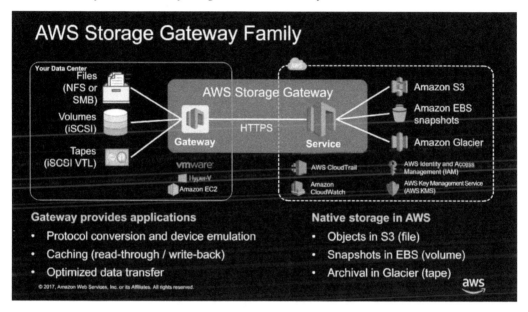

The AWS Storage Gateway works in conjunction with VMware of (as one example) on the on premises server. It then connects to the AWS SG service, which then enables the services on AWS.

AWS CodeDeploy

AWS CodeDeploy is a deployment service but not only to compute services such as Amazon EC2, AWS Lambda but also to on-premises servers.

This is covered in the following quotation.

> *"AWS CodeDeploy makes it easier for you to rapidly release new features, helps you avoid downtime during application deployment, and handles the complexity of updating your applications."[312]*

---

311 https://aws.amazon.com/storagegateway/
312 https://aws.amazon.com/codedeploy/

CockroachDB/AWS RDS

With multiple databases or database copies being deployed in various regions in the cloud and on-premises, several approaches have come forward to manage this issue.

For instance, both CockroachDB and Spanner are sold on the concept of "horizontal scalability." This is very different from vertical scalability, which is more commonly discussed and is how large a database can become without losing its initial performance characteristics.

Cloud Spanner: The best of the relational and non-relational worlds

	CLOUD SPANNER	TRADITIONAL RELATIONAL	TRADITIONAL NON-RELATIONAL
Schema	✓ **Yes**	✓ Yes	✗ No
SQL	✓ **Yes**	✓ Yes	✗ No
Consistency	✓ **Strong**	✓ Strong	✗ Eventual
Availability	✓ **High**	✗ Failover	✓ High
Scalability	✓ **Horizontal**	✗ Vertical	✓ Horizontal
Replication	✓ **Automatic**	⟳ Configurable	⟳ Configurable

How Cloud Spanner compares to other database categories (according to Google).[313]

Both AWS RDS and CockroachDB allows one copy of the database (called a node) to be on premises, with other nodes of the database to reside in the cloud, with the nodes kept in synch and therefore allowing full distribution of the database. A combination of nodes makes ups a cluster. AWS RDS and CockroachDB can be used on the public cloud or the private cloud, and hence is presented as also supporting hybrid clouds. The difference between the two approaches is that AWS RDS employs a master-slave model, where one database is the master and copies changes to the slave databases. CockroachDB operates under a design where all the nodes are equal.

---

313 https://cloud.google.com/spanner/

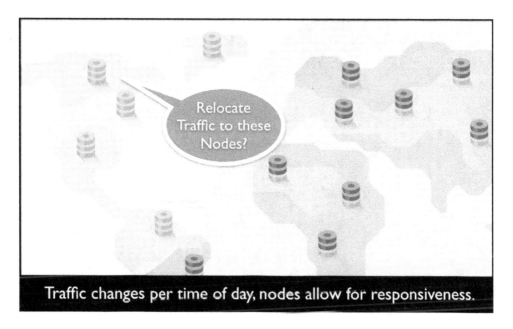

Traffic changes per time of day, nodes allow for responsiveness.

(Initial image from CockroachDB)

This places the node closest to the customer. For a company with an on-premises node, having a multi-node database like Cockroach DB in the cloud can serve users in regions of the world where the company has no data center. This has a meaningful impact on speed, and is a perfect example of one of the benefits of a hybrid cloud, even for companies that plan to keep their on-premises location or locations.

This "need for speed" is covered in the following quotation.

> *"This problem is compounded by the fact that latencies quickly become cumulative. If your SLAs allow for a 300ms round trip between an app and a database, that's great––but if the app needs to make multiple requests that cannot be run in parallel, it pays that 300ms latency for each request. Even if that math doesn't dominate your application's response times, you should account for customers who aren't near fiber connections or who live across an ocean: those 300ms could easily be 3000ms, causing requests to become agonizingly slow.*
>
> *If you need a gentle reminder as to why this matters for your business, Google and Amazon both have oft-cited studies showing the financial implications of latency. If your site or service is slow, people will take their attention and wallets elsewhere."*[314]

---

314 Scaling Databases with Multi Region Deployments, Cockroach Labs

Node failure?

- **Traditional RDBMS** goes down
- **NoSQL** risks inconsistency
- **CockroachDB** offers high availability & consistency

The big selling point of multi-node databases is both the ability to keep an application up during a failure of one of the nodes. After the failure, when the node that failed is brought back up, it is automatically synchronized with the other good nodes.[315]

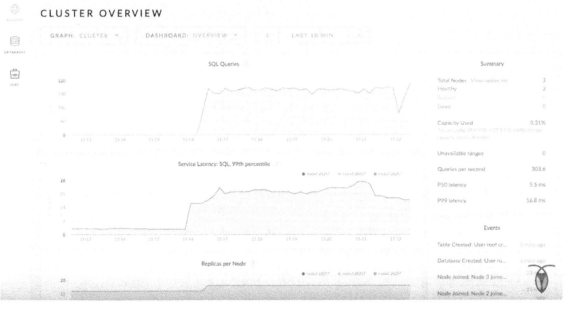

The example from the CockroachDB website shows a node as "suspect," in the upper right hand corner of the user interface. Of course with CockroachDB one (or more) of the nodes can be on premises.

---

315 https://www.cockroachlabs.com/docs/stable/

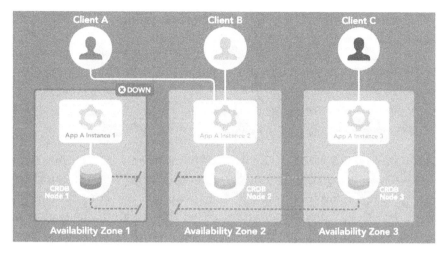

In addition, CockroachDB will allocate the traffic that would ordinarily be directed to Availability Zone 1 to Availability Zone 2. Client A is not directed back to Availability Zone 1 until the changed data from Node 2 and Node 3 (which would be kept in sync) is updated to Node 1.[316] This means the database is "inherently high availability." That is, no special configuration is necessary to make it high availability.

This is a simulation which shows how multiple nodes interact with one another.[317]

---

316 Building High Availability Services with CockroachDB, Cockroach Labs, Sean Loiselle
317 https://www.cockroachlabs.com/blog/database-evolution/

We have been discussing this in the context of database failure, but it applies to the overall availability zone as is covered in the following quotation.

> *"Individual datacenters and entire regions also fail, and many teams are caught by surprise when they do. To survive these kinds of failures, you should employ a strategy similar to the one you adapted for networking and availability zone failures: spreading your deployment to more geographies."*[318]

In addition to unplanned downtime, this works the same way for planned downtime. This improves the ability to bring down a node for maintenance, bring the node back up, and have CockroachDB takes care of all of this. For those that use DropBox and synch across multiple computers, the principle is similar. All of the copying and synchronizing takes place without the user worrying about how that is done. All the user sees that that (after a few minutes if the computer is recently turned on and connected to the WiFi) the files on another computer are the same as the files on the presently used computer.

Although CockroachDB/Spanner is one approach. AWS RDS has a different approach, which is explained in the following quotation.

> *"DB instances using Multi-AZ deployments may have increased write and commit latency compared to a Single-AZ deployment, due to the synchronous data replication that occurs. You may have a change in latency if your deployment fails over to the standby replica, although AWS is engineered with low-latency network connectivity between Availability Zones. For production workloads, we recommend that you use Provisioned IOPS and DB instance classes (m1.large and larger) that are optimized for Provisioned IOPS for fast, consistent performance."*[319]

SQL presents a fundamental problem to horizontally scaled databases. This is the fact that the data in the database has to be available on a single server. Without this, it will not be possible to perform JOIN requests. However, with the cloud, either standard or hybrid, there are multiple instances or nodes of duplicate databases. This is explained in the following quotation.

> *"Relational databases scale well, but usually only when that scaling happens on a single server node. When the capacity of that single node is reached, you need to scale out and distribute that load across multiple server nodes. This is when the complexity of relational databases starts to rub against their potential to scale. Try scaling to hundreds or thousands of nodes, rather than a few, and the complexities*

---

318 Building High Availability Services with CockroachDB, Cockroach Labs, Sean Loiselle
319 https://docs.aws.amazon.com/AmazonRDS/latest/UserGuide/Concepts.MultiAZ.html

become overwhelming, and the characteristics that make RDBMS so appealing drastically reduce their viability as platforms for large distributed systems."[320]

AWS RDS uses a master-slave copy scenario where one master is copied to the other slave nodes. CockroachRB, the open source versions of Google Cloud Spanner is, in theory, treats all of the nodes as if they are equal. AWS outlines the problem with this in the following quotation.

> *"In a Multi-AZ deployment, Amazon RDS automatically provisions and maintains a synchronous standby replica in a different Availability Zone. The primary DB instance is synchronously replicated across Availability Zones to a standby replica to provide data redundancy, eliminate I/O freezes, and minimize latency spikes during system backups. Running a DB instance with high availability can enhance availability during planned system maintenance, and help protect your databases against DB instance failure and Availability Zone disruption."*

The reason for this is there are have multiple master-servers, collisions of data will be unavoidable.

Also, performance on read/write will depend on the number of servers. With the master-slave design, that problem is eliminated. However, this means that the databases are not genuinely independent. They rely upon the master database. And the slave databases only provide read access, not write access.

Luckily, any database has about 5% of write requests and 95% of read requests. So, with the single master you provide a full server only for write requests. In the case where a change is made, that change sent to the master directly (that is bypassing the slave). This is considered far more robust than the CockroachDB approach of synchronizing multiple SQL databases.

---

320 https://readwrite.com/2009/02/12/is-the-relational-database-doomed/

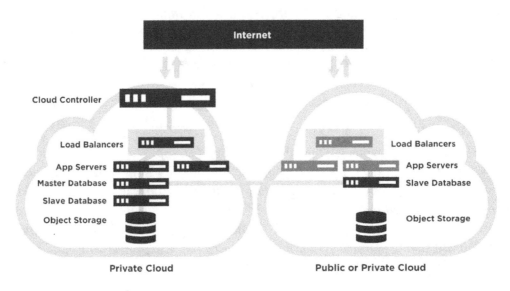

Figure 8 – Hybrid Cloud Warm Disaster Recovery Scenario

Notice in this graphic, displays the standard master-slave database model. What can be a Public Cloud contains the slave database, while the master stays in the Private Cloud which is normally on premises.[321]

Both approaches support a hybrid cloud. And many people think the AWS RDS/Cloud SQL approach is more practical, but this may change as technology continues to advance.[322] It should also be considered that this problem goes away if a NoSQL database is used. This is why NoSQL faster and have no problems with replications.

We know of many projects where NoSQL works like a real-time DB for application and then data in **parallel transformed into a SQL database**. For programmers NoSQL is more beneficial during run-time.

---

321 https://assets.rightscale.com/uploads/pdfs/Designing-Private-and-Hybrid-Clouds-White-Paper-by-RightScale.pdf

322 *"If you have a DB instance in a Single-AZ deployment and you modify it to be a Multi-AZ deployment (for engines other than SQL Server or Amazon Aurora), Amazon RDS takes several steps. First, Amazon RDS takes a snapshot of the primary DB instance from your deployment and then restores the snapshot into another Availability Zone. Amazon RDS then sets up synchronous replication between your primary DB instance and the new instance."* - https://docs.aws.amazon.com/AmazonRDS/latest/UserGuide/Concepts.MultiAZ.html

AWS & OpenStack and CloudStack

Up to this point, we have discussed using AWS services and software to control the on-premises environment. However, open source cloud management projects like OpenStack and CloudStack allow AWS to be accessed, as well as any on-premises resources. This ability to connect to any cloud and any on-premises resources from one UI is sometimes called a "single pane of glass."

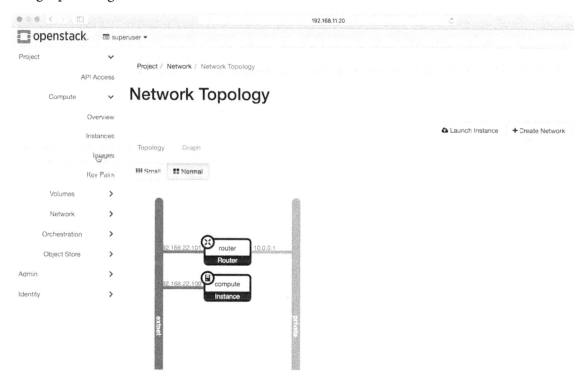

OpenStack is truly impressive. We recommend watching this specific video which shows how quickly things can be setup in OpenStack.[323]

OpenStack can control AWS, Google Cloud and other cloud resources, and it also runs on VMware, as explained by VMware.

> *"VMware Integrated OpenStack is a VMware supported OpenStack distribution that makes it easy to run an enterprise grade OpenStack cloud on top of VMware virtualization technologies. VMware Integrated OpenStack is ideal for many different use cases, including building a IaaS platform, providing standard,*

---

323 https://www.youtube.com/watch?v=pWFyFtGPVdA

OpenStack API access to developers, leveraging edge computing and deploying NFV services on OpenStack."[324]

What AWS's Hybrid Strategy is Pointed Towards

With AWS pushing into on-premises, this means that AWS is not only offering services that run on its infrastructure, but has extended its services to run on customer's infrastructure. Some have argued that IBM and Oracle have the advantage when it comes to offering hybrid cloud. This is due to IBM and Oracle already being on premises in their customer's accounts. However, neither of these companies demonstrate much of an intuitive understanding of the cloud. They do not offer the ease of use that AWS offers, and once you use AWS for on-premises, you can, of course, use AWS's cloud services.

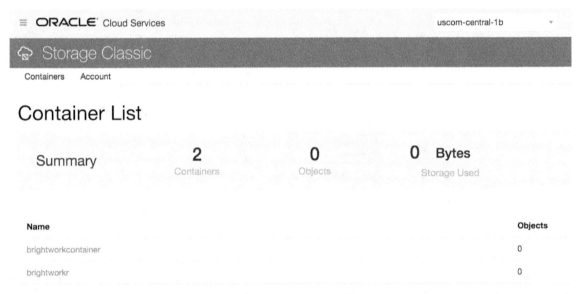

The Oracle Cloud appears to have similar issues to the SAP Cloud, as it shows low usability, indicating that like SAP, Oracle is getting little feedback as to what should be improved.

Oracle has had a long time to figure out the cloud, and they don't appear to be making progress. Oracle resources have continually told us to "try out the Oracle Cloud." We have. And we do not want to use it. We suggest Oracle resources that suggest using the Oracle Cloud try it for themselves first, before being frustrated when told it is not usable. One has to have the software to be part of the hybrid cloud future. AWS and Google Cloud do.

---

324 https://www.vmware.com/products/openstack.html

AWS offering for on premises is an attempt to put a "straw" into on-premises environments.

That is they will entice on-premises customers with free items (that cost AWS little to offer) that will make on-premises customer increasingly comfortable with the cloud. As time passes and as more AWS services are used, it will become increasingly difficult for these on-premises customers to justify investments into more on-premises overhead.

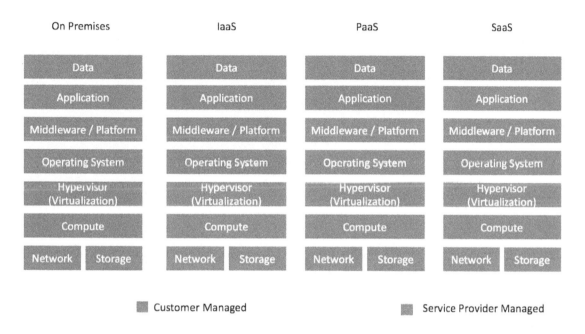

(Graphic from the book Hybrid Cloud for Architects: Build Hybrid Cloud Solutions Using AWS and OpenStack)[325]

This is the future desired state for IaaS providers. They see the hybrid cloud as an intermediate state to taking over the infrastructure of customers.

This is proposed by Elias Khnaser in the following quotation.

> *"The public cloud will host most workloads, and you will have just the most important things in the private cloud. So you are going to justify putting something in the private cloud versus putting something in the public cloud, as the prices fall as well."[326]*

---

325 https://www.amazon.com/Hybrid-Cloud-Architects-solutions-OpenStack-ebook/dp/B076H91F7Q/
326 https://www.youtube.com/watch?v=b9WQ4Fms-Ho

Their roadmap shows a large amount of collaboration to make the VMWare Cloud on AWS a success.[327]

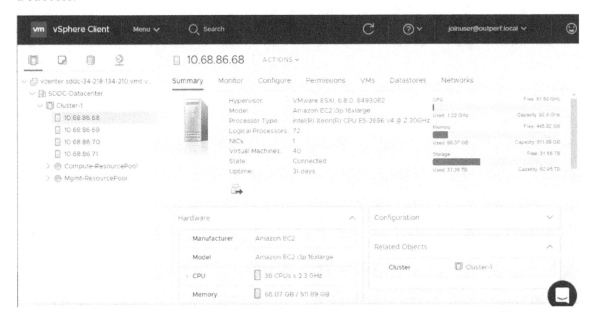

The caveat explained by House of Brick is that there may be restrictions and may require a legal review by each Oracle customer planning on leveraging this new offering due to licensing restrictions.[328]

> *"From these indications, it seems like a strong possibility that the VMware Cloud on AWS is in compliance with the requirements of the Licensing Oracle Software in the Cloud Computing Environment document published by Oracle. We will be doing more internal analysis of this possibility, as well as consulting with our legal partners, and the legal teams of the clients we are working with. Once we feel confident in making a more definitive statement, we will do so at that time." –* ***House of Brick Technologies***

Conclusion

VMware Cloud for AWS is a may of melding on-premises environments with AWS. This will improve SAP, and Oracle environments as VMware Cloud for AWS can serve as a "straw" into these on-premises environments that not only provides access to AWS services but

327 https://cloud.vmware.com/vmc-aws/roadmap

328 http://houseofbrick.com/running-oracle-in-a-public-or-hybrid-cloud/

allows AWS services to be used to manage on-premises resources. The overall announcement of VMware Cloud For AWS is a recently announced product as per the time of this book's publication and is something whose full effect has yet to be discovered.

VMware Cloud for AWS fits directly into the hybrid cloud, which is how different clouds and on-premises environments interact with one another. Also, we addressed the topics of OpenStack and CloudStack which allow the control of not only AWS but provide a single pane of glass on all resources (cloud and on-premises). AWS's clear intent is to manage more and more of customer's overall stack. Currently, AWS has the bulk of their services towards the bottom of the stack (Network, Storage, Computer, Virtualization, and Operating System) but it is clear they will increase their top of the stack services in the future.

Chapter 13: Case Studies

In this chapter we will go through the case studies we were able to obtain related to the use of cloud services.

Case Study #1: Migrating Our Brightwork Explorer Application to AWS

Brightwork Research & Analysis recently engaged in a development effort to create an application that could help companies monetize forecast error (rather than using the typical forecast error measurements) and which calculated parameters for MRP systems.

The software addresses two basic problems.

1. Forecast accuracy measurements are often not performed in companies in a way that enables the company to focus on what to improve, and the forecast error measurements used usually are too abstract and divorced from the financial impact can end up with the wrong items receiving the emphasis for forecasting improvement.

2. In all the cases that we have seen over decades of working with MRP systems, they have had poorly optimized parameters (things like safety stock, reorder point and economic order quantity) MRP systems (usually executed within ERP systems) do not have good ways of managing these parameters.

We consider the application that was developed to be a "Jiffy Lube" for forecasting and supply planning systems, allowing for an external analysis in a flexible tool, that then can provide values that help those supply planning and demand planning systems to work better.

Because of our background in SAP, the Brightwork Explorer was first targeted towards companies that ran SAP ERP or SAP advanced planning tools. But the application is vendor neutral as all systems regardless of the vendor use similar inputs that are calculated by the

Brightwork Explorer. At this point, we were relying on CSV file import and export and were considering an interface to a particular application as a future development.

We named this application the Brightwork Explorer, and we thought it would be instructive to describe our experience in migrating our application to AWS.

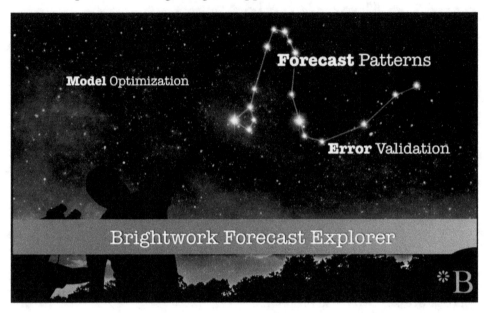

What the application does is less important in this story than how we decided to leverage AWS.

The Development of the Brightwork Explorer

We began the development of the Brightwork Explorer locally. The development occurred over video conferences with the coding performed in real time from interaction with the designer and business process owner with the developer logged into and coding on the designer and business process owner's computer, and with some of the work performed by the developer on his computer. After the application was ready to be shared with users, the development was migrated to AWS. We chose PostgreSQL as our database and S3 to store upload files. We also started with a small server configuration to begin, as we would be breaking the application in with a small number of customers and even beginning with smaller test files.

Important Benefits from Using AWS for Our Application

There were a few critical business models that we decided to follow was to offer a cloud application.

This had three important benefits.

1. *Lower Barrier to Implementation*: We would never have to worry about getting a customer to implement our software on their server. They would **not have to buy** the software, but could first test it to see if it was **a fit for their needs**. This allowed us to make the software available to far more customers.

2. *Upgradeability and Reduced Maintenance Overhead*: We planned to make many upgrades to the software, particularly in the first year, and would never have to worry about previous versions of our software "floating around" eating up maintenance efforts and we could make our changes directly to our multi-tenant application.

3. *Accessibility*: We could directly access any client's data so that we could provide support. This significantly reduced our overhead. This was also true for companies that used the software. The Brightwork Explorer creates simulation versions, and those simulation versions can be shared among various users within one company.

Brightwork MRP & S&OP Explorer

| Basic Options | | Intro | Forecast Accuracy | Inventory Calculation | Stock Breakdown | Constraints | Costs | Reference | | Export |

Inventory Calculation

Show 10 entries   Search:

	Sku	Whse	Service Level Code	Lead Time As A % Of A Month	Average Late Lead Time Variability	Safety Stock	Total Days Supply Stock	Total Average Stock	EOQ Or EPQ	Production Or Procurement Orders Per Month	Reorder Point
0	98804	AL04	A	0.13	0.27	59.31		59.38	0.24	4.49	13.19
1	98804	AZ17	A	0.13	0.85	78.56		83.24	1.06	66.38	27.63
2	98804	CA05	A	0.77	0.70	49.66		73.59	1.87	33.43	64.02
3	98804	CA20	A	0.13	2.20	43.49		50.77	1.43	76.53	25.71
4	98804	CO11	B	0.20	0.60	6.94		12.37	0.97	55.88	11.28
5	98804	FL14	B	0.60	1.94	34.39		42.86	0.90	31.40	18.46
6	98804	FL16	B	0.27	0.73	45.82		50.69	6.01	6.09	11.54
7	98804	FL19	B	0.13	1.40	4.72		6.32	5.44	4.42	3.43
8	98804	FL29	C	0.73	1.24	278.10		284.86	8.81	2.09	13.51
9	98804	FL45	C	0.78	0.58	309.18		334.17	20.96	3.41	49.99

Showing 1 to 10 of 18 entries   Previous 1 2 Next

product_A_service_level	0.9
product_B_service_level	0.85
product_C_service_level	0.8
product_D_service_level	0.75
product_E_service_level	0.7
product_F_service_level	0.65

Summary

Total Inventory Dollars	$2,129,487
Total Cost to Carry	$532,372
Total Order Cost	$3,704
Total Planned Profit	$811,307
Total Pallet spots	94.70
Total Labor Consumption	4,735.15

Each time a combination of settings is saved in the Brightwork Explorer, it is saved as a simulation. This is a combination of settings that results in an aggregate number of values for inventory, costs, profits, pallet spot consumption, and several other critical items. The application allows simulations to be saved so others can review them.

After we decided on the cloud, AWS was the natural choice for us. This is the configuration we leveraged for the Brightwork Explorer. Those were the initial reasons for moving the Brightwork Explorer to AWS. However, for our purposes, we could have also used Google, but our developer for the Brightwork Explorer was more familiar with AWS, having used AWS for several applications in the past.

How Did the Brightwork Explorer on AWS Work in Practice?

All of these beginning reasons turned out to be true, once we deployed the application we received extra benefits that we did not list above.

Easy Collaboration With Our Developer

We are not in the same country as our developer, so AWS became a shared space for us to collaborate.

- As it is our application, we controlled our AWS account and paid the AWS billing, but provided our developer with an account.

- If we needed another developer to add something, we could create a new account for them to allow them access.

- We had several types of collaboration. One was the collaboration with our customers. This was feedback provided by using the Brightwork Explorer application.

- From this feedback, we determined what changes we need to be made.

- We were testing a new application and "guinea pigging" our first customers (and telling them this, and not charging them for accessing the application in its early state).

One of the areas of change that we needed was the ability to delete simulations. We told the developer to make this change at 12:00 PM and the change was applied, along with a second change related to date management at 2:02 PM the changes had been made. We refreshed the screen, and we were able to access the changes. There was no downtime.

Scalability

The second area of benefit from using AWS was scalability. We were going to be initially testing the software with just a few companies. Therefore, there was little need to pay very much for a higher performance and volume system on AWS because of the limited use.

- So we kept our costs low in the beginning.

- We will be able to scale the Brightwork Explorer to any size as new customers come on board.

- This also allowed us to test the response from the market with minimal financial investment.

Conclusion on This AWS Case Study Experience

From multiple dimensions, we were quite pleased with our experience in setting up our application on AWS or Google Cloud.

- Previously the Brightwork Explorer had been in a series of R and Python scripts that we ran on projects. And without a reasonably easy way to deliver the business logic through something like AWS or Google Cloud, we most likely would have **never developed** the application.

- The effort involved maintaining such an application would have been overwhelming, and the Brightwork Explorer is only one of the things we work on, so we could not having it consume that much of our time. Indeed, if we had to distribute on-premises versions of the Brightwork Explorer, we would have lost interest in investing in the application and commercializing it for broader distribution for what we think is an essential calculation for forecasting and supply planning systems.

Overall, we are quite pleased with our AWS experience. It is a small application and certainly not an example of anything that leveraged advanced features of AWS, but it allows us to get our requirements met quickly and to begin deploying to anywhere. While reviewing an AWS document on migration, we found the following quotations.

> *"Democratize advanced technologies: Technologies that are difficult to implement can become easier to consume by pushing that knowledge and complexity into the cloud vendor's domain. Rather than having your IT team learn how to host and run a new technology, they can simply consume it as a service. For example, NoSQL databases, media transcoding, and machine learning are all technologies that require expertise that is not evenly dispersed across the technical community. In the cloud, these technologies become services that your team can consume while focusing on product development rather than resource provisioning and management.*
>
> *Go global in minutes: Easily deploy your system in multiple Regions around the world with just a few clicks. This allows you to provide lower latency and a better experience for your customers at minimal cost."*

We found both of these proposals to be true of our implementation on AWS.

Case Study #2: Real Time MRP: Setting Up MRP in AWS

At one particular FMCG manufacturer, a make to order model was followed. In make to order the purchase order for inbound materials comes after the sales order is received. During the implementation of SAP ERP it becomes obvious enough that standard functionality will not fit requirements and contradicts to scope that was sold to the customer.

This company assumed immediate confirmation of incoming orders when the sales manager has to be able to confirm the exact order specification with the exact nearest delivery date. This was viewed as too stringent of a requirement by the consulting firm, but all attempts of the consulting firm to persuade the customer to change the business requirements didn't succeed. The core problem the company faced was the absence of functionality that could answer how many of product A could be produced in the future. The standard approach was to follow the following path:

- Create Sales Order → Run MRP → Capacity Planning for PP Order → Run MRP for Components

To execute these steps, each sales manager required up to 30-40 minutes. It also had the negative consequence that it required the constant involvement of plant managers to perform capacity planning. After every phone call, a sales manager was not able to take the next phone call until all MRP runs were complete. Therefore, during the day the manager was able to handle only 15-16 phone calls, and due to the low number of calls per manager versus the total number of calls necessary to meet demand, the company did not have enough managers to handle the capacity.

Another problem was in related to concurrency. That is while the first sales manager would run through all of their steps, the second manager was not able to start their MRP routine, This was due to shared raw materials and plant capacity. Therefore the response time to every incoming client's call dramatically increased, which lead to customers being put on hold, and which further resulted in several of them turning to competitors to have their orders fulfilled.

The bottleneck was a combination of the MRP runtime, along with improved capacity planning. The company needed a real time MRP solution that had a maximum possible yield for every product for given time horizon. Taking in account that in standard ERP we had nothing to offer, and that ERP in SAP was quite cumbersome both in terms of the software design and limited to the on premises hardware.

The Custom MRP Solution Built on AWS

To work around the limitation of MRP as run in ERP, the decision was made to build a solution as a third-party web-service deployed in AWS. This MRP application was called Real Time MRP.

Once development started on Real Time MRP, the development team was able to leverage any AWS resource that they wanted. They decided on using the following AWS services.

- *AWS Elastic Beanstalk*: This provided easy to scale virtual machines. Two types were used: first – for web application content, second – for MRP calculation workers.

- *AWS Amazon MQ*: This provided a predefined message broker to manage statuses of products in real time (actual/in progress).

- *AWS DynamoDB*: This provided an extremely fast NoSQL database.

Getting the Data from SAP to AWS and Back

The integration between SAP and AWS was performed with the Brisk Data Pipeline. This is important because SAP is generally known as the most difficult vendor in which to integrate. Moreover, using SAP standard integration tools like SAP PI/PO are expensive and troublesome to use. Furthermore, while SAP has been pushing customers to the SAP Cloud and the SAP Cloud Platform Integration add-on component (which is part of the Custom App Professional Edition which runs between $4600 and $15,000 per month), there is little evidence of this component being used on SAP projects. And secondly, the overall SAP Cloud is a liability. The problem with all of SAP's integration solutions is the bottleneck is the server, and it is more logical to access AWS servers rather than rely upon SAP servers. This provides far better scaling, pipeline optimization as well as data reuse.

As with the SAP integration solutions the Brisk Data Pipeline also works on top of SAP JCo and C/C++ library. However, on the implementation, Brisk was used with a 100% programming approach. This is where all of the integration logic compiled to bytecode and produce zero overhead. Brisk also can work with any data cache, scale my servers horizontally or do whatever I want to do.

Below is code that provides REST API to real life SAP system from Amazon AWS t2.micro instance.

```
1   @RestController
2   public class MaterialMasterController {
3
4       @GetMapping("/material")
5       public BAPI_MATERIAL_GETALL getMaterial(@RequestParam String matnr){
6           BAPI_MATERIAL_GETALL input = new BAPI_MATERIAL_GETALL();
7           String normalized = ("000000000000000000" + matnr).substring(matnr.length());
8           input.setMATERIAL(normalized);
9
10          BapiJCoAdapter adapter = new BapiJCoAdapter(JCoEnvironmentSettings.getInstance());
11          return adapter.callBapi(input);
12      }
13  }
```

This is everything needed to write to open single API to SAP BAPI. It requires only a couple of hours or days through the Integration Framework to build integration part that easily *outperforms any SAP PI/PO implementations in 100-150 times while working on 7$ Amazon AWS server.*

Accessing Scalable and Specialized Hardware Resources

Because AWS was used, it meant the solution could be **easily** scaled. This means that as much capacity as was necessary could be allocated against the processing. And that furthermore the most appropriate type of processing capacity could be applied against the MRP run. That is versus using the ERP hardware at the on-premises location that was primarily sized for transaction processing rather than for MRP processing.

The performance improvements naturally expected to be good, and they ended up being quite impressive and allowed the MRP processing time meet the customer requirements.

- Overall, the response time was reduced from 30-40 minutes to a matter seconds. (Which should tell us something about how efficiently MRP was being processed in SAP.)

- The average data latency was between 200-230 milliseconds.

- Denis Myagkov developed the MRP logic. It was also not standard MRP logic, or anything like the MRP logic that is in SAP ERP. Denis was (and is) of the view that MRP logic needs to be customized per client. An identical MRP logic will nearly always need adjustments to meet customer requirements. Interestingly, nearly all MRP run from in SAP ERP uses SAP's standard logic without any adjustment.[329]

The Business Outcome

Salespeople accessed SAP with a custom web application that provided maximum possible production capacity for products two weeks out from the order request date. In this way, the manager was able to confirm this to the customer with only the smallest time lag, and then to update the quantity from the customer in the application's web interface.

---

329 We will not get into the detail of Denis' approach for the MRP logic other to say that it is based on Kolmogorov–Zurbenko where the model is applied to every new event arranged in FIFO order. Using it requires going heavy on compute resources. But by doing so it enabled Real Time MRP to meet the customer requirement for a near immediate response time for the user. Real Time MRP is also triggered by events.

Real Time MRP's Processing Sequence

Right after manager updated quantity in web application it automatically triggered the following sequence:

1. Creation of Sales Order in SAP ERP via RFC (remote function call).

2. Recalculation of maximum values for every dependent material (common components or capacity) with database update. Calculation problem was represented as a quite simple system of linear inequalities with maximization problem.

3. During all calculations process, all materials were marked with 'lock' status using AMQ.

4. To operate with the actual data from SAP system like material consumption or replenishments, on ERP side implemented user extensions in specific processes that notified remote server via RFC.

Conclusion

Real-Time MRP was able to be free of the limitations of SAP ERP. SAP ERP could never have met the customer requirements laid out in this case study. This is true of either the business logic of the performance requirements. With the Real-Time MRP application the performance was greatly enhanced, and the MRP logic was customized to the requirements.

The nice thing about the solution is that it can be connected to any SAP ERP system, and SAP customers usually have MRP that has both poor performance characteristics and are not customized for specific requirements of different manufacturing environments.

In most cases when a company does make a change in this area, they purchase a separate external system to run supply planning, which also means using the standard design of the supply planning method available within that application as well, and the procedure does not run on an optimized AWS server. However, with Real-Time MRP, a company can obtain performance and MRP customization from a lightweight and far less expensive solution.

Note: As a related note, for years now Brightwork Research & Analysis has been proposing how inefficient and limiting it is to run MRP from within ERP systems, This topic is covered this in the book How to Repair Your MRP System.[330] This was part of the general overestimation of ERP systems that lulled companies into thinking they could get competent functionality for all of their needs from one system.

---

330 http://www.brightworkr.com/scmfocuspress/supply-books/repairing-mrp-system/

Case Study #3: Cloud Forecasting on AWS

A different FMCG wholesale company from the previous case study maintained roughly 2500 SKUs.

During the sales process, SAP promised the customer that SAP provided "best in class" forecasting mechanisms. SAP stated that the forecasting functionality in SAP's ERP system would easily replace any existing tools and algorithms client used in production. The contract that was eventually signed stipulated that SAP would implement forecasting algorithms similar to or better than the client's existing algorithms.

The project was begun under these assumptions. However, during blueprinting, consultants came to the project management office to escalate a problem. The customer's existing tool for material forecasting was MATLAB. Unfortunately, nobody within the SAP team had a clue how to match MATLAB's functionality.

The client asked for the following items to be present in SAP forecasting

1. Representation of forecast function as a linear combination of multiple functions. For instance a combination of multiple sinusoidal functions with exponentiation smoothing.

2. A way to assemble multiple functions with given weights to improve the probability of estimation.

3. A transparent model of how the algorithm filled in missing values.

4. The ability to apply to superimpose a sales history from one product to a new, that had no sales history.

5. A transparent mechanism how to include promotions in the statistical forecast.

Understanding SAP's Promise Versus MATLAB

MATLAB is an advanced program for mathematics. There is no way for SAP ERP forecasting to match what MATLAB has to offer. The forecasting functionality was added to SAP ERP many years ago and is only in very rare cases enabled. Even SAP DP which is SAP's specialized forecasting system, which was not in scope, would have had no hope of matching or exceeding the forecasting methods available in MATLAB. Although, on the other hand, MATLAB is not typically used to forecast the number of SKUs that the customer was using it for.

The entire scenario laid out by SAP was an example of how SAP oversells its solutions into customers. It was heavily influenced by SAP salespeople who were saying anything to get the deal sold. However, it is typical for the understanding of forecasting methods to be so thin in companies that they are not able to draw distinctions between what method are available in various systems.

The Cloud Forecasting Solution

From the beginning the agreement with the client was that the team would build a platform for implementation of models, but not for the actual forecasting model calculations. There also was a lengthy debate on the project regarding the approach of implementation between programming versus client management.

Ultimately the decision was made to place the cloud forecasting system on AWS.

The following AWS services were used.

1. *AWS Kinesis*: This to get all updates for materials (refurbishments, consumption).

2. *AWS Lambda*: This triggered by Kinesis for models implementation. By using Lambdas, the company was able to implement they Math functions in Python instead of MATLAB. Python is the go-to language for applying math functions to support an overall program. MATLAB and the language R tend to be more for the analytics stage when the analyst is testing hypothesis.

3. *AWS RDS*: Using PostgreSQL to store the historical data.

4. *AWS Elastic Beanstalk*: Used as a remote RFC server for on-premise SAP ERP.

How the Solution Worked at a High Level with the AWS Components

1. SAP ERP sent RFC calls to a remote cloud server with details on every transaction related to specific materials.

2. Elastic Beanstalk imported data to Kinesis and to database.

3. Kinesis invokes Lambdas with custom-made forecasting functions.

SAP Attempts to Undermine the Custom Solution

Yet again, and as we covered in the section on SAP ABAP, SAP proposed that the customer use their ABAP programming language to build this solution. This was immediately rejected by the customer due to ABAP's "disturbing syntax and development tools."

That ended up being a good decision, because ABAP would have been a poor choice for both forecasting and for the cloud.

SAP's Habit of Force Fitting ABAP into the Most Inappropriate Places

Therefore having been caught lying about what SAP ERP could do in forecasting, once the decision was made to create something custom, SAP still recommended using ABAP to build the solution. ABAP as a language is both a bad fit for cloud, and it has no history of being used for the solution described in this case study. Python, on the other hand, was a natural choice for this solution. Python can natively call a large number of statistical functions, and an enormous number of mathematical and statistical programs are written Python. SAP knew this but continued to recommend ABAP as ABAP is a tool for maintaining account control. This is yet another example of how SAP does recommends ABAP when it is entirely inappropriate for the task.

Conclusion

- The cloud forecasting solution that supported this SAP customer's expectations was built in two months.

- The monthly AWS costs for production use averaged less then 100 dollars.

This case study demonstrated an effective and proven custom solution for forecasting. However, it also illustrated why it is so dangerous to listen to SAP or SAP proponents on anything related to either the cloud or to development. SAP continuously will promote their solutions, which are a poor fit for the cloud. In this example, they recommended ABAP, without the slightest concern for whether ABAP was an appropriate language for cloud or performing statistical functions. SAP was unconcerned as to the functionality provided by ABAP, or the long-term cost of maintaining a custom application developed is a less appropriate language for the customer. If this same project occurred to today, SAP would undoubtedly have attempted to push the development to their SAP Cloud, which again, would have been a bad choice and would have undermined the development.

One undeniable reason why SAP Cloud would also be a bad choice is that in addition to it being extremely difficult to use, SAP Cloud does not support most of the AWS services that were accessed as part of the solution. SAP sales reps are taught to redirect everything back to SAP, and the benefits of the recommended SAP offering vis-à-vis competitive offerings are not factored into the equation.

This case study will repeat itself many times into the future, as SAP fights against using AWS and Google Cloud unless they can intermediate and add an upcharge to the AWS, Google Cloud or Azure services. SAP Cloud is designed as that upcharge device. And SAP's consulting partners will help SAP redirect cloud interest in their clients to the "SAP Cloud Upcharger."

This is why it is the view of the three authors of this book that SAP's advice and the advice of SAP consulting partners on matters related to the cloud should be disregarded.

Conclusion

AWS and Google Cloud are changing the game for enterprise software in a way that people with work experience only in on-premises software will have a hard time processing. This is explained in the following quote from Andy Jassy, CEO of AWS.

> *"...we were adding lots of software developers at Amazon in 2002 and 2003, we noticed that projects were still taking us the same amount of time to complete as when we had fewer resources. This was surprising to us, and counter to what teams predicted. When we investigated, we found that virtually every team was spending several months and people resources recreating the same infrastructure software pieces (compute, storage, database, analytics, machine learning etc.). It turned out that teams were spending 80% of their time on the undifferentiated heavy lifting of infrastructure and just 20% of their time on what differentiated their ideas. We wanted to flip that equation on its head to let Amazon teams invent and experiment more quickly. And we figured if a strong technology company like Amazon had this challenge, it was likely that a lot of other builders at small and large companies (governments!) would too."*[331]

And AWS is correct!

This inefficiency has also negatively impacted SAP and Oracle environments since they started being SAP and Oracle environments. In their history SAP and Oracle never attempted to increase efficiency. The entirety of SAP's focus on speeding projects has been to introduce one marketing program after another claiming that the new invention sped projects. That is SAP's primary focus has been in convincing customers that SAP software can be implemented faster than it can in reality. We covered this exact topic in the article How to Best Understand the Faux SAP RDS.[332]

The truth is that SAP and Oracle projects have not changed much over decades with the same implementation model, designed around maximizing consulting billing hours in a

---

331 https://www.amazon.com/Enterprise-Cloud-Practices-Transforming-Legacy-ebook/dp/B00XWT5MAO/
332 http://www.brightworkr.com/sapprojectmanagement/2017/06/best-understand-faux-sap-rds/

one-off "job shop" implementation strategy.[333] Instead, their strategy was to take a **high** margin model, with high margin consulting and **high** overhead software and databases, and market that approaches to as many companies as possible.

The result?

SAP and Oracle customers have the highest TCO and SAP, and Oracle have developed into the most difficult vendors to work with. Analysis of commentary around SAP and Oracle with respect to the cloud shows that the explanation of how the cloud is counter to SAP and Oracle's account control is nearly completely absent.

While SAP and Oracle followed a one-off high overhead model, AWS and Google Cloud are more like the rise of mass production in a time when only short production runs were possible. This is explained in the following quote from Seeking Alpha.

> *"The "raw material" for what this company sells continues to plunge in price. Without a lengthy discussion regarding the costs of servers and storage and switches, I think most people understand just how significantly the cost of those components is dropping. And on the pricing side, this company is selling some value added services and that trend is sure to continue. I commented about the initiative that Amazon has launched in data visualization."*

Cloud is often presented as almost waste free, while on premises is widely acknowledged as quite wasteful. In on-premise environments much software is purchased that is little used. The typical hardware is oversized and has a very low average usage. There is most certainly less wasted in the cloud, but there is wasted, as is explained in this graphic.

---

333 In fact, due to maturity issues with applications like S/4HANA being released far too early, SAP projects are in some cases lengthening. Our study of S/4HANA implementations is available at this link. - http://www.brightworkr.com/saphana/2017/04/25/s4hana-implementation-study/

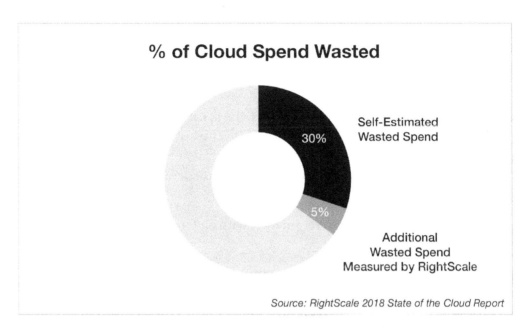

% of Cloud Spend Wasted

30% — Self-Estimated Wasted Spend

5% — Additional Wasted Spend Measured by RightScale

Source: RightScale 2018 State of the Cloud Report

According to Rightscale 76% of the cost of cloud is compute, while another 15% is database. Combined these make up 91% of cloud costs, hence these are the areas to focus cost optimization attention.[334]

The Transition of Thought Leadership from SAP and Oracle to AWS and Google Cloud

For a time Oracle provided a distinctly differentiated product to the market in their Oracle database. For a time SAP provided a distinctly differentiated ERP system. These two developments gave those companies great power. However, at this point, those products are not anywhere as distinct as when they were first introduced. Also, SAP and Oracle have grown into difficult vendors to manage with enormous senses of entitlement over the IT budget and with both vendors pushing the envelope as to what is legal to achieve their all-consuming revenue objectives.

Furthermore, if you implement SAP and Oracle's products as they and their consulting partners stipulate, the result is the highest TCO in the industry. SAP and Oracle want this TCO hidden and IT analysts and SAP and Oracle consulting partners are only too happy to help SAP and Oracle keep this information on the "down low." As was found by Vinnie Mirchandani, in our coverage earlier in the book, attempts at quantification of such costs

334 https://www.rightscale.com/blog/cloud-cost-analysis/aws-costs-how-much-are-you-wasting

are not appreciated or supported by the major IT analysts. SAP and Oracle want pricing secret, so that pricing can never be determined without a lengthy interaction with their sales representatives. AWS and Google Cloud are offer price transparency because they aren't software vendors, but service providers.

AWS and Google Cloud offer a menu of options, the prices are communicated to customers in real time for various services configuration.[335] The customer chooses, and AWS and Google Cloud are happy to make money from any of them. We spin up AWS and Google Cloud services without ever talking to an AWS and Google Cloud sales rep, and you know what?

We don't miss them. In fact, if we never interact with an Oracle or SAP sales rep again, that would be a good thing.

The following quote from Denis Myagkov further illuminates this.

> *"I think that SAP's and Oracle's myth department is propelling they database solutions without any context. It's pretty weird to compare one database with another and not mention of its application. Any database is only a way to store some data somewhere and somehow and here we have the huge gap – what system will be consumer of they databases?*
>
> *AWS and Google act like good merchants, they simply propose an assortment of different databases for developers. Maybe I'm wrong, but I prefer to choose tools for the task, but not vice versa."*

And this is the issue. When we debate SAP, but more Oracle DB resources, what we get back is how deep the Oracle database is in this or that, how it is used by the World Data Center for Weather or some other upper tier case studies (with all of the upper tier case studies open

---

335 Most of AWS and Google's services are open source. This means leveraging the work of hundreds of thousands of people, who were not paid. However, while Google has a good history of giving back to the open source community, AWS does not. AWS has a history of taking from open source, but offering secrecy in return. Some believe this is from Bezos' trading background. This is simply taking from the common area, and monetizing it for personal profit. Without open source projects AWS would for all intents and purposes not exist. This taking from the common area is a constant problem in our economic system with banks receiving massive support from the government (banks could not exist without fractional reserve banking – a power granted by the government), pharmaceuticals siphoning off tax research dollars from NIH funded research performed in universities. AWS is widely known to follow military type secrecy internally. There is also a problem with this, by keeping their additions secret, they make their overall software less sustainable. This is a mark against AWS and a credit to Google Cloud. Google showed with Kubernetes how a private company can add to open source and also benefit. - https://forums.theregister.co.uk/forum/1/2014/01/22/amazon_open_source_investigation/

source databases ignored). However, the database is part of the IaaS, and the IaaS enables the database to do things, **or it sets the boundaries for what is possible** (for example horizontal scalability, which is multi-location and based upon the IaaS).

Should anyone be surprised?

Because the database is what SAP and Oracle have to sell, as they have not figured out IaaS beyond having offerings that function more as propaganda (that makes Wall Street think there is something there, make it seem like they are hip and cool, etc..) and that lead the industry in licenses purchased for shelfware.

Oracle loves promoting bare metal. Unsurprisingly, bare metal is what Oracle is offering, as they cannot do the sophisticated things with multitenancy, etc. that AWS or Google Cloud can do. This is equally true of SAP, which for their internally developed products are designed to work on dedicated rather than virtualized servers. Bare metal is hosting; it is not cloud. If hosting were the answer, IBM and CSC would be rising, instead of being companies that barely anyone talks about with respect to the cloud.

Let us say that a salesperson wants to sell you an engine out of context with the value it provided to you. They could discuss its technical specifications. For example, it could be a very powerful engine (a selling point the salesperson chooses to emphasize) It may product 1000 horsepower. It may have a fantastic compression ratio, and so on. However, what about how it fits within the car and the daily use of that car? The salesperson can go into a lengthy soliloquy discussing very narrow characteristics of the engine. Pretty soon, if you listen to that salesperson, you will put that engine in your economy car. After all, it's a great engine! Sports car advertisements are similar in that they sell a dream of a car, out on an open country road, that provides a very different experience in traffic, where you might prefer more leg room and an automatic. The car may go 200 mph, but by the way, the speed limit is 65 mph. 45 to 55 mph with traffic. That is the danger in listening to a salesperson who has something to sell and only that particular thing to sell.

Hasso Plattner engaged in this type of context free selling when SAP introduced its HANA database. First, nearly everything he said about HANA was not true as we covered in the article When Articles Exaggerate SAP S/4HANA Benefits.[336] However, let's say for a moment it was all true. Even if true, it would not improve the condition of the user as Hasso and SAP have proposed. Also, it certainly would not be worth the price, maintenance overhead, and indirect access implications.

---

336 http://www.brightworkr.com/saphana/2016/04/07/when-articles-exaggerate-sap-hanas-benefits/

SAP and Oracle both like to pretend the car/road or the IaaS is **immaterial to the discussion**, and that the primary focus should be what they have to offer, which are applications and databases. And only commercial databases and applications, of course, no open source databases or applications are to be considered.

The Move Away from Proprietary Hardware

A critical component of AWS and Google Cloud is the ability to move away from proprietary hardware. AWS and Google Cloud have amazing economies of scale in hardware and data center technology and management. How could a company put together a hardware setup that is competitive on price or flexibility with AWS/Google Cloud? Those data centers have untold economies of scale. It's like mass production, versus a job shop for an IT department. If we look at a big company, say Chevron, they are still not going to have the scale or competence of AWS/GCP. Does anyone look to Chevron for technology? Of course not.

Global Infrastructure

When you spend $10 billion every single year on your on DCs as AWS and Google do, you get a unique volume discount suppliers, so the unit price goes way down.

The Mass Production Movement of IaaS

The history of manufacturing is frequently misunderstood. Standards of living in countries that went through the industrial revolutions, after the introduction of mass production. Before that time, things were made in smaller batches, and only the wealthy had many manufactured items due to their high cost. While craftsmen working away in a workshop may be romantic, it is also inefficient. For efficiency, mass production is necessary. This means bringing scale and automation into the equation.

There is a similar analogy here with on-premises versus cloud implementation. SAP and Oracle consulting firms show up at a client site and perform implements as a job shop. Every implementation is a "one-off." Productivity is low, which means employment is high, and each company buys their hardware, and many projects go and on, without leveraging the immediate things that can be accessed by cloud. If we currently performed manufacturing this way, the costs for everyday items would extremely high.

That is the point of the cloud, and it is "already built." One just has to leverage what is out there to use for one's purposes. Of course, there are adjustments; there is still a configuration of applications. However, the more one can leverage prebuilt items, the faster the software can be deployed, and the more testing can be performed on the included (and excluded) components. The on-premises model, which is highly directed around "building consulting practices" is the inefficiency problem that keeps inflating TCO. It's also an opportunity for cloud vendors and companies with automation capabilities like AWS and Google to sharply reduce the TCO associated with product maintenance, upgrades, security, patching, and so on.

Leveraging the Cloud

AWS and Google Cloud allows everyone to do things that just weren't anywhere near possible just a few years ago. We frequently can't believe what we are able to access and test in both AWS and Google Cloud, and at such a low cost. Every company that uses enterprise software should be thinking about how to learn more about AWS and Google Cloud to figure out how to best apply their services for their unique situation. This book has been focused on SAP and Oracle environments, but only because that is the background of the authors. AWS and Google Cloud's services are universal in their applicability and of course work on Infor or any other application vendor's environments. However, SAP and Oracle environments can benefit so much from AWS and Google Cloud because they are so limited by the entire SAP and Oracle set of restrictive technologies, mindset, and presentation that customers should passively accept SAP and Oracle's advice.

How to Contact Us

We hope you enjoyed the book. As this book should have made clear, we think AWS and Google Cloud is something that should be leveraged by SAP and Oracle accounts. It is just of question of how much is right for each company, and of course how fast. AWS and Google Cloud allow companies to do things that are not possible using on-premises solutions, or using SAP or Oracle's cloud. When faced with questions, we usually move to ask how one can leverage AWS or Google Cloud to answer that question. There are so many areas of SAP and Oracle accounts that we see that could leverage either AWS or Google Cloud. We can explain the options available in AWS and Google Cloud and get SAP and Oracle environments integrated with either AWS or Google Cloud. We provide everything from creating the financial business case, cost optimization of AWS and Google Cloud services versus your needs, evaluation of your on-premises design and its applicability to the cloud, prioritization analysis, cloud technology evaluations to cloud strategy.

Secondly, this book is going to grow and be added to in the future. If you have a story that you think is pertinent to this book, reach out to us. We can probably provide you with feedback and potentially add the information as a quotation to the future updates to the book.

There are several ways to contact us.

If you have a comment that you would like to see publicly commented upon, head over to the book page at Brightwork Research & Analysis, and leave a comment and we will respond. This is a good place to add questions about future editions of the book. http://www.brightworkr.com/scmfocuspress/how-to-leverage-aws-and-google-cloud-for-sap-oracle/

If you are interested in consulting services contact us at info@brightworkr.com. If you have a question for one of the three authors, we have our author emails and LinkedIn profiles in the author section of the book.

Author Profiles

Shaun Snapp

Shaun Snapp is the managing editor for Brightwork Research & Analysis. He is a long time SAP consultant and researcher. Brightwork covers a variety of topics, but has a strong focus on SAP. Brightwork has increasingly been focused on researching how to combine AWS and Google Cloud services with SAP on-premises environments.

Shaun Snapp's Linked In Profile:
https://www.linkedin.com/in/shaunsnapp/

Ahmed Azmi

Ahmed is an analyst at Brightwork Research and Analysis, a senior advisor for the minister of information technology and a member of the advisory board at the national telecommunication regulatory authority. Previously, he held senior leadership positions at Sybase, HP, Oracle, and SAP. Ahmed is a contributing member of the international executive association. A guest speaker at Dubai Gitex, Flat6labs, and DTEC. And a featured author on Armatic.com, and Autodeploy.net.

Ahmed Azmi's Linked In Profile:
https://www.linkedin.com/in/ahmedazmi/

Mark Dalton

Mark's deep commitment to creating transformational outcomes using enterprise software for customers has been a driving force throughout his career. Working at JD Edwards Mark was able to see how great organizations focus on the customer, and developed the first multi-channel business intelligence platform across the organization. That experience has guided how Mark views the importance of organizational alignment of sales, customer support, product development, and marketing to enable a superior customer experience.

Mark Dalton's LinkedIn Profile:
https://www.linkedin.com/in/markdaltonautodeploy/

This Book was Reviewed in Parts for Technical SAP Validation by the following.

Denis Myagkov

Denis is a solution architect with more than 15 years of experience in delivering complex and unique solutions for the clients who wants to get maximum from their SAP Systems. Denis has developed a number of solutions that help improve SAP by leveraging AWS.

Denis Myagkov's LinkedIn Profile:
https://www.linkedin.com/in/denismyagkov/

Previous Books by Shaun Snapp

If you liked this book, you may like these other books from one of the same authors.

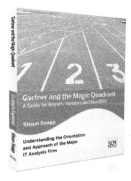

Gartner and the Magic Quadrant:
A Guide for Buyers, Vendors and Investors

Enterprise Software Selection: How to
Pinpoint the Perfect Software Solution
Using Multiple Sources of Information

Enterprise Software TCO: Calculating
and Using Total Cost of Ownership in
Decision Making

Enterprise Software Project Risk
Management: How to Control the Risk
Factors on IT Projects

The Real Story Behind ERP: Separating
Fiction from Reality

The Real Story Behind Two Tiered ERP:
Separating the Marketing from the
Usable Strategy

Supply Chain Forecasting Software

Promotions Forecasting: Techniques for
Forecast Adjustments in Software

Setting Forecast Parameters in Software:
Alpha, Beta, Gamma, etc..

Lean and Reorder Point Planning:
Implementing the Approach the Right
Way in Software

Repairing Your MRP System

Inventory Optimization and Multi-Echelon Planning Software

Safety Stock and Service Level: A New Approach

Sales and Operations Planning in Software

Process Industry Manufacturing Software: ERP, Planning, Recipe, MES & Process Control

Superplant: Creating a Nimble Manufacturing Enterprise with Advanced Planning Software

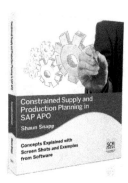

Constraint Based Supply and
Production Planning in SAP APO

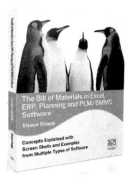

Bill of Materials in Excel, Planning,
ERP and PLM/BMMS Software

Capacity Management in MRP,
APS & S&OP Software

Multi-Method Supply Planning
in SAP APO

Planning Horizons, Calendars and
Timings in SAP APO

Setting Up the Supply Network
in SAP APO

Replenishment Triggers: Setting Systems
for Make to Stock, Make to Order &
Assemble to Order

Supply Planning with MRP, DRP
and APS Software

www.ingramcontent.com/pod-product-compliance
Lightning Source LLC
LaVergne TN
LVHW062304060326
832902LV00013B/2045